THE ODYSSEY EQUATION

THE ODYSSEY EQUATION

How to be prepared for
any future that finds you

AMAR B. SINGH

Anecdote
Publishing House
For the love of quality reading!

anecdotepublishinghouse.com
champreaders.com

Anecdote Publishing House
2nd Floor 2/15 Lane no. 2 Ansari Road, Daryaganj-110002
Email: info@anecdotepublishinghouse.com
Website: anecdotepublishinghouse.com

Published by Anecdote Publishing House

First Edition 2025

ISBN 978-81-988015-3-1
MRP ₹ 399

Book Promoted and Marketed by Champ Readers Pvt. Ltd.
Editorial Process: Meraki
Cover design by: Rishikumar Thakur
Layout by: OGAI Technologies Pvt Ltd
Printed by Thomson Press (India) Ltd, New Delhi

To

The Original Unshakeable People

My parents,

Bajrang B. Singh & Savitri Singh

"No one can make you feel inferior without your consent."

– Eleanor Roosevelt

"You are the sky. Everything else is just the weather."

– Pema Chodron

"Between stimulus and response there is a space. In that space is our power to choose our response. In our response lies our growth and our freedom."

– Viktor Frankl

"I am not what happened to me, I am what I choose to become."

– Carl Jung

"The greatest glory in living lies not in never falling, but in rising every time we fall."

– Nelson Mandela

"You are not a drop in the ocean. You are the entire ocean in a drop."

– Rumi

"The world is full of magic things, patiently waiting for our senses to grow sharper."

– W.B. Yeats

"This being human is a guest house. Every morning a new arrival."

– Rumi

"Peace comes from within. Do not seek it without."

– Buddha

For all those living in the shadow of uncertainty – may this approach transform your relationship with the unknown, revealing that preparation isn't about predicting the future, but developing the capacity to dance gracefully with whatever arrives.

$$\Delta + \psi \longrightarrow \infty$$

CONTENTS

CHAPTER SUMMARIES

Chapter 0: Why You Need to Become Unshakeable

Explores the increasing complexity and uncertainty of modern life that make traditional approaches to resilience inadequate. Introduces the three-layer framework as a comprehensive solution and explains why this integrated approach is essential in today's world.

Chapter 1: The Foundation of Strategic Resilience

Introduces Layer 1, explaining why strategic thinking matters and the limitations of reactive approaches. Presents the Strategic Delta Method as a framework for navigating complex situations through multiple pathways and contingency planning.

Chapter 2: Strategic Delta in Action

Demonstrates practical applications of the Strategic Delta Method across various life domains. Shows how to identify critical paths, create contingencies, and apply these principles to career, relationships, and health challenges through real-world examples.

Chapter 3: Quantum Principles for Practical Results

Introduces quantum thinking as a complement to traditional strategic approaches. Explains key principles like the observer effect, superposition, and quantum tunnelling, showing how they expand possibilities beyond conventional cause-and-effect thinking.

Chapter 4: The Quantum Delta Method

Combines strategic planning with quantum flexibility to create a synthesis that thrives amid uncertainty. Explains the four components—quantum assessment, quantum outcomes, quantum pathways, and quantum execution—through practical case studies.

Chapter 5: Mastering Layer 1
Addresses common obstacles to strategic mastery such as analysis paralysis, strategic abandonment, confirmation bias, method rigidity, and false dichotomy thinking. Provides metrics for measuring progress and explains why strategies alone aren't enough.

Chapter 6: Beyond Strategy
Marks the transition to Layer 2 by exploring the inherent limitations of strategic approaches. Shows how even perfect plans can fail due to factors beyond our control and introduces mental resilience as a complementary capacity to strategic thinking.

Chapter 7: Drawing Lines on Water
Uses the metaphor of attempting to create fixed patterns on flowing water to illustrate the futility of rigid expectations. Explores flow states, adaptability, and practical approaches to working with reality's fluid nature rather than against it.

Chapter 8: Quantum Uncertainty as a Strength
Transforms our relationship with uncertainty from threat to asset. Shows how quantum perspectives on probability, possibility, and emergence can create opportunities precisely because the future isn't fixed in predetermined patterns.

Chapter 9: Resilience Through Acceptance
Distinguishes between genuine acceptance and passive resignation, showing how radical acceptance creates freedom for effective action. Provides practical approaches to cultivating acceptance that becomes a foundation for both peace and purposeful engagement.

Chapter 10: Mastering Layer 2
Integrates the components of mental flexibility into a cohesive approach to master life's challenges. Explores the harmony

between planning and acceptance, the dance of awareness and action, and signs indicating readiness for Layer 3 exploration.

Chapter 11: The Nature of Consciousness
Begins the exploration of Layer 3 by examining consciousness not as an abstract philosophical concept but as the foundation in which all experience arises. Introduces the observer and the observed, quantum entanglement and non-duality, and the nature beyond the separate self.

Chapter 12: Time as an Illusion
Explores how our conventional understanding of time creates unnecessary vulnerability and how a different relationship with time can transform what can "fuck with you." Examines the eternal now, spooky action at a distance, and freedom from outcome attachment.

Chapter 13: The Paradox of Doing
Addresses the apparent contradiction between action and the recognition that the doer is itself an appearance within consciousness. Explores action without an actor, the dance of consciousness, the flow of purpose, and how this paradox manifests in daily life.

Chapter 14: True Resilience
Examines the quantum nature of personal growth, how to create conditions for crossing thresholds of consciousness, and the paradoxical wisdom of embracing "not knowing." Shows how integration across all three layers creates complete resilience.

Chapter 15: Living Across All Layers
Provides practical guidance for integrating all three layers in daily life. Explores recognising your default layer, expanding your range, layer-appropriate responses, and the foundation approach to integration.

Appendix A: The Three-Layer Assessment
A practical tool for readers to assess their current development across all three layers in different life domains, with scoring guidance and interpretation.

Appendix B: Practice Guide for the Three Layers
Provides specific practices for cultivating each layer, ranging from strategic methods and mental flexibility techniques to contemplative approaches for philosophical transcendence.

Appendix C: Reading List by Layer
A curated list of books and resources aligned with each layer, providing readers with guidance for further exploration.

WHY I WROTE THIS BOOK

I never set out to write a book using mathematical symbols. As someone who has spent years helping people and organisations navigate change, I always focused on practical methods, straightforward strategies, and using accessible language. Mathematics seemed far too abstract for the deeply human challenges of preparation and resilience.

Yet, during a particularly tumultuous period in my own life—unexpected transitions, uncertain outcomes, and the familiar anxiety that accompanies significant change—I found myself sketching three symbols on a notepad: Δ, Ψ, and ∞. In that moment, I realised these symbols captured perfectly what I had been teaching and learning about preparation in an unpredictable world.

The equation $(\Delta + \Psi) \rightarrow \infty$ emerged not from academic theory but from lived experience. It represents the journey I've witnessed countless times—in others and in myself. We begin seeking strategic methods to control change (Δ). We discover the necessity of mental resilience to implement those methods effectively (Ψ). And eventually, somewhat to our surprise, we find ourselves approaching a perspective that transcends both strategy and psychology (∞)–one where preparation isn't about controlling outcomes but about developing a fundamentally different relationship with change itself.

My professional path has been anything but linear. With degrees in engineering, law, and business, I've moved between seemingly disconnected worlds: from the intense calculations of investment banking to the creative chaos of marketing; from the raw industrial power of iron making to the nuanced art of strategy and sales. Along the way, I've written books exploring psychology, philosophy, technology, spirituality, and religion.

This boundary-crossing approach wasn't planned. It emerged naturally from an insatiable curiosity and a refusal to accept artificial limitations on what I could learn or where I could contribute. Each new domain enriched my understanding of the others, creating a web of insights that would have been impossible to achieve through specialisation alone.

Yet as I've watched the modern professional landscape evolve, I've observed something that deeply concerns me: an increasing retreat into specialisation driven by fear rather than passion. I see brilliant minds narrowing their focus not because they've found their true calling, but because they're seeking security in an uncertain world. I witness organisations building deeper silos rather than broader capabilities. I notice educational systems that reward narrow expertise while penalising the courageous explorer.

The result is a profound limitation in how we approach problems, opportunities, and life itself. When we specialise out of fear, we sacrifice the cross-pollination of ideas that drives true innovation. We forfeit the adaptability that thrives in changing conditions. Most tragically, we diminish the richness of our own experience—the deep satisfaction that comes from connecting disparate dots and seeing patterns invisible to the specialist's eye.

This isn't just a professional concern. It's a human one too. The quality of life available to the adaptable, multidimensional thinker is fundamentally different from that of the fearful specialist. The former sees possibilities where the latter sees threats. The former builds capabilities that transcend any single future, while the latter gambles everything on predictions that may never materialise.

I wrote this book because I believe we need a new approach—one that honours depth while embracing breadth; one that prepares us not for a single predicted future but for many possible futures; one that transforms fear into preparation and anxiety into adaptability.

This book presents a framework that might initially seem counterintuitive in our age of specialisation and prediction. Rather than offering certainty, it embraces uncertainty. Rather than promoting mastery in a single domain, it advocates for adaptable excellence across multiple possible futures. Rather than promising a clear path forward, it provides tools for navigating in fog.

But there is more.

My professional background had equipped me with strategic methods and frameworks—approaches that worked brilliantly in controlled conditions but often faltered when reality threw its inevitable curveballs. I watched as smart, capable people (including myself) create excellent plans only to fall apart when those plans met unexpected obstacles.

This observation launched me on a decade-long exploration that ultimately transformed not just my professional work but my entire understanding of human resilience. What began as research into better strategic methods evolved into something far more comprehensive.

The first revelation came when I recognised that strategic approaches alone, no matter how sophisticated, would always have limitations. This wasn't a failure of the methods but simply the reality of living in a complex, interconnected world where complete control is impossible. This insight led me to explore mental resilience—the capacity to navigate uncertainty with equanimity when even the best strategies reach their limits.

But the most profound shift came from an unexpected personal crisis that pushed me beyond both strategic methods and mental resilience. During a period when everything I'd relied on seemed to collapse simultaneously—family health challenges, professional setbacks, and relationship difficulties converging in a perfect storm—I stumbled into a question I hadn't previously considered: What if the very foundation of my vulnerability—my sense of being a separate self, moving through threatening circumstances—wasn't as solid or fundamental as I'd assumed?

This question opened a door to the third layer of becoming unshakeable—a recognition that beneath the practical strategies and mental flexibility lies a more fundamental resilience based on understanding the nature of identity itself. This wasn't abstract philosophy but a practical insight with profound implications for how I experienced life's challenges.

As I integrated these three layers in my own life and shared them with others, I witnessed transformations that far exceeded what any single approach could have achieved. People who had reached the limits of strategic methods alone discovered new dimensions of resilience through mental flexibility. Those who had developed both strategic approaches and mental resilience found even deeper freedom through questioning the nature of the self that seemed vulnerable to life's challenges.

I wrote this book because I believe this three-layer approach offers something uniquely valuable. Most personal development resources focus exclusively on either practical strategy, psychological resilience, or philosophical understanding. Few integrate all three into a comprehensive journey that honours each layer's unique contribution.

Throughout this book, you'll encounter a central metaphor: the spotlight and the dancer. This isn't just a literary device; it's a fundamental principle that explains why some people and organisations thrive under pressure while others crumble. The spotlight doesn't create quality—it amplifies what already exists. Your performance in critical moments is largely determined by the work you've done when no one was watching.

This book distils what I've learned from working with leaders facing disruption, individuals navigating life transitions, and organisations adapting to rapidly changing landscapes. The frameworks, practices, and perspectives shared here have been tested in real-world conditions of uncertainty, complexity, and high stakes.

I've structured the journey through conversations at the beginning of each chapter between Avika and Jai, two characters representing many of the bright, capable people I've worked with on the one hand, and on the other, those whose mentorship and guidance I've been fortunate to receive throughout my own journey. Their dialogues illustrate how these concepts move from intellectual understanding to practical application to lived experience. These aren't just decorative elements; they're deliberate teaching tools designed to help you grasp abstract ideas through concrete examples. Each chapter also has several examples of people using strategies across the three layers to transform their lives. These examples use a few imaginary names across the book for different examples.

My hope is that this book serves as both a compass and a companion as you navigate your own changing landscape. The world will continue to transform at an accelerating pace. The future will remain fundamentally unpredictable. But with the right approach—one that integrates strategic intelligence, mental resilience, and a larger perspective—you can be genuinely prepared for any future that finds you.

This is not a book about controlling the uncontrollable. It's about developing the strategic awareness, mental flexibility, and wisdom to move through change with both effectiveness and peace. It's about recognising that true preparation isn't about knowing exactly what will happen—it's about cultivating the ability to respond skilfully to whatever does.

The approach I share in these pages draws from diverse traditions and disciplines—strategic methodologies, psychological research, contemplative practices, and philosophical inquiries that span cultures and centuries. I've done my best to present these ideas in practical, accessible language without diluting their transformative potential.

As you read, I encourage you to approach these explorations not as abstract concepts but as invitations to direct experience. The true value of this journey emerges not from intellectual understanding alone but from embodying these insights in your daily life. Try the exercises, experiment with the perspectives, and notice what emerges from your own exploration.

Welcome to *The Odyssey Equation*. May your journey through these pages help you navigate your journey through life.

With gratitude,
Amar B. Singh

ACKNOWLEDGEMENTS

Creating a book is like embarking on a journey across uncharted waters—what begins as a solitary vision eventually requires a constellation of guiding stars to reach its destination. This book would not exist without the many brilliant lights which illuminated my path.

First, I must express my deepest gratitude to my family, whose unwavering support created the foundation from which this work could emerge. Your patience during the long hours, your honest feedback when it was needed the most, and your belief in this project when mine occasionally wavered, made all the difference.

To my teachers and mentors—those who taught me and those whose wisdom I've encountered through their writings—thank you for the seeds of insight that have grown into the three-layer framework presented in these pages.

My heartfelt appreciation goes to the many individuals who generously shared their stories of becoming resilient, truly unshakeable, across different domains of life. Your willingness to reveal both your struggles and breakthroughs brings these abstract principles to life. While some names have been changed to protect privacy, your contributions form the living heart of this book.

To my first readers—Sanjeev and Amit—thank you for your time and effort as I worked on the early drafts and providing me invaluable feedback that helped me refine this work. Your perspectives showed me blind spots I couldn't see and possibilities I hadn't imagined.

Special appreciation goes to the wisdom traditions that have informed Layer 3 of this work, particularly the teachings preserved in the *Ashtavakra Gita* and other non-dual texts. These ancient insights prove as relevant today as they were thousands of years ago.

I would like to express my heartfelt gratitude to Sagar from Ancedote Publishing for bringing my work into print, to Meraki for her thoughtful and meticulous editing, to Rishikumar Thakur for designing such a beautiful cover, to Arivazhagi Balasundaram for the book's elegant design, and to Matt Preschern for his insightful foreword. Your dedication and creativity have shaped this book into what it is today—thank you all for being part of this journey.

Finally, my deepest gratitude to you, the reader, for bringing your attention and engagement to these pages. A book only fulfils its purpose when it finds resonance in the mind and heart of its reader. May this work serve your journey toward becoming truly unshakeable across all dimensions of your life.

FOREWORD

Matt Preschern is a technology investor and former Chief Marketing Officer with 25+ years of leadership experience at global corporations including IBM, HCL Technologies, Forcepoint, and NTT Ltd.

Named among the top 20 most influential CMOs by Forbes, Matt brings a unique boundary-crossing perspective, integrating engineering, marketing, and business insights to help organisations navigate complexity and change.

I had just returned from a vacation in Dubai, energized and ready to fly to Austin, Texas. Ready to re-emerge again as an IT-Executive and excited about the journey ahead. The world is my oyster, so what could go wrong?

What started as a sharp pain in my right ear as the flight descended, led to an urgent ER visit, quickly turned into the kind of "nightmare" one hears about, but usually does not happen to one self. The pain evolved into vertigo, complete loss of balance, almost like motion sickness on steroids and subsequently to an 80%+ hearing loss on my right side. To this day, "I'm on the beach" with a slight ringing in my ears that has not subsided - my constant companion, 24x7. At the time, I couldn't walk straight. I couldn't concentrate, at times struggling to form coherent sentences.

It became increasingly clear that this might be a permanent state of being.

As someone who had been no stranger to sports injuries and surgeries – Achilles, knees, shoulders, concussions – I thought I understood physical challenges. But this was different. I can't even put it into words how profoundly it challenged my entire being, my sense of who I was, my belief in my ability to navigate life's obstacles.

Here was a situation that no amount of strategic planning could have prevented and no degree of mental toughness could simply power through. And in that seemingly desperate situation, a doorway opened into what this book describes as Layer 3 – a fundamental shift in how I related to life itself.

But my journey to that moment had already taken me through the first two layers the author so brilliantly describes.

The Chess Master Phase

When I arrived in the United States as a young immigrant with very little to start with, I quickly learned that survival required a combination of strategic thinking and mental flexibility. Nothing ever played out as planned or anticipated. Like a chess master, I had to predict moves several steps ahead, structure my responses carefully, and often adjust my plans or move to plan B or even plan C. This is what this book identifies as Layer 1 – the Strategic Delta approach to resilience.

I became obsessed with contingency planning. Every personal, every career move, every business decision, every financial choice was mapped out with multiple scenarios. If Plan A failed, I had Plans B through Z ready to deploy. This strategic approach served me well. It helped me build a successful career, navigate complex business environments, and create the kind of security I had not needed growing up.

But life, as it turns out, doesn't always play by the rules of chess.

When Strategy Takes a Punch

Mike Tyson once said, "Everyone has a plan until they get punched in the mouth." I discovered the truth of this statement when I encountered situations that no amount of strategic planning could have anticipated or controlled. Market crashes that defied all predictive models. Personal crises that appeared out of nowhere. Health challenges that couldn't be strategized away.

This forced me to develop what this book calls Layer 2 – mental toughness and flexibility. I had to learn to work with uncertainty instead of fighting it. Rather than being paralyzed when my carefully laid plans crumbled, I developed the capacity to stay present, think clearly under pressure, and find opportunities in chaos.

This layer taught me to make lemonade out of lemons – to transform setbacks into comebacks, obstacles into opportunities. It was a profound evolution from my chess-master approach. I thought I had reached the pinnacle of resilience.

I was wrong.

When Everything Changes in an Instant

In those months of uncertainty following my health crisis, something remarkable happened. My mind, exhausted from years of constant planning and controlling, finally began to quiet. In that silence, something deeper emerged – an inner wisdom, an intuitive knowing that guided me more effectively than any strategic framework ever had.

I began to understand what tennis players experience when they enter "the zone" – that flow state where they play without limits, where action happens effortlessly, where they're no longer fighting the game but dancing with it. I realized that the wave is not separate from the ocean, and that true resilience comes not from resisting life's uncontrollable nature, but from recognizing our fundamental unity with it.

From Lemonade to Never Wasting a Crisis

Everything happens for a reason. This transformation didn't make me passive or fatalistic. Instead, it enhanced every aspect of my leadership and decision-making. I still use strategic thinking, but now it's informed by deeper wisdom. I still apply mental toughness, but it's tempered by acceptance and flow. The integration of all three layers has taken me from merely "making lemonade out of lemons" to "never letting a good crisis go to waste."

More importantly, it has given me access to what the author calls "total resilience" – the kind of *unshakeability* that doesn't depend on controlling outcomes but comes from a deep understanding of who you really are and how life actually works.

Why This Book Matters Now

In our current era of unprecedented change and uncertainty, the old models of resilience are proving inadequate. We need more than just strategic thinking or mental toughness, though both are essential. We need an integrated approach that recognizes the full spectrum of human capacity for navigating challenge and change.

What makes "The Odyssey Equation" extraordinary is its refusal to offer simplistic solutions. The author doesn't promise that life will become easy or that you'll never face difficulties. Instead, he provides a comprehensive framework for developing the kind of resilience that actually works when everything else fails.

The three-layer system isn't theoretical – it's a practical roadmap built on real understanding of how humans actually grow and develop. You can't skip layers or take shortcuts. Each builds upon the previous one, creating a foundation that becomes genuinely unshakeable.

A Personal Invitation

If you're reading this book, chances are you've already discovered that conventional approaches to resilience have their limits. Perhaps you've mastered strategic thinking but found yourself overwhelmed when your plans fell apart. Maybe you've developed mental toughness but still feel like you're fighting life rather than flowing with it.

This book offers something different – a path to total resilience that honors both the practical realities of modern life and the deeper truths about human consciousness and potential. It's an invitation to become not just strategically smart or mentally tough, but truly unshakeable in the most profound sense of the word.

The journey through all three layers isn't always comfortable, but it's absolutely worth it. On the other side lies a freedom and effectiveness that most people never experience – the ability to remain grounded and purposeful regardless of external circumstances.

The author has done something remarkable here: he's created a bridge between ancient wisdom and modern necessity, between practical strategy and profound transformation. This isn't just another book about resilience – it's a comprehensive guide to unlocking the full spectrum of human potential for navigating an uncertain world.

Looking back at my own journey through that health crisis that challenged my entire being, I can honestly say I wish I had this book during those difficult months. It would have provided the roadmap I was desperately seeking – not just for surviving the crisis, but for transforming it into a gateway to deeper wisdom and total resilience.

Thank you for including me in this initiative of sharing true resilience with the world. This book doesn't just offer hope – it offers a proven path forward.

Read it. Apply it. And discover what it truly means to be unshakeable.

Matt Preschern

INTRODUCTION

The Nature of True Resilience

Life doesn't ask for our permission before changing. It doesn't wait until we're ready before presenting challenges, opportunities, or crises. In a world of accelerating complexity and uncertainty, how do we prepare for a future we cannot predict?

We live in an age that worships specialisation. "Find your niche," we're told. "Become the world's expert in an increasingly narrow slice of knowledge." This advice made perfect sense in the 20th century's relatively stable economic landscape. But in today's world, where AI can master specialised tasks with frightening speed and global connections, when a disruption on one side of the planet immediately affects the other, specialisation alone has become a liability.

Enter the modern polymath—not the unreachable ideal of Leonardo da Vinci, but a practical, contemporary version. Today's polymath isn't someone who knows everything about everything, but rather someone who:

- Builds bridges between different domains of knowledge.
- Recognises patterns across seemingly unrelated fields.
- Maintains flexibility in their career and life choices.
- Cultivates diverse networks and perspectives.
- Embraces continuous, curiosity-driven learning.

This book outlines three powerful methods that together form a comprehensive approach to developing the polymath mindset:

1. **Strategic Delta Methods:** Identifying and bridging the gaps between different domains of knowledge and skill to create unique value combinations that can't be easily replicated or automated.
2. **Quantum Rules of Navigation:** Learning to operate effectively in conditions of fundamental uncertainty by developing your ability to think probabilistically, recognise patterns, and maintain multiple perspectives simultaneously.
3. **Quantum Delta:** The integration of the first two methods to create an approach to life and work that's both strategically sound and intuitively responsive allowing you to make calculated leaps into new territories while maintaining your core stability.

I developed these methods through years of working with friends, colleagues, entrepreneurs, artists, and professionals in transition. What began as a set of mentoring and coaching tools evolved into a comprehensive philosophy for navigating our increasingly volatile world. The methods have been battle-tested in real-world conditions and refined through both successes and failures.

But what happens when we expand our perspective? What happens when we realise that even being a polymath with the best strategies may not be enough, that life is bigger than our plans?

This is the three-layer journey we'll explore together:

Layer 1: Strategic Control – Learning to direct your spotlight intentionally through practical methods and strategies.

Layer 2: Mental Preparedness – Recognising that much of the stage remains in darkness and developing the resilience to navigate uncertainty.

Layer 3: Philosophical Transcendence – Realising you are the light itself, transcending the illusion of separation that makes you vulnerable in the first place.

This book offers an answer in the form of an equation: $(\Delta + \Psi) \rightarrow \infty$

It may look like abstract mathematics, but within these three symbols lies a practical, powerful system for navigating any future that finds you.

Δ (Delta) is the symbol mathematicians use to represent change. In our equation, it represents strategic methods—the practical tools, frameworks, and approaches that help us anticipate, plan for, and adapt to change. This is where we begin our journey, by becoming students of change itself, learning to read its patterns and prepare for its movements before they arrive.

Ψ (Psi) is the symbol used in psychology and quantum physics to represent the mind and mental states. In our equation, it represents mental resilience—the internal resources, perspectives, and cognitive flexibility that allow us to remain centered regardless of external circumstances. This is the second stage of our journey, where we turn our attention inward to strengthen the one territory we can truly influence: our own minds.

∞ (Infinity) represents the unlimited and boundless. In our equation, it represents seeing ourselves as waves in an infinite ocean—recognising our connection to something larger than ourselves and finding peace in that recognition. This is where our journey leads, not through direct effort, but through the integration of strategic methods and mental resilience.

The equation tells us something important: we don't achieve infinity through effort alone. Instead, it emerges naturally when we combine delta (strategic methods) and psi (mental resilience). The arrow in the equation (→) represents tendency or approach. We don't conquer infinity—we approach it, gradually and naturally, through the work we do in the first two dimensions.

***

Most books on resilience focus exclusively on Layer 1—giving you tools and tactics without addressing the deeper mindset shifts that truly lead to resilience. Other books might jump straight to Layer 3, offering profound philosophical insights that, while beautiful, can feel impossible to apply in your everyday life.

This book is different. We'll journey through all three layers, giving you practical strategies while progressively deepening your understanding of what it truly means to be unshakeable.

The words in this book are for those who have been told to "pick a lane." For the ever ambitious, creative soul. For the mid-career professional sensing the ground shifting beneath their feet.

For the young planning their future in a world where many of tomorrow's jobs don't exist yet.

And finally, it's for anyone who suspects that the conventional wisdom about career, learning, and success may be dangerously outdated; for those who don't just want to survive in this volatile world—they want to position themselves to thrive because of it.

In the following chapters we'll dive deep into each method, providing concrete examples, practical exercises, and strategic frameworks you can apply immediately. We'll examine real-world case studies of individuals and organisations that embody the unshakeable approach, and we'll tackle real challenges and objections to pursuing the polymath path.

Whether you're facing career transitions, relationship challenges, health concerns, or simply the everyday uncertainty of modern life, *The Odyssey Equation* provides a comprehensive system for becoming not just resilient, but truly prepared for any future that finds you.

Let's begin the journey.

PROLOGUE

Why You Need to Become Unshakeable

The vulnerability of modern life. Rising complexity and uncertainty. Introducing the three-layer solution.

"I don't get it," Jai said, stirring his coffee absently "Some people just seem... unaffected by things that would completely throw me off."

Avika looked up from her notebook. "You mean like Menka from marketing? The way she handled that product launch disaster last month was incredible. While everyone was panicking, she just... navigated through it."

"Exactly!" Jai pointed his spoon at her. "It's not that she doesn't care or doesn't feel things. She just has this... I don't know..."

"Unshakeable quality?" Avika suggested. "Like she can face whatever comes up without losing her centre?"

"Yes! That's it. And I want to understand how to develop that. Because honestly, I'm tired of feeling like I'm at the mercy of whatever life throws at me."

Avika closed her notebook and leaned forward. "I think it's more than just one skill or technique. From what I've observed, it seems to happen in layers."

"Layers?" Jai raised an eyebrow.

"Yes. Like there's a foundation of practical strategies, but then something more on top of that... and maybe something even deeper beneath it all."

THE DANCER δ

The theatre was empty now. The audience had filed out nearly an hour ago, but I lingered, unable to leave after witnessing such a transformative performance. At eighteen, I had never seen contemporary dance that moved me like this—bodies navigating changing patterns of light with such precision and adaptability.

"Did you enjoy the show?"

I turned to find a woman in her sixties watching me from the aisle. Her silver hair was pulled back in a neat bun, and despite her age, she carried herself with the unmistakable posture of a dancer.

"I'm sorry," I stammered. "I should probably go. I just—"

"Stay," she said, sitting several seats away. "I choreographed the piece. I'm always curious about what makes someone remain seated in an empty theatre."

"Your name is Elisa," I said, recognising her from the programme. "The performance was... I don't have the right words for it."

She nodded, seemingly satisfied with my inadequate description.

"I kept thinking about the spotlights," I continued. "How they kept changing, and how the dancers always knew where to go, even when the light shifted unexpectedly."

"That's actually the point of the entire piece," she said, looking genuinely surprised. "Most people focus on the dancers. You focused on the relationship between the dancers and the changing light."

"Is that wrong?"

"Quite the opposite. The piece is called 'Delta' for a reason."

"Like the river delta?" I asked.

"Like the mathematical symbol for change," she corrected. "In calculus, delta represents the difference between two states. It's the fundamental unit of transformation."

I nodded, mathematics had always been my strength.

"The spotlights in my choreography represent the changing circumstances of life," she continued. "They shift constantly, sometimes gradually, sometimes suddenly. The question is: how do we respond to delta? Do we resist it, ignore it, or learn to work with it?"

"The dancers seemed to know where the lights would move before they changed," I observed.

"That's strategic anticipation," she said with a smile. "The first skill of navigating change. The dancers study the patterns of the light, learn to read subtle cues, prepare for multiple possibilities. They don't know exactly where the spotlight will move, but they've developed a relationship with change itself."

"But there were moments when the lights changed randomly," I said. "How did they handle that?"

"By mapping variables and calculating trajectories," she replied. "They know that even seemingly random changes follow patterns if you zoom out far enough. Each dancer recognises the key variables shaping their environment and prepares for various scenarios.

I thought about my own life, how reactive I was to every unexpected change, always caught off guard, always scrambling to adjust.

"The problem for most of us," Elise continued, as if reading my thoughts, "is that we're trying to build permanent solutions in an impermanent world. We want the spotlight to stay fixed, or at least to move in predictable ways. But that's not the nature of life."

"So what's the answer? Just accept that everything constantly changes?"

"Not just accept it—master it," she said. "Delta isn't your enemy. It's the medium you work with, like a sculptor works with clay or a musician works with sound."

She stood, gathering her things.

"The first step in preparing for any future is learning to read the patterns of change," she said. "That's delta. But it's only the beginning of the journey."

"What's the next step?" I asked.

She paused, considering me with a curious expression.

"Perhaps you'll come to my studio sometime and find out," she said, handing me a business card with an address. "The second part requires more than just a conversation."

As she walked away, I looked down at the simple embossed card. Below her name was a single line:

The Odyssey begins with delta, but it doesn't end there.

LAYER 1

STRATEGIC CONTROL

THE DELTA DOMAIN

δ

THE DELTA DOMAIN (Δ)

Change is the only constant. From market fluctuations to technological disruptions, from personal transitions to global transformations, we live in a world defined by delta—the mathematical symbol for change. Yet most of us were never taught how to navigate this fundamental reality.

In this first section, we explore the Delta Domain—the strategic methods that allow us to anticipate, understand, and prepare for change before it arrives. This isn't about prediction in the fortune-telling sense. Rather, it's about developing a mathematical relationship with change itself, learning to read its patterns and calculate its trajectories.

Delta thinking transforms our relationship with the future. Instead of seeing change as a threat to be feared or controlled, we learn to see it as information—valuable data that, when properly analysed, becomes our strategic advantage. Through mapping variables, calculating trajectories, conducting honest diagnostics, and shifting from reaction to anticipation, we build the first part of our equation.

The chapters ahead will equip you with practical frameworks for navigating uncertainty with confidence. As you work through these concepts, remember that mastering delta isn't about eliminating uncertainty—it's about developing a strategic relationship with it. This is where our journey toward preparedness begins.

ONE

The Foundation of Strategic Resilience

Why strategy matters. The limits of reactive thinking. Introducing the Strategic Delta Method.

"So, you're saying the first step is having actual strategies?" Jai asked, spreading papers across Avika's dining table. "I thought becoming 'unshakeable' would be more about mindset or attitude."

Avika pointed to the notes she'd made. "That comes later. But without practical methods to navigate challenges, mindset alone isn't enough. It's like wanting to be calm during a storm while your boat has holes in it."

"Makes sense," Jai nodded. "So, this Strategic Delta Method you mentioned... how exactly does it work?"

"Instead of having just one plan that can fail, you develop multiple viable paths toward your goal," Avika explained, drawing diverging lines on a blank page. "Like a river delta with many channels to the ocean instead of a single vulnerable stream."

Jai stared at the diagram. "I've never approached problems that way. Usually, I just try to find the 'right' solution and stick with it until it either works or fails completely."

"And how's that working out for you?" Avika asked with a knowing smile.

Jai laughed. "Point taken. So strategic resilience isn't about having one perfect plan..."

"It's about having multiple viable paths and the wisdom to navigate between them," Avika finished.

A goal without a plan is just a wish.
– Antoine de Saint-Exupéry

Have you ever watched someone navigate a crisis with such calm competence that it seems almost superhuman? While others panic, they methodically assess the situation, identify options, and take decisive action.

That's the first layer of becoming unshakeable—the ability to strategically respond rather than reactively flail. And the good news? This isn't some inborn talent. It's a set of skills anyone can develop.

Why Strategy Matters?

Let me tell you about two friends who faced the same challenge—unexpected layoffs during an economic downturn.

Priya had no strategic approach. When she lost her job, she immediately fell into panic mode. She frantically applied to dozens of positions regardless of fit, took the first offer that came along (at a significant pay cut), and found herself miserable six months later.

Alex, on the other hand, took three days to process his emotions before developing a strategic response. He assessed his skills, researched growing industries that might value his expertise, reached out to his network with specific requests, and created a system to track applications and follow-ups. Within two months, he had multiple offers and ultimately secured a position with better compensation and growth potential than his previous job.

Same external circumstance, dramatically different outcomes—all because one responded strategically while the other reacted emotionally.

Now, to be clear, emotions aren't the enemy. They provide valuable information and energy. But when emotions drive your actions without strategic consideration, they often lead to short-sighted decisions that create more problems than they solve.

I witnessed this contrast during a leadership offsite of a technology company facing market disruption. Smita, the marketing director, spent the entire first day venting about unfair competition and impossible targets. She was reacting emotionally, which felt temporarily satisfying but produced no actionable direction.

Partha, the operations leader, took a different approach. He acknowledged the challenging circumstances but quickly shifted to a strategic stance: "Given these new market conditions, what options do we have? What unique advantages can we leverage? What specific steps would move us toward stability and growth?"

By the end of the offsite, Partha's team had developed concrete plans while Smita's group was still processing frustration. The contrast couldn't have been clearer—strategic approaches create forward momentum in situations where reactive responses lead to stagnation.

This doesn't mean suppressing emotions or ignoring legitimate concerns. It means channelling the energy of emotions into strategic frameworks that generate effective action rather than circular thinking.

The Limits of Reactive Thinking

Most people live in reactive mode, bouncing from one situation to another without a clear strategic framework. This reactive approach has several critical limitations: *It's emotionally expensive.*

Constantly reacting to circumstances keeps your nervous system in a heightened state, depleting your energy and making clear thinking more difficult.

I saw this play out with a college junior who came to me after nearly burning out as a newly promoted manager. "I'm constantly putting out fires," he told me during our discussion. "Every day brings a new crisis that requires immediate attention. I never get ahead of the problems."

He was stuck in reactive mode, and the toll on his wellbeing was evident—disrupted sleep, persistent anxiety, and diminishing job satisfaction. His emotional resources were depleted by the constant state of reactivity.

It's inherently short-term.

Reactive thinking focuses on immediate relief rather than long-term outcomes. It's like treating symptoms while ignoring the underlying cause.

Gini experienced this limitation in her approach to relationship conflicts. She would react to each disagreement with her partner as an isolated incident, seeking quick resolution without addressing the patterns that generated recurring tensions.

"I was always focused on ending the current argument," she explained. "But I never stepped back to understand why we kept having the same fight in different forms."

This short-term orientation created temporary peace but allowed underlying issues to fester, ensuring that similar conflicts would continue emerging in new disguises.

It surrenders power unnecessarily.

When you're constantly reacting, you position yourself as the effect rather than the cause in your own life story.

Krishna, a small business owner, initially approached market challenges reactively – responding to competitor moves, customer complaints, and economic shifts as if they were forces beyond his influence.

"I felt like a leaf being blown around by winds I couldn't control," he told me. "Every morning I'd wake up wondering what new problem would dictate my day."

This stance unnecessarily surrendered his agency, placing him in a position of weakness even in areas where he could potentially exercise significant influence.

It creates predictable patterns.

Reactive behaviour becomes predictable over time, making you vulnerable to manipulation by those who recognise your patterns.

Shrishti, a negotiation consultant, pointed this out during a corporate training: "When you're purely reactive, you become easy to read—and therefore easy to manage. People learn which buttons to push to get predictable responses from you, which places you at a significant disadvantage in any negotiation or collaborative process."

Manoj, an old friend, who came to me after his business nearly failed, put it this way: "I spent three years playing whack-a-mole with problems. Every day was just reacting to whatever crisis popped up. I was working harder than ever but making no real progress."

This reactive cycle isn't just exhausting—it's fundamentally disempowering. And it's the opposite of being unshakeable.

Introducing the Strategic Delta Method

The Gap Map: Charting Your Delta Territories

In mathematics, the Greek letter delta (Δ) represents change or difference between two values. In the context of becoming unshakeable, your "delta gaps" are the strategic spaces between different domains of knowledge, skill, and experience—spaces that, when bridged, create unique value and resilience.

On a chilly October morning in 2001, Steve Jobs took the stage at Apple's Cupertino headquarters to unveil a new product.

The tech industry was still reeling from the dot-com crash, and most companies were playing it safe. But Jobs wasn't announcing an incremental improvement to existing technology. Instead, he revealed the iPod—a product that would help transform Apple from a struggling computer manufacturer into one of history's most valuable companies.

What made the iPod revolutionary wasn't any single technological breakthrough. Rather, it was Apple's ability to bridge critical delta gaps between previously separate domains: consumer electronics, music distribution, user interface design, and miniature storage technology. While competitors had created MP3 players before, none had successfully integrated these domains into a cohesive experience.

"Creativity is just connecting things," Jobs later explained. "When you ask creative people how they did something, they feel a little guilty because they didn't really do it, they just saw something. It seemed obvious to them after a while. That's because they were able to connect experiences they've had and synthesise new things."

This perspective—that extraordinary value often emerges from connections between domains rather than advancements within them—forms the foundation of the Strategic Delta approach.

The Power of the Gap

Let me introduce you to Mira, whose story illustrates this principle perfectly.

Mira began her career as a nurse, working in intensive care for seven years. When she decided to pursue an MBA, her friends thought she was abandoning her medical knowledge. Instead, Mira specifically focused on healthcare administration and data analytics during her programme.

After graduating, rather than taking a typical hospital management role, she joined a healthcare technology startup developing AI solutions for predicting patient deterioration in ICUs. Her unique combination—clinical experience, business training, and a working understanding of data analytics—made her invaluable in translating between doctors, engineers, and business stakeholders.

When the pandemic hit and the startup struggled, Mira was quickly recruited by a major healthcare system to lead their digital transformation initiatives at twice her previous salary. While specialists in either healthcare or technology were being laid off, Mira's unique position straddling these domains made her more valuable than ever.

The key to Mira's unshakeable career wasn't maximum depth in any single area. It was her strategic position at the intersection of multiple domains—what I call the delta gap.

Let me give you another example, Angela Duckworth, psychologist and author of *Grit: The Power of Passion and Perseverance*, observed a similar pattern in her research on high achievers. "Many of the most successful people I've interviewed combine at least two skills or interests, and their careers live in the intersection," Duckworth notes. This intersectional positioning—developing capability combinations rather than maximum specialisation—creates distinctive value that pure specialists struggle to match.

The Four Types of Delta Gaps

Not all gaps between domains are equally valuable. Through research and working with people over several years, I've identified four types of delta gaps with particular strategic potential:

1. Knowledge Translation Gaps

Gaps between fields where experts need to share knowledge, but don't speak the same language or use the same methods.

Neil deGrasse Tyson exemplifies someone who has built an extraordinary career bridging knowledge translation gaps. While Tyson holds a doctorate in astrophysics—making him a legitimate specialist in that domain—his distinctive value comes from his ability to translate complex scientific concepts for general audiences.

"The good thing about science is that it's true whether or not you believe in it," Tyson famously observed. This perspective—focusing on accessibility rather than complexity—guides his approach to knowledge translation.

Tyson's position in bridging the gap between astrophysics and public understanding has created value that neither pure scientists nor pure communicators could generate independently. This translational capability—making specialised knowledge accessible across domain boundaries—represents one of the most valuable delta gap types.

Similarly, Malcolm Gladwell has built his career bridging gaps between academic research and popular understanding. Though not conducting original research himself, Gladwell's value comes from his ability to identify, synthesise, and translate scientific findings into compelling narratives accessible to general audiences.

"The key to good decision making is not knowledge... it's understanding," Gladwell notes. This distinction—between specialised knowledge and broadly accessible understanding—highlights the value of translation gaps.

2. Innovation Gaps

Spaces where techniques, tools, or ideas from one domain could solve problems in another but haven't yet been applied there.

Elon Musk has repeatedly identified and exploited innovation gaps throughout his career. When founding SpaceX, Musk recognised that approaches from software development and manufacturing could transform space launch technology—a domain that had remained relatively unchanged for decades.

"The path to the CEO's office should not be through the CFO's office, and it should not be through the marketing department. It needs to be through engineering and design," Musk observed. This perspective—prioritising innovation capability over traditional business functions—guides his approach to innovation gaps.

By applying rapid prototyping methodologies, vertical integration, and software-driven design to rocketry, Musk created value that neither traditional aerospace companies nor tech firms could generate independently. This innovation transfer—applying tools and techniques across domain boundaries—represents another valuable delta gap type.

Chef José Andrés similarly bridged innovation gaps when founding World Central Kitchen, which applies restaurant industry logistics and culinary expertise to disaster relief. Traditional disaster response organisations struggled with food quality and distribution efficiency, while restaurants excelled at these challenges in normal conditions. Andrés identified this innovation gap and created extraordinary value by transferring restaurant capabilities to disaster contexts.

"Food relief is not just a meal that keeps hunger away... it's a plate of hope," Andrés explains. This perspective—seeing food service as humanitarian infrastructure rather than mere sustenance—emerged directly from his innovation gap positioning.

3. Integration Gaps

Spaces where multiple specialised functions need to be synthesised into coherent systems or strategies.

Tim Cook's extraordinary success as Apple's CEO demonstrates the value of integration gaps. While Steve Jobs excelled at product vision and design, Cook's distinctive value comes from his ability to integrate diverse functions—supply chain, manufacturing, finance, and retail—into coherent systems that deliver on Apple's product promises.

"We believe that we need to own and control the primary technologies behind the products we make," Cook explains. This perspective—focusing on systematic integration rather than isolated excellence—guides Apple's approach under his leadership.

Cook's position bridging gaps between specialised functions has created value that individual domain experts could not generate independently. This integration capability—synthesising diverse specialties into coherent systems—represents a third valuable delta gap type.

Jessica Jackley similarly bridged integration gaps when co-founding Kiva, which integrates microfinance, social media, and international development into a coherent system for addressing poverty. Traditional development organisations excelled in programme implementation but struggled with direct funding mechanisms, while financial institutions had lending capabilities but limited reach in developing regions. Jackley identified this integration gap and created extraordinary value through systematic combination.

"There is a connection between money and happiness, but it works in surprising ways," Jackley notes. This perspective—seeing financial tools as mechanisms for human connection rather than mere transactions—emerged directly from her integration gap positioning.

4. Experience Gaps

Spaces where lived experience or cultural knowledge creates unique perspectives on professional domains.

Oprah Winfrey's unprecedented media success demonstrates the value of experience gaps. While many media professionals possessed technical broadcasting skills, Winfrey's distinctive value came from combining professional capability with lived experiences that gave her unique perspective on topics affecting her audience.

"Turn your wounds into wisdom," Winfrey advises. This perspective—transforming personal experience into professional insight—guides her approach to experience gaps.

Winfrey's position bridging gaps between professional media and diverse lived experiences created value that neither traditional broadcasters nor community leaders could generate independently. This experiential integration—combining professional capability with personal perspective—represents a fourth valuable delta gap type.

Bryan Stevenson, founder of the Equal Justice Initiative, similarly bridges experience gaps between legal expertise and direct understanding of marginalised communities. Traditional legal advocacy often lacked authentic connection to affected populations, while community organisations sometimes lacked technical legal capabilities. Stevenson identified this experience gap and created extraordinary value through personal integration.

"Each of us is more than the worst thing we've ever done," Stevenson observes. This perspective—seeing legal justice through a humanistic rather than purely procedural lens—emerges directly from his experience gap positioning.

The most valuable delta gaps generally share three characteristics:

- They exist between domains that are related enough to inform each other but separate enough that few people bridge them.
- They involve domains experiencing significant change or growth.
- They connect areas where miscommunication or lack of integration creates substantial costs.

Finding Your Unique Delta Gaps

Identifying your potential delta gaps begins with mapping your current knowledge, skills, and experiences. But not in the traditional "skills inventory" approach that produces generic lists. Instead, ask yourself these more revealing questions:

Q1. What domains do you have insider knowledge of?

Not just what you know, but where you understand the unstated rules, language, and culture.

Howard Schultz's transformation of Starbucks emerged directly from his insider knowledge across multiple domains. While working for a housewares company selling coffee equipment, Schultz developed insider understanding of both American retail and Italian coffee culture. This unique combination—seeing opportunities invisible to those with single-domain insider knowledge—allowed him to reimagine coffee retail in ways that created extraordinary value.

"Risk more than others think is safe. Dream more than others think is practical," Schultz advises. This perspective—taking calculated risks based on cross-domain insight—emerges from recognising unique insider knowledge combinations.

Q2. Where do you regularly notice miscommunication or missed opportunities between experts?

Dr. Atul Gawande identified his delta gap when he noticed persistent miscommunication between surgical specialists that created life-threatening errors. Despite being a surgeon himself, Gawande recognised that the problem wasn't insufficient expertise but rather inadequate integration between specialised domains.

"Better is possible. It does not take genius. It takes diligence. It takes moral clarity. It takes ingenuity. And above all, it takes a willingness to try," Gawande explains. This perspective—focusing on systematic improvement rather than individual brilliance—guided his development of surgical checklists that dramatically reduced complications and mortality.

Gawande's position bridging gaps between surgical specialties, systems thinking, and communication created value that pure medical specialists could not generate independently. This integration—systematising coordination across specialised domains—emerged directly from noticing miscommunication patterns.

Q3. What problems do you understand differently because of your unique combination of experiences?

Sara Blakely's creation of Spanx emerged directly from her unique combination of experiences. Having worked as a fax machine salesperson while performing stand-up comedy on the side, Blakely brought outsider perspective to women's apparel—a domain dominated by industry veterans with traditional fashion backgrounds.

"Don't be intimidated by what you don't know. That can be your greatest strength and ensure that you do things differently from everyone else," Blakely advises. This perspective—treating the outsider's viewpoint as an advantage rather than a limitation—shaped her revolutionary approach to shapewear.

Blakely's position bridging gaps between consumer experience, sales knowledge, and product development created value that fashion industry specialists failed to generate despite greater domain expertise. This experiential combination—seeing opportunities invisible to single-domain experts—represents another valuable delta gap identification approach.

Q4. What unusual juxtapositions exist in your background that others might consider unrelated?

Lin-Manuel Miranda's creation of *Hamilton* emerged directly from unusual juxtapositions in his background. By combining deep knowledge of hip-hop music with passion for American history—domains rarely connected—Miranda created a revolutionary theatrical experience that neither traditional composers nor historians could have envisioned.

"I think the most interesting art comes from people who are exploring different lanes at the same time," Miranda observes. This perspective—deliberately cultivating unusual domain combinations—guides his creative approach.

Miranda's position bridging gaps between contemporary music, traditional theater, and historical narrative created value that specialists in any single domain could not generate independently. This juxtapositional thinking—connecting seemingly unrelated fields—represents a powerful delta gap identification approach.

Q5. In what contexts have you been the "translator" between different types of experts?

Brené Brown's extraordinary impact emerged from her position as translator between academic research and practical application. As a social work researcher studying vulnerability and shame, Brown initially presented her findings in traditional academic formats. Her breakthrough came when she began translating this research into accessible frameworks that resonated with diverse audiences.

"Vulnerability is not winning or losing; it's having the courage to show up and be seen when we have no control over the outcome,"

Brown explains. This perspective—focusing on human connection rather than academic precision—guides her translational approach.

Brown's position bridging gaps between rigorous research and practical application created value that neither pure academics nor self-help authors could generate independently. This translational capability—making specialised knowledge actionable across domains—represents another valuable delta gap identification approach.

The Delta Gap Canvas

To help identify your most promising delta gaps, I've developed a simple but powerful visual tool called the Delta Gap Canvas. Draw three overlapping circles representing:

1. Your Knowledge Domains: Fields where you have formal training or substantial self-education
2. Your Experiential Background: Industries, cultures, and environments you've been immersed in
3. Your Skills & Abilities: What you can actually do (as opposed to what you know in theory)

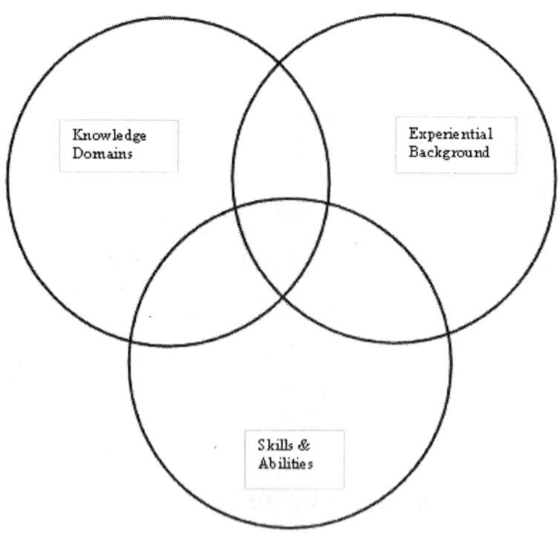

In the areas where these circles overlap, list the specific elements from each category that combine in interesting ways. These intersections often reveal your most promising delta gaps.

***

Case Study: Rajat's Delta Gap Canvas

For example, consider Rajat—an engineer at a technology company with prior experience in marketing and investment banking, who began his career on the assembly line of an automobile company.

His educational qualifications apart from his engineering degree also include an MBA and a LLB degree. He also has certifications in human psychology and basic philosophy.

The Venn-diagram shows an example of Delta Gaps between knowledge, experience, and skills, for Rajat.

Knowledge domains are engineering, business, laws, psychology, philosophy, spirituality.

Experiential background is technology marketing, corporate strategy, investment banking, production operations.

Skills are counselling, mentoring, writing, public speaking.

Intersection of Knowledge and Experience:

- Business Strategy Consulting
- Technical Writing/Documentation
- IP/Patent Strategy
- Change Management
- Production Engineering

Intersection of Knowledge and Skills:

- Educational Content Creation
- Ethics Training
- Personal Development Coaching
- Philosophical Writing
- Technical Communication

Intersection of Experience and Skills:

- Executive Coaching
- Marketing Communication
- Leadership Development
- Financial Advisory
- Operations Training

Intersection of Knowledge, Experience, and Skills:

- Tech Ethics Consulting
- Business Transformation Leadership
- Financial/Business Education
- Corporate Wellbeing Programs
- Technical Leadership Development

Let's take a moment to understand the elements emerging out of intersections and the logic for those:

a) Knowledge ∩ Experience (without Skills)

1. Business Strategy Consulting: Leveraging your business knowledge and corporate strategy experience.
2. Technical Writing/Documentation: Combining engineering knowledge with technology marketing.

3. IP/Patent Strategy: Using your legal knowledge in technology contexts.
4. Change Management: Applying psychology knowledge to corporate strategy.
5. Production Engineering: Engineering knowledge applied to production operations.

b) Knowledge ∩ Skills (without Experience)

1. Educational Content Creation: Converting your knowledge domains into written/spoken content.
2. Ethics Training: Philosophy knowledge combined with mentoring and public speaking.
3. Personal Development Coaching: Psychology and spirituality knowledge with counselling skills.
4. Philosophical Writing: Your philosophy knowledge expressed through writing.
5. Technical Communication: Engineering knowledge paired with writing/speaking skills.

c) Experience ∩ Skills (without Knowledge)

1. Executive Coaching: Using corporate strategy experience with counselling/mentoring skills.
2. Marketing Communication: Technology marketing experience with writing/speaking skills.
3. Leadership Development: Corporate strategy experience with mentoring skills.
4. Financial Advisory: Investment banking experience with counselling skills.
5. Operations Training: Production operations experience with mentoring/speaking skills.

d) Knowledge ∩ Experience ∩ Skills (central overlap)

1. Tech Ethics Consulting: Engineering/philosophy + technology experience + counselling/speaking.

2. Business Transformation Leadership: Business knowledge + corporate strategy + mentoring/speaking.
3. Financial/Business Education: Business/laws + investment banking + writing/speaking.
4. Corporate Wellbeing Programmes: Psychology/spirituality + corporate experience + counselling.
5. Technical Leadership Development: Engineering + operations experience + mentoring/speaking.

These intersections reveal Rajat's most promising differentiated opportunities where you can leverage unique combinations of your knowledge, experience, and skills to create distinctive value.

Let's take an example of Dr. Paul Farmer, who revolutionised global health through Partners in Health. Farmer combined medical knowledge (infectious disease expertise), experiential background (immersion in Haitian communities), and unique skills (cross-cultural communication and systems design) to create healthcare delivery models that traditional medical specialists could not envision.

"The idea that some lives matter less is the root of all that is wrong with the world," Farmer observed. This perspective—seeing health through both medical and social justice lenses simultaneously—emerged directly from his position at the intersection of multiple domains.

Farmer's unique location on the delta gap canvas—where medical knowledge, cultural experience, and systems thinking overlapped—created value far beyond what specialised expertise in any single domain could have produced.

For example, a former colleague named Chetan mapped:

- Knowledge Domains: Computer science, environmental science
- Experiential Background: Growing up in rural Mexico, Silicon Valley tech culture

- Skills & Abilities: Programming, data visualisation, storytelling

In the overlaps, he identified potential delta gaps including "using technology to address agricultural challenges in developing regions" and "communicating environmental data to non-technical stakeholders through visual storytelling."

Chetan eventually established a consulting practice that helps environmental nonprofits harness data and technology, positioning himself at this high-value intersection.

Evaluating Strategic Potential

Not all identified delta gaps are worth pursuing. To evaluate which have the greatest strategic potential, assess them against these four criteria:

1. Scarcity: How few people currently bridge this particular gap?

When evaluating delta gap scarcity, consider not just the rarity of individual components but the combination itself. Many people have healthcare experience, and many have data science skills, but few possess both with sufficient depth to create meaningful integration.

Whitney Wolfe Herd identified a scarce delta gap when founding Bumble. While many executives had experience in either technology platform development or women's social dynamics, Herd's distinctive value came from deeply understanding both domains simultaneously. This scarce combination—technical capability paired with gendered social insight—allowed Bumble to create dating app features that competitors hadn't envisioned.

"I always say that you can't be what you can't see," Herd notes. This perspective—recognising how representation shapes possibility—guided her identification of a scarce but valuable delta gap.

2) Demand Trajectory: Is the need for this particular integration growing, stable, or declining?

When evaluating demand trajectory, consider not just current value but directional change. Some delta gaps may have limited present value but rapidly increasing importance as domains evolve.

Andrew Ng recognised a delta gap with extraordinary demand trajectory when he began connecting machine learning with practical business applications. While many researchers possessed theoretical AI knowledge, and many executives understood business needs, Ng's distinctive value came from bridging these domains just as technological capabilities were making practical applications viable.

"AI is the new electricity," Ng observes. This perspective—seeing how fundamental technological shifts create integration opportunities—guided his identification of a delta gap with explosive demand trajectory.

3) Transferability: If conditions change, how adaptable are the integration skills you'll develop?

When evaluating transferability, consider whether the integration capabilities themselves—not just the specific domain knowledge—would retain value in different contexts.

Arianna Huffington demonstrated transferability when pivoting from political commentary to digital media to wellness technology. While the specific domains changed, her integration capabilities—connecting cultural insight with audience development, content creation, and business strategy—retained value across these transitions.

"We need to accept that we won't always make the right decisions—that sometimes we'll mess up badly. Failure isn't the opposite of success; it's a part of it," Huffington explains. This perspective—seeing integrative learning across attempts rather than binary outcomes—guides effective transferability assessment.

4) Personal Engagement: How deeply interested are you in both sides of this gap?

The last criterion is particularly important. Becoming truly unshakeable requires sustained learning and adaptation. This is far easier when you're genuinely interested in the domains you're bridging.

José Andrés exemplifies this principle through his work bridging culinary arts and humanitarian response. While these domains might seem unrelated, Andrés' deep personal engagement with both food and social justice created sustainable motivation that purely strategic considerations couldn't maintain.

"Food relief is not just a meal that keeps hunger away... it's a plate of hope," Andrés explains. This perspective—finding personal meaning in domain integration—sustains engagement through inevitable challenges.

Based on these criteria, we could start developing a view of which strategic delta gap should Rajat start pursuing. While we don't know his personal inclination, we can take a view based on scarcity, the market demand trajectory, and transferability potential.

From Gap Analysis to Strategic Action

Once you've identified promising delta gaps, the next step is developing a strategic plan to position yourself within them. This doesn't mean abandoning your existing expertise—rather, it means strategically expanding in directions that create valuable combinations. There are three primary approaches:

1. The Adjacent Expansion: Building knowledge or skills in a domain closely related to your current expertise, creating immediate combinatorial value.

Reid Hoffman exemplifies adjacent expansion through his career development. After leadership experience at PayPal, Hoffman could have specialised further in payments technology. Instead, he strategically expanded into social networks—a domain adjacent to his existing expertise—creating LinkedIn as a professional connection platform that payments specialists couldn't envision.

"The fastest way to change yourself is to hang out with people who are already the way you want to be," Hoffman advises. This relational perspective—using social connections to accelerate capability development—guides effective adjacent expansion.

The financial analyst learning data science to enhance financial modelling, the teacher acquiring video production skills to create educational content, and the architect studying psychology to design for human experience—all exemplify adjacent expansion strategies.

2. The Strategic Leap: Acquiring knowledge or experience in a seemingly unrelated field that, when combined with your current expertise, creates unexpected value.

Stewart Butterfield exemplifies strategic leaping through his unusual career path. Originally trained in philosophy, Butterfield entered technology development and eventually founded Slack—a company valued at $27 billion when acquired by Salesforce. His philosophical background, seemingly unrelated to software development, actually provided distinctive perspective on communication patterns that shaped Slack's revolutionary approach.

"The experience of the team and the character of the people is just as important as their talents," Butterfield observes. This humanistic perspective—seeing technology through philosophical rather than purely technical lens—emerged directly from his strategic leap across domains.

The lawyer studying design thinking to create innovative legal service delivery, the engineer developing public speaking skills to lead organisational change, or the healthcare provider studying business strategy to transform service delivery models all exemplify strategic leap approaches.

3. The Excavation: Formalising and developing "hidden" knowledge you already possess from past experiences or personal interests.

Issa Rae exemplifies excavation through her groundbreaking series Insecure. Rather than pursuing traditional entertainment industry paths, Rae formalised her observational knowledge of Black women's experiences into the web series *The Misadventures of Awkward Black Girl,* which eventually led to her HBO success.

"I'm rooting for everybody Black," Rae famously stated. This perspective—explicitly centering experiences often marginalised in mainstream entertainment—guided her excavation of hidden knowledge into formal creative expression.

The marketing executive with a lifelong gaming hobby developing expertise in gamification strategies for consumer engagement, the finance professional with immigrant experience creating cross-cultural financial literacy programs, or the software developer with musical background designing unique audio interfaces all exemplify excavation approaches.

For most people, the adjacent expansion offers the most immediate returns, while strategic leaps create more distinctive long-term positioning. The ideal approach often combines elements of all three, creating a unique constellation of capabilities that evolves over time.

Beyond Skills: The Identity Shift

Perhaps the most challenging aspect of bridging delta gaps isn't acquiring new knowledge—it's expanding your identity to encompass multiple domains without feeling like an impostor in any of them.

Traditional career advice encourages clear, singular professional identities: "I'm a lawyer" or "I'm an engineer." The delta gap approach requires comfort with more complex identities: "I bridge legal and design thinking to create more human-centered compliance systems."

This identity shift from specialist to integrator can be psychologically challenging. Many people feel they don't have "permission" to claim expertise across domains, or worry they'll be seen as dilettantes.

The reality is quite different. Research by organisational psychologists shows that those who successfully integrate multiple domains often gain rather than lose credibility—precisely because their unique positioning makes them irreplaceable in specific contexts.

Indra Nooyi navigated this identity shift successfully throughout her career. Rising from product manager to CEO of PepsiCo, Nooyi consistently resisted narrow specialist identity in favour of integrative self-definition.

"Just because you are CEO, don't think you have landed. You must continually increase your learning, the way you think, and the way you approach the organisation," Nooyi advises. This developmental perspective—seeing identity as evolving integration rather than fixed specialisation—guides effective delta gap positioning.

Similarly, Partha Chang transformed the culinary world by refusing traditional chef identity constraints. Combining formal culinary training with authentic Asian-American cultural experience and disruptive entrepreneurial approach, Chang created Momofuku—a restaurant group that redefined contemporary dining.

"I've learned, as a rule of thumb, never to ask whether you can do something. Say, instead, that you are doing it. Then fasten your seat belt," Chang suggests.

This action orientation—defining identity through integration activity rather than prior permission—characterises successful delta gap navigators.

I first witnessed the power of this approach when working with Sagar, an entrepreneur whose primary business had been devastated by regulatory changes. When we met, he was oscillating between denial and despair—either believing the changes wouldn't really affect him or feeling that his business was doomed.

"I've spent twelve years building this company," he told me during our initial consultation. "I can't imagine doing anything else, but I don't see how we survive these new regulations."

Instead of focusing on his existing business model (a single vulnerable path), we developed a delta of possibilities—multiple channels that could lead toward his broader goal of creating value in his industry.

"What if instead of seeing this as the end of your business, we view it as a forced evolution?" I suggested. "Let's create multiple potential paths forward rather than trying to preserve a single approach that's becoming increasingly vulnerable."

Over the following weeks, Sagar developed three distinct strategic directions:

1. Modifying his current business model to comply with new regulations.

2. Developing a complementary service that wasn't affected by the regulatory changes.
3. Creating a consulting practice to help others navigate the new regulatory landscape.

The key insight was developing these paths simultaneously rather than sequentially. Instead of putting all his energy into saving his existing model (Path 1), Sagar allocated resources to all three directions, allowing them to develop in parallel.

When it became clear that the modified business model (Path 1) would be significantly less profitable under new regulations, Sagar wasn't devastated. He had already made progress on Paths 2 and 3, which were showing promising results. Within a year, his business had transformed into a hybrid model combining elements of all three paths—more resilient and ultimately more profitable than his original approach.

"If I had focused exclusively on saving my original business model, I would have fought a losing battle until I ran out of resources," Sagar reflected. "By developing multiple paths simultaneously, I discovered opportunities I couldn't have seen from my initial perspective."

This is the essence of the Strategic Delta Method—creating multiple viable channels toward your goals rather than relying on a single vulnerable path.

The Strategic Delta Method has Four Core Components:

Situation Assessment

Before taking action, accurately assess your current reality. This seems obvious, but most people skip this step, operating on assumptions rather than facts.

Effective assessment includes:

- Gathering objective data rather than relying solely on perceptions.
- Identifying key stakeholders and their interests.
- Recognising both constraints and resources.
- Honestly evaluating your own role in creating the current situation.

When Salina's small business was losing money, her initial assumption was that she needed more customers. But when she performed a proper situation assessment, she discovered something surprising: her most profitable clients were actually a small subset of her customer base. The majority of customers were costing her money due to high service demands and low profit margins.

This accurate assessment completely changed her strategy. Instead of pursuing more customers, she restructured her offerings to attract more of the profitable client type while gracefully transitioning away from the unprofitable ones.

"Without that honest assessment, I would have worked harder to acquire more of the very customers who were draining my resources," Salina told me. "Taking time to really understand the situation rather than rushing to solutions was critical."

Outcome Definition

Many people jump straight to solutions without clearly defining what "success" actually looks like. This is like setting off on a journey without a destination in mind—you'll certainly go somewhere, but it's unlikely to be where you actually want to be.

Effective outcome definition:

- Focuses on end results rather than methods
- Includes measurable criteria for success
- Considers both short-term and long-term horizons
- Aligns with your deeper values and priorities

Brajesh, an IT manager facing a major system migration, initially defined his goal simply as "complete the migration with minimal disruption." But when pressed to define his desired outcome more precisely, he realised several additional criteria were important: maintaining security standards, creating documentation for future migrations, and using the opportunity to train junior team members.

This clearer outcome definition led to a completely different approach to the project—one that accomplished the technical goal while also building team capability and organisational knowledge.

"By defining success more comprehensively, I realised the project wasn't just about moving systems but about strengthening our entire IT foundation," Brajesh explained. "This broader definition guided decisions throughout the process in ways my initial narrow focus wouldn't have."

Pathway Multiplication

This is where the "delta" concept really comes alive. Instead of identifying a single path forward, deliberately develop multiple viable approaches.

Most people naturally gravitate toward the first workable solution they find. This is a cognitive bias called "satisficing"—settling for the first satisfactory solution rather than exploring potentially better options.

Strategic thinkers, by contrast, force themselves to develop multiple pathways even when the first option seems perfectly adequate.

When Aisha was considering a career change from engineering to design, her initial plan was straightforward: get an advanced degree in her desired field, then seek entry-level positions. But by applying pathway multiplication, she identified three additional approaches: 1) leveraging her existing skills in a transitional role that bridged both industries, 2) starting with project-based work to build a portfolio without additional credentials, and 3) partnering with an established professional to create a joint venture.

By exploring all four pathways simultaneously rather than committing to just one, she discovered that the third option—project-based work—yielded results much faster than her original plan would have.

"If I had committed to my original plan of getting another degree, I would have spent two years and significant money before making any progress," Aisha told me. "By developing multiple pathways, I discovered a much more efficient route to my goal."

Strategic Execution

The final component transforms planning into results through disciplined implementation. Strategic execution includes:

- Breaking chosen pathways into concrete next actions.
- Establishing clear timelines and accountability measures.
- Building in regular review points to assess progress.
- Developing specific triggers for pathway adjustment or abandonment.

This last point is crucial. Many people develop plans but then stick with them long after it's clear they're not working. Strategic execution includes predetermined conditions for when to persist, when to adjust, and when to abandon a particular approach altogether.

Jasdeep, a product manager, built this directly into his launch plan for a new software feature. The plan included specific metrics that would trigger different responses: if adoption reached a certain threshold by a specific date, the team would accelerate development; if adoption fell below a different threshold, they would gather user feedback and make adjustments; and if adoption remained extremely low despite adjustments, they had a predefined point at which they would sunset the feature and reallocate resources.

"Having these decision triggers defined in advance made difficult decisions much clearer when the time came," Jasdeep explained. "We didn't waste time debating what to do because we'd already established the conditions for different responses while we were thinking clearly, before emotional investment clouded our judgment."

This strategic execution approach meant that emotions and sunk costs didn't drive decisions—clear, predetermined criteria did.

Building Your Strategic Foundation

The Strategic Delta Method forms the cornerstone of Layer 1: Resilience. It provides a structured framework for navigating complex situations without being at the mercy of circumstance or emotional reactivity.

As you integrate this method into your approach to challenges, you'll develop what I call "strategic intuition"—the ability to naturally think in terms of multiple possibilities rather than linear progressions. This capacity becomes a fundamental aspect of resilience, allowing you to navigate uncertainty with confidence rather than anxiety.

Menka, a leadership consultant who adopted this method after a period of career uncertainty, described its impact: "Developing multiple pathways fundamentally changed my relationship with uncertainty. Instead of seeing the unknown as a threat, I began to view it as a field of possibilities where multiple viable options could emerge. This shift didn't just change my external results—it transformed my internal experience from anxiety to confident exploration."

This shift from reactive to strategic thinking doesn't happen overnight. It requires deliberate practice and a willingness to challenge habitual patterns. But with consistent application, these approaches become second nature—a foundation of resilience that serves across diverse situations.

In the next chapter, we'll explore how to apply the Strategic Delta Method to specific situations across different domains of life—from career transitions to relationship challenges to health goals—giving you concrete tools to immediately enhance your ability to shape circumstances rather than being shaped by them.

TWO

Strategic Delta in Action

Identifying critical paths. Creating multiple contingencies. Practical applications in career, relationships, and health.

"I'm trying to apply this multiple-path approach to my career situation," Jai said, spreading three documents on the coffee shop table. "Path one: negotiate for the position I want in my current company. Path two: develop specialised skills for a lateral move to the Thompson project. Path three: build my consulting credentials for potential independent work."

Avika looked impressed. "You're actually doing it! But the real question is—are you pursuing these simultaneously or just keeping them as backup plans?"

Jai frowned. "Is there a difference?"

"Huge difference," Avika said, pointing to his documents. "Backup plans only activate after your main plan fails—which means lost time and momentum. Strategic Delta means advancing all viable paths simultaneously, even if at different paces."

"That sounds... exhausting," Jai admitted.

"Less exhausting than starting from scratch after a single plan fails," Avika countered. "Besides, I've noticed these paths often support each other in unexpected ways."

"Like how?" Jai asked.

"Well, developing consulting credentials might actually strengthen your negotiating position at your current job," Avika pointed out. "And specialised skills for the Thompson project could enhance your consulting portfolio. They're not isolated—they're interconnected."

Jai sat back, considering. "So rather than hedging my bets, I'm creating a network of possibilities that strengthen each other..."

"Exactly. Now you're thinking in deltas rather than lines."

In the previous chapter, we introduced the Strategic Delta Method as the foundation of Layer 1: Resilience. Now it's time to see this approach in action—applying these principles to real-world situations across different domains of life.

The beauty of the Strategic Delta Method is its versatility. Whether you're navigating career transitions, relationship challenges, health goals, or financial decisions, the same framework applies. Let's explore practical applications that you can adapt to your specific circumstances.

Identifying Critical Paths

The first step in applying Strategic Delta is identifying the critical paths—the essential routes that lead toward your desired outcome. This isn't about finding a single "correct" path but recognising multiple viable routes.

I witnessed the power of this approach while working with Menka, whose tech startup failed after two years of intensive effort. When we first met, she was devastated. She had poured everything into one approach, and when it didn't succeed, she felt completely lost.

"I feel like I've hit a dead end," she told me during our initial session, her voice heavy with disappointment. "I invested everything in this one path, and now I have no idea where to go next."

"That's precisely the limitation of single-path thinking," I replied. "When that one route is blocked, it feels like there's nowhere to go. But what if we develop multiple paths toward your broader goals?"

As we explored Menka's deeper motivations, we discovered that her ultimate aim wasn't specifically to run a startup but to create innovative solutions in her field. With this broader goal in mind, we mapped out three distinct approaches:

1. Joining an established company in an innovation role.
2. Partnering with a complementary founder for a new venture.
3. Consulting while developing a scaled-down version of her original concept.

"The key," I explained, "is to develop these paths simultaneously rather than sequentially. Don't put all your energy into Path 1 and only explore Path 2 if the first one fails. Advance all three in parallel, even if at different paces."

Menka embraced this approach, allocating specific time each week to developing all three paths. She updated her resume and began networking for corporate innovation roles (Path 1), created a list of potential co-founders with complementary skills (Path 2), and reached out to her network about consulting opportunities (Path 3).

Within weeks, this multi-path approach began yielding unexpected synergies. A consulting conversation led to an introduction to a potential co-founder. An interview for a corporate role revealed industry needs that informed how she refined her product concept.

"I had defined success so narrowly that when that specific path didn't work out, I had no alternatives," Menka explained in a follow-up session. "It was like driving with blinders on—when my road ended, I couldn't see any other ways forward. Now I have multiple routes developing simultaneously, and they're actually strengthening each other in ways I never anticipated."

By developing these paths simultaneously rather than sequentially, Menka created a delta of possibilities rather than a single vulnerable pathway. When her consulting work unexpectedly connected her with a potential partner who shared her vision, she was prepared to recognise and develop this opportunity precisely because she wasn't fixated on a single route.

> *Try This:* For an important goal you're pursuing, map at least three completely different paths that could lead to success. These shouldn't be minor variations but fundamentally distinct approaches. For each path, identify the first three concrete actions you could take to begin exploring it.

Creating Multiple Contingencies

Beyond developing multiple primary paths, Strategic Delta involves creating contingencies for when obstacles arise. This isn't pessimistic thinking—it's realistic preparation that creates resilience.

Rishabh implemented this approach when planning a career transition from corporate finance to entrepreneurship. Rather than simply quitting his job to launch his business (a single vulnerable path), he created contingencies at multiple levels.

"I think I'm ready to leave my job and start my own business," he told me during our first coaching session. His excitement was palpable, but so was a subtle undercurrent of anxiety.

"That's an exciting step," I acknowledged. "Before you make the leap, let's develop some contingency plans—not because I doubt your success, but because creating backup options actually allows you to take bold steps with greater confidence."

Together, we developed a network of contingencies:

Financial Contingencies

Primary Path: Business reaches profitability within six months.

- Contingency 1: Part-time consulting work if profitability timeline extends.

- Contingency 2: Specific savings threshold that would trigger a re-evaluation.
- Contingency 3: Pre-arranged possibility to return to former employer if needed.

Market Reception Contingencies

Primary Path: Initial service offering gains traction

- Contingency 1: Alternative service package ready if primary doesn't resonate.
- Contingency 2: Different market segment identified if original target doesn't respond.
- Contingency 3: Pivot plan developed if entire concept needs rethinking.

I also encouraged Rishabh to define specific triggers for each contingency—objective conditions that would activate these backup plans rather than subjective feelings that might lead to premature abandonment or stubborn persistence.

"If monthly revenue hasn't reached $3,000 by the four-month mark, I'll activate the consulting contingency," Rishabh decided. "If I haven't signed at least five clients within the first three months, I'll introduce the alternative service package. And if my savings drop below $15,000, I'll have a serious conversation with my former employer."

These predefined triggers meant Rishabh wouldn't have to make difficult decisions under the emotional pressure of the moment. The contingency network meant that when his business took longer than expected to become profitable, Rishabh didn't face a binary succeed-or-fail scenario. He activated his consulting contingency, which not only provided income but ultimately led to valuable client relationships for his main business.

"Having these contingencies in place gave me the confidence to take the leap," Rishabh explained during a follow-up session six months later. "I knew that even if things didn't go according to plan—and they definitely didn't—I wouldn't crash. I'd have multiple ways to adjust course."

This contingency planning doesn't diminish your commitment to success. On the contrary, it enables bolder action precisely because you've created safety nets that allow you to take calculated risks.

> *Real-World Application:* For an important initiative in your life, identify the three most likely challenges you might encounter. For each potential obstacle, develop at least two specific contingency responses. Then set clear triggers—objective conditions that would activate each contingency rather than leaving it to subjective judgment in the moment.

Practical Applications in Career

The job market has transformed dramatically in recent decades. The concept of a straightforward, predictable career path has given way to a more complex landscape of constant change, disruption, and opportunity. This environment makes Strategic Delta particularly valuable.

Priya applied these principles when her industry began experiencing significant technological disruption. Rather than clinging to a traditional career path that was becoming increasingly vulnerable, she developed a delta of possibilities.

"I've built my career in this industry for fifteen years," Priya told me during our first session. "But these new technologies are eliminating roles like mine. I'm worried about my future."

"Instead of seeing this as a threat to a single career path, what if we develop multiple potential directions?" I suggested. "Let's create a career delta that gives you several viable options as the industry evolves."

Together, we mapped three distinct paths:

Path 1: Vertical Advancement: Continuing in her current company but focusing on developing skills that would remain relevant despite automation trends.
Path 2: Horizontal Expansion: Building expertise in an adjacent field where her existing knowledge would be valuable but wouldn't face the same technological threats.
Path 3: Entrepreneurial Venture: Developing a specialised consulting practice addressing the transition challenges her industry was facing.

Instead of pursuing these paths sequentially (the traditional approach), Priya advanced them simultaneously. She sought projects within her company that built relevant skills, took courses in the adjacent field on evenings and weekends, and began developing relationships that could support a consulting practice.

When her company unexpectedly announced layoffs, Priya wasn't devastated—she had already made progress on multiple paths. She accelerated her consulting plan, leveraging both her traditional expertise and her newly acquired adjacent skills.

"If I had waited until the layoffs to start developing alternatives, I would have been competing with everyone else from my company for the same opportunities," she noted during our follow-up conversation. "By creating my delta in advance, I was six months ahead of where I otherwise would have been."

This approach transforms career vulnerability into opportunity—not through wishful thinking but through strategic development of multiple viable paths.

Try This: In your career context, identify skills or relationships you could develop now that would support multiple possible future paths. Focus particularly on "intersection skills" that would be valuable across different potential directions rather than only on a single track.

Practical Applications in Relationships

Relationships present unique strategic challenges. Unlike career or finance, they involve another person with their own intentions, perceptions, and autonomy. Yet Strategic Delta principles can still create more resilient connections.

Jaimin and Leila applied this approach to address communication issues that had created recurring conflicts in their marriage. When they first came to me for couples counselling, they were frustrated by their inability to break negative patterns despite genuine effort from both sides.

"We keep having the same fights in different forms," Jaimin explained during our initial session. "We try to resolve each specific issue, but the underlying pattern just emerges in new ways."

"Rather than focusing on individual conflicts, let's develop multiple paths toward improved communication," I suggested. "Instead of putting all your energy into a single approach that might not work for both of you, let's create several routes toward your shared goal."

Together, we developed three distinct pathways:

Path 1: Structured Communication: Implementing specific tools like scheduled check-ins, speaker-listener techniques, and predetermined "timeouts" during heated moments.

Path 2: Individual Development: Each partner working with a therapist on personal patterns that contributed to communication breakdowns, independent of the relationship dynamics.

Path 3: Environmental Design: Modifying their physical and digital environments to reduce stress triggers that often preceded conflicts (including work schedule adjustments, space reconfiguration, and technology boundaries).

By pursuing these approaches simultaneously rather than sequentially, Jaimin and Leila created synergies that wouldn't have emerged from a single-path approach. Their individual therapy work (Path 2) helped them utilise the structured communication tools more effectively (Path 1), while their environmental adjustments (Path 3) created conditions where both other approaches could succeed more easily.

"Before, we'd try one approach until it failed, then try something else," Jaimin explained during a follow-up session three months later. "This created a pattern of repeated disappointment. With multiple paths developing simultaneously, we could see progress somewhere even when we faced setbacks in other areas."

This multi-path approach creates resilience in relationships by ensuring that obstacles on any single path don't derail your overall progress toward connection and understanding.

> *Real-World Application:* For a relationship challenge you're facing (romantic, family, friendship, or professional), identify at least three distinct approaches that could improve the situation. For each approach, define a specific action you could take within the next 48 hours to begin developing that path.

Practical Applications in Health

Health goals often fail due to single-path thinking. We fixate on one approach—a particular diet, exercise regimen, or medication—and when that path encounters obstacles, progress stalls. Strategic Delta offers a more robust alternative.

Smita applied this method to address chronic fatigue that had resisted previous solutions. When we first met, she was frustrated by her lack of progress despite trying numerous approaches sequentially.

"I've tried everything," she told me, the exhaustion evident in her voice. "Special diets, supplement regimens, different medical approaches. Each one seems promising initially, but then either stops working or creates new problems."

"Instead of pursuing one approach at a time, what if we develop multiple paths simultaneously?" I suggested. "This would give us several routes toward improvement rather than betting everything on a single method."

Together, we developed three distinct paths:

Path 1: Physiological Optimisation: Working with medical professionals on hormone balance, nutrient levels, and sleep quality. This included specific testing protocols and targeted interventions based on results.

Path 2: Energy Management: Implementing systems to track, conserve, and strategically deploy her limited energy. This included activity logging, energy-based scheduling, and environmental modifications.

Path 3: Psychological Resilience: Developing practices to address how her relationship with fatigue might be affecting her experience of it, including mindfulness techniques, cognitive reframing, and purpose-focused engagement.

By advancing these paths simultaneously, Smita created progress even when individual approaches hit limitations. When her hormone interventions (Path 1) showed minimal initial impact, she wasn't devastated because her energy management strategies (Path 2) were already creating noticeable improvements in her daily functioning.

"What surprised me most was how these paths influenced each other," Smita noted during our three-month review. "The psychological approaches changed how I implemented the physiological ones, while the energy management strategies gave me more resources for the psychological work."

This integrated approach created a resilience that no single method could provide. When one path encountered obstacles, progress on other paths maintained momentum and often suggested adjustments that improved the challenging approach.

> *Your Turn:* For a health challenge you're facing, identify three distinct paths that could lead to improvement. Make sure these paths operate on different levels (e.g., physical, behavioural, psychological) rather than being variations of the same approach. For each path, identify a metric that would help you track progress.

***

Case Studies of Success

To further illustrate the power of Strategic Delta in action, let's examine two case studies of individuals who transformed challenging situations through this approach.

A. Career Reinvention After Industry Collapse

Partha had spent fifteen years building expertise in print media when digital disruption decimated his industry. Layoffs were widespread, and traditional positions were disappearing faster than professionals could retrain.

"My entire career foundation was crumbling," Partha told me during our first session. "The skills I've spent decades developing suddenly seem irrelevant, and I don't know where to turn next."

Many of Partha's colleagues pursued a single path: desperately seeking the dwindling number of traditional roles still available. This created a highly competitive environment with diminishing opportunities.

Partha took a different approach, creating a Strategic Delta with multiple paths:

Path 1: Expertise Translation: Identifying how his editorial skills could transfer to digital content environments, focusing on quality and depth as differentiators in a space often prioritising volume and speed.

Path 2: Complementary Capability Development: Building new technical skills specifically in data visualisation and multimedia storytelling—areas where his narrative expertise could combine with new capabilities to create distinctive value.

Path 3: Industry Network Leverage: Developing a consultancy helping traditional media professionals and organisations navigate digital transition—turning his experience of industry disruption into a service.

By pursuing these paths simultaneously, Partha created momentum even as individual paths encountered obstacles. When his initial attempts at expertise translation (Path 1) yielded limited results, his progress in data visualisation (Path 2) opened unexpected opportunities in analytics-driven content.

Within eighteen months, Partha had established a new career identity at the intersection of editorial excellence and data storytelling—a position that actually offered more security and satisfaction than his previous role in the declining print industry.

"If I had focused exclusively on trying to preserve my traditional career path, I would have been competing with everyone else for an ever-shrinking pool of jobs," Partha reflected during our final session. "By developing multiple paths simultaneously, I discovered opportunities at the intersection of seemingly different domains that I couldn't have seen from my initial perspective."

B. Health Transformation Through Multiple Pathways

Ekta had struggled with chronic pain for years, seeing numerous specialists and trying various treatments with limited success. The traditional medical approach—sequential testing and intervention—had left her feeling hopeless after multiple disappointments.

"Every time a treatment fails, I have to start over from scratch with a new approach," Ekta explained during our first consultation. "It's exhausting and demoralising to keep getting my hopes up only to face another dead end."

Using Strategic Delta principles, we developed a multi-path approach:

Path 1: Medical Exploration: Continuing to work with selected medical professionals but taking a more active role in research and treatment selection, focusing on practitioners open to collaborative approaches.

Path 2: Functional Systems: Addressing fundamental inputs to her physical system—nutrition, movement, sleep, stress—through systematic experimentation and personalised protocols rather than generic recommendations.

Path 3: Pain Psychology: Exploring how her relationship with pain affected her experience of it, including pain neuroscience education, mindfulness-based pain management, and purpose-focused engagement strategies.

This multi-path approach created breakthrough possibilities that a single path couldn't have achieved. While medical interventions alone had yielded limited results, the combination of targeted medical approaches, system-based lifestyle modifications, and psychological tools created a transformative effect.

"It wasn't that any single approach solved everything," Ekta explained during our six-month review. "It was the interaction between them that created possibilities I hadn't experienced before. The psychological work made the medical interventions more effective, while the functional systems created a foundation where everything else could work better."

Within a year, Ekta had reduced her pain levels by over 70% and regained activities she had believed were permanently lost to her condition.

"Before, I was always waiting for the one treatment that would solve everything," she reflected. "Now I understand that complex challenges rarely have single-point solutions. It's the integration of multiple approaches that creates true transformation."

Your Strategic Delta Plan

Now it's time to apply these principles to your own situation. Here's a step-by-step process for creating your Strategic Delta plan:

1. **Define Your Desired Outcome:** Be specific about what success looks like but focus on results rather than methods. What are you ultimately trying to achieve, regardless of how you get there?
2. **Identify Multiple Critical Paths:** Develop at least three fundamentally different approaches to achieving your outcome. These should not be minor variations but distinct pathways leveraging different mechanisms, resources, or principles.
3. **Map Initial Actions for Each Path:** For each path, identify the first 2-3 concrete actions you could take to begin developing that route. Focus on actions that provide information or create optionality rather than requiring major commitments.
4. **Create Contingency Networks:** For each path, identify

potential obstacles and specific contingency responses. Set clear, objective triggers for when these contingencies would activate.

5. **Identify Synergy Opportunities:** Look for ways in which your different paths might support each other. Are there resources, relationships, or capabilities that would enhance multiple paths simultaneously?
6. **Establish Progress Metrics:** Determine how you'll measure advancement along each path. These metrics should be observable and specific rather than subjective assessments.
7. **Schedule Regular Reviews:** Set specific times to assess progress across your entire delta, adjust approaches based on emerging information, and potentially develop new paths as the situation evolves.

***

Swastik, a business leader who implemented this process during a period of industry transformation, described its impact: "The Strategic Delta approach completely transformed my relationship with uncertainty. Instead of seeing change as a threat to my single business model, I began viewing it as an opening for multiple possible adaptations. This shift didn't just change our external results—it fundamentally altered my internal experience from anxiety to curious exploration."

> *Real-World Application:* Take a current challenge you're facing and work through these seven steps to create your own Strategic Delta plan. Don't rush this process—quality thinking at this stage creates more robust strategies that can withstand real-world complexity.

Conclusion: Beyond Single-Path Thinking

The examples and applications in this chapter demonstrate a fundamental shift from traditional single path thinking to

Strategic Delta approaches. This shift creates resilience not by making individual paths foolproof (an impossible standard) but by ensuring that obstacles on any single path don't derail your entire progress.

This multi-path orientation transforms vulnerability into opportunity across all domains of life—from career development to relationship challenges to health goals. By developing multiple viable routes toward your desired outcomes, you create a resilience that doesn't depend on perfect execution of any single approach.

As you implement these principles in your own life, you'll develop what I call "strategic intuition"—the ability to naturally think in terms of multiple possibilities rather than linear progressions. This capacity forms a cornerstone of **Layer 1 resilience**—creating a foundation of strategic control even amid complexity and change.

In the next chapter, we'll explore how quantum principles can further enhance your strategic effectiveness, introducing elements of possibility and creative influence that traditional planning approaches often miss.

THREE

Quantum Principles for Practical Results

Introduction to quantum thinking. Breaking deterministic patterns. The observer effect in your daily life.

"You lost me at 'quantum,'" Jai said, making air quotes with his fingers. "Isn't that just complicated physics that has nothing to do with real life?"

Avika laughed. "That's what I thought too until I saw how these principles actually play out in everyday situations. Remember Pranay from sales?"

"The guy who somehow turned that disaster with the Johnson account into an even bigger opportunity? Yeah, what about him?"

"He doesn't know he's applying quantum principles, but that's exactly what he's doing," Avika explained. "Instead of seeing reality as fixed paths of cause and effect, he operates as if multiple possibilities exist simultaneously until someone makes a choice that collapses them into one outcome."

Jai looked sceptical. "That sounds nice in theory, but—"

"But nothing," Avika interrupted. "Think about it. When the Johnson contract fell through, most people saw only one reality: failure. Pranay somehow held multiple possible realities in mind simultaneously—including ones where this apparent failure opened doors that success would have kept closed."

Jai considered this. "And because he saw those possibilities..."

"He could take actions that made those better possibilities more likely to materialise," Avika finished. "That's quantum thinking in action. Not mysterious or mystical—just a fundamentally different way of relating to what's possible."

When most people hear "quantum physics," they think of complex equations and abstract concepts far removed from daily life. But what if I told you that quantum principles could help you get that promotion, improve your relationships, or even find peace during chaotic times?

Let me tell you about my friend Raj. For years, he approached his career like a billiard ball on a pool table—following a straight, predictable path based on cause and effect. He did everything "right" according to conventional wisdom: got the degree, put in long hours, followed the corporate ladder precisely... and felt increasingly stuck and frustrated.

"I was doing everything by the book," Raj told me during our first coaching session. "But I kept hitting walls. The more I pushed in my predetermined direction, the more resistance I encountered."

Raj's experience illustrates the limitation of purely Newtonian thinking—approaching life as if it operates like classical physics—with objects following predictable trajectories based on initial conditions and applied forces. This mechanical worldview dominated Western thought for centuries and still shapes how most of us approach challenges.

But at the quantum level—the realm of atoms and subatomic particles—reality operates according to profoundly different principles. And while we don't experience quantum effects directly in our macroscopic world, the underlying paradigm offers powerful metaphorical tools for approaching life's complexities.

This is where Raj's story took an interesting turn. Through our work together, he began applying three core quantum principles to his approach:

The Observer Effect: You Change What You Observe

In quantum physics, the act of observation affects the particle being observed. The famous double-slit experiment demonstrates that electrons behave differently when observed than when not observed—shifting from wave-like behaviour to particle-like behaviour based on measurement.

In practical terms, this means your attention itself is a creative force. What you focus on not only determines what you see but influences what becomes possible.

Raj began intentionally observing opportunities rather than limitations. Instead of focusing on why his ideas wouldn't get approved, he started noticing which decision-makers seemed open to innovation and which organisational needs aligned with his proposals.

"I realised I had been creating self-fulfilling prophecies," Raj explained during a follow-up session. "By focusing exclusively on obstacles, I was actually strengthening those very barriers. When I shifted my attention to potential openings, I began seeing possibilities that had been there all along—they just weren't visible through my previous lens."

Within weeks, he found champions for his proposals that had been "impossible" before. Nothing in the external environment had changed—what shifted was what Raj chose to observe and thus bring into focus.

***

Sarita, a healthcare leader, applied this principle during a challenging hospital merger. Rather than focusing on the inevitable conflicts between different organisational cultures (which many of her colleagues were fixated on), she deliberately directed her attention toward examples of successful integration and complementary strengths.

"My colleagues thought I was being naively optimistic," Sarita told me. "But I wasn't ignoring problems—I was just choosing to observe patterns that might support solutions rather than only seeing evidence that confirmed our fears."

This selective attention allowed Sarita to identify integration pathways that others missed. While colleagues who focused exclusively on conflicts encountered exactly the resistance they expected, Sarita discovered collaborative possibilities that created unexpected breakthroughs.

The observer effect doesn't mean denying reality or engaging in magical thinking. It acknowledges that your habitual observations shape both your perceptions and the unfolding of situations. By consciously directing your attention, you influence which possibilities come to fruition.

> *Try This:* For the next three days, deliberately observe evidence of what's working in your life rather than what's broken. Write down at least three positive observations each day. Notice how this simple shift in attention begins to change your experience.

Superposition: Multiple Possibilities Exist Simultaneously

Quantum particles can exist in multiple states simultaneously until measured—what physicists call "superposition." The famous thought experiment of Schrödinger's cat illustrates this principle: until observed, the cat exists in a superposition of states, both alive and dead simultaneously.

While macroscopic objects like cats don't actually exist in superposition, this principle offers a powerful metaphor: situations in your life contain numerous potential outcomes that haven't "collapsed" into reality yet. By recognising these multiple possibilities, you expand beyond limited either/or thinking.

When Raj's department faced budget cuts, rather than assuming the worst (layoffs, increased workload), he recognised multiple possibilities existed. He prepared for different scenarios and proactively proposed a restructuring that actually improved his position.

"Before, I would have seen only two possibilities: either things stay the same or they get worse," Raj explained. "By recognising that multiple scenarios could unfold, including ones I hadn't yet imagined, I could prepare for various outcomes while influencing which one materialised."

Swastik, a relationship therapist, applies this principle with couples trapped in seemingly binary conflicts. "Most relationship struggles occur because each partner sees only two possibilities—either I get what I need or I don't," Swastik told me. "When they recognise that multiple possibilities exist beyond this limited either/or framing, creative solutions often emerge that neither person initially imagined."

Swastik helps couples identify these superpositions of possibility by asking: "What are at least five different ways this situation could develop, including scenarios neither of you has considered?" This simple question often breaks the deadlock of binary thinking, revealing options that satisfy both partners' underlying needs.

Superposition thinking doesn't guarantee your preferred outcome will materialise. What it does is expand the field of possibilities beyond the limited set your conventional thinking normally perceives. By recognising that situations exist in a state of multiple potentials rather than predetermined outcomes, you gain both strategic advantage and psychological flexibility.

> *Real-World Application:* Next time you face uncertainty, list at least five possible outcomes—including ones that seem unlikely but positive. For each, identify one small action you could take to make that outcome more probable. This breaks the pattern of assuming the worst-case scenario will automatically unfold.

Quantum Tunnelling: Breaking Through Seemingly Impenetrable Barriers

In quantum physics, particles can occasionally pass through barriers that should be impenetrable according to classical physics. This phenomenon, called quantum tunnelling, occurs because at the quantum level, particles behave according to probability distributions rather than fixed positions.

As a metaphor, quantum tunnelling suggests that apparent barriers in your life may be more permeable than they appear—and that approaches that seem "impossible" according to conventional thinking occasionally succeed through pathways invisible to linear reasoning.

Raj applied this principle when facing a seemingly insurmountable career obstacle—he lacked the "required" ten years of experience for a position he knew he could excel in. Rather than accepting this barrier as absolute, he found an unexpected path through it by creating a detailed proposal showing how his unique background created advantages the standard candidate wouldn't offer.

He got the job.

"According to conventional thinking, I shouldn't have even tried—the barrier of formal requirements was 'impenetrable,'" Raj told me afterward. "But by focusing on probabilities rather than certainties, I recognised there might be paths through this barrier that weren't immediately obvious."

Ekta, a nonprofit director, applied quantum tunnelling to funding challenges. When traditional grant applications repeatedly failed, she developed an unconventional approach that bypassed normal funding channels. Instead of pursuing foundation grants directly, she created strategic partnerships with funded organisations, gaining resource access without competing in oversaturated grant pools.

"Everyone told me it was impossible to launch our programmes without major grant funding," Ekta explained. "But by looking for tunnels through the barrier rather than trying to climb over it, we found pathways that others couldn't see."

Quantum tunnelling doesn't suggest all barriers are illusory or that blind optimism will magically overcome obstacles. Rather, it recognises that apparent impossibilities occasionally yield to approaches that exploit hidden permeabilities in seemingly solid barriers. By maintaining experimental openness rather than accepting limitations as absolute, you occasionally discover paths that conventional thinking would miss.

> *Your Turn:* What barrier are you accepting as absolute in your life right now? A financial limitation? A relationship dynamic? Educational requirements? How could you "tunnel through" rather than trying to climb over it?

Breaking Deterministic Patterns

The most powerful aspect of quantum thinking is that it breaks deterministic patterns—the rigid cause-and-effect chains we assume control our lives.

Sarita, a single mom struggling with overwhelming anxiety, always followed the same pattern: **stress → comfort eating → guilt → more stress**. Quantum thinking helped her see this wasn't a fixed chain but a pattern she could interrupt at any point.

"I had been treating my responses as if they were as inevitable as billiard balls colliding," Sarita told me during our work together. "If stress appeared, I believed comfort eating would automatically follow, and then guilt, and then more stress—around and around in a predictable cycle."

Through quantum principles, Sarita began creating what I call "quantum interventions"—tiny pattern breaks that created new possibilities. Sometimes this meant simply pausing for three deep breaths when stress began. Other times it meant calling a friend instead of opening the refrigerator. Each small intervention created branching possibilities that weren't available in her previous deterministic worldview.

"I realised I wasn't a mechanical system following inevitable cause-effect patterns," Sarita explained. "At each moment, multiple possibilities existed, and even tiny interventions could shift which one materialised."

Within months, her anxiety levels had decreased by half, and she'd developed new response patterns that served her better.

Leo, a business leader, applied this pattern-breaking to organisational challenges. His company had fallen into predictable response cycles when facing market threats—reacting with either aggressive competition or anxious retrenchment, neither of which was serving them well.

"We were stuck in deterministic thinking—believing that certain triggers would inevitably produce particular responses," Leo explained. "By introducing deliberate pattern interrupts, we discovered we had far more choice than we'd realised."

These organisational pattern breaks included simple interventions like changing who participated in strategic meetings, altering the physical environment where decisions were made, and introducing new information sources into planning processes. These small changes disrupted the automatic cause-effect chains that had been limiting their responses.

Quantum pattern-breaking doesn't require dramatic transformations. Often, the most effective interventions are small disruptions at key points that create space for new possibilities to emerge. By recognising that you exist in probability fields rather than deterministic chains, you gain the freedom to experiment with pattern interrupts that shift potential outcomes.

Quantum Thinking in Your Daily Life

You don't need a physics degree to apply quantum principles. Try these simple practices:

A. Question Certainty

When you catch yourself saying "That's just how it is" or "It always happens this way," pause and ask, "Is that really true? What other possibilities exist?"

Ekta applied this when repeatedly encountering the same conflict with her teenager. "I had been treating our arguments as inevitable—as 'just how things are between us,'" she told me. "By questioning this certainty, I created space to experiment with different approaches that eventually shifted our entire relationship dynamic."

B. Create Superpositions

Intentionally hold multiple possibilities in mind rather than narrowing to a single expected outcome. This keeps you flexible and open to opportunities.

Pranay practiced this during job negotiations. Rather than fixating on a single desired outcome, he consciously held multiple possible scenarios in mind—different compensation structures, role configurations, and even the possibility of walking away for a better opportunity. This mental superposition allowed him to navigate the negotiation with unusual flexibility, ultimately securing an arrangement better than his initial target.

C. Use Pattern Interrupts

Break habitual responses with small, unexpected actions. Take a different route to work. Respond to criticism with curiosity instead of defence. Eat dessert first occasionally!

Smita implemented this with family holiday gatherings that had fallen into predictable conflict patterns. Simple interventions—changing seating arrangements, introducing new activities, altering the timing of potentially contentious discussions—disrupted patterns that had seemed fixed for decades, creating space for new, more positive dynamics to emerge.

D. Embrace Probability

Instead of thinking in absolutes ("I'll never get hired"), think in probabilities that you can influence ("If I apply these quantum principles, I can increase my chances of finding the right position").

Jaimin practiced this during a career transition. Rather than seeing each rejection as evidence of inevitable failure, he viewed his job search as a probability field he could influence through multiple small adjustments to his approach. This perspective kept him experimenting and adapting rather than becoming discouraged by initial setbacks.

Jai, a struggling entrepreneur, applied these principles when his business faced bankruptcy. Instead of seeing failure as inevitable, he recognised it as just one possibility in a field of many. He used pattern interrupts to break his spiral of panicked decision-making, questioned his certainty about what customers wanted, and explored multiple potential business models simultaneously.

Today, his company is thriving—but in a completely different industry than where he started. As he told me, "Quantum thinking didn't just save my business; it showed me that what I thought was the 'end' was actually a portal to something better."

Practical Quantum Applications

Let's explore how quantum principles can be applied to specific life situations:

A. Career Advancement

Sarita felt stuck, overlooked for promotions despite strong performance. Through quantum observation, she realised she'd focused only on formal paths, missing informal influence opportunities. By building relationships with decision-makers and adding unexpected value, she uncovered new promotion routes. Within six months, she earned a promotion and a new role created for her unique skills.

"I'd been tunnel-visioned on the traditional ladder," Sarita said. "Shifting my focus revealed multiple unseen paths."

B. Relationship Transformation

Swastik and Seema were trapped in a conflict cycle with predictable responses. Quantum interventions introduced small pattern interrupts—like pausing before replies or changing physical posture—that disrupted their dynamics. These shifts opened new possibilities, gradually transforming their interactions.

"We treated conflicts like predictable physics," Swastik said. "Realising we existed in possibility fields gave us unexpected freedom.

C. Health Improvement

Pranay's weight management followed a rigid calories-in/calories-out model, causing frustrating relapse cycles. Quantum principles helped him see health as a probability field influenced by many factors. Small routine changes and multiple strategies replaced the single-method approach, transforming his results and mindset.

"I stopped forcing my health like a machine and started influencing it through small adjustments," Pranay explained.

D. Financial Navigation

Ekta faced overwhelming debt with only two traditional options: long-term payments or bankruptcy. Quantum thinking revealed multiple possibilities. She found "tunneling" opportunities, combined partial solutions, and challenged assumptions about creditors. In eighteen months, she resolved debts expected to take a decade.

"Rejecting deterministic either/or thinking uncovered solutions traditional methods missed," Ekta said.

Integrating Quantum and Strategic Approaches

Quantum principles don't replace the Strategic Delta Method we explored in previous chapters—they enhance it. While Strategic Delta creates multiple pathways toward your goals, quantum thinking expands what you perceive as possible within each path.

These approaches work synergistically:

- Strategic Delta ensures you're not dependent on a single vulnerable route.
- Quantum principles ensure you're not limited by deterministic thinking within each route.
- Together, they create a resilience that neither approach alone can provide.

Raj, whom we met at the beginning of this chapter, integrated both approaches in his career development. He maintained multiple professional paths (Strategic Delta) while applying quantum principles within each path—questioning certainties, creating superpositions of possibility, implementing pattern interrupts, and recognising opportunities for quantum tunnelling through apparent barriers.

"The Strategic Delta Method gave me multiple routes to explore," Raj reflected. "Quantum principles expanded what I could perceive and influence within each route. Together, they transformed not just my external results but my internal experience of the journey."

This integration creates a foundation for the most robust form of Layer 1 resilience—the ability to shape circumstances through both multiple pathways and expanded possibilities within each path.

Conclusion: Expanding Your Possible

Quantum principles offer more than just interesting scientific concepts—they provide practical tools for expanding what you perceive as possible in your life. By questioning deterministic thinking, recognising multiple simultaneous possibilities, creating pattern interrupts, and finding unexpected pathways through apparent barriers, you develop a relationship with reality that transcends conventional limitations.

As you practice these approaches, you'll likely notice something interesting: what initially requires conscious application gradually becomes a natural way of perceiving. You'll begin automatically questioning certainties, recognising multiple possibilities, and identifying potential pattern interrupts without deliberate effort.

This evolution from technique to perception represents the integration of quantum thinking into your worldview—a fundamental shift from Newtonian determinism to quantum possibility. When this shift occurs, you've developed a core aspect of Layer 1 resilience: the capacity to perceive and influence possibilities invisible to conventional thinking.

In the next chapter, we'll explore how to combine these quantum principles with strategic methods in a powerful synthesis—the Quantum Delta Method—that creates unprecedented resilience in navigating life's complexities.

FOUR

The Quantum Delta Method

Combining strategic planning with quantum flexibility. Creating robust plans that adapt to uncertainty. Case studies of success.

"So, if I understand correctly," Jai said as they walked through the park, "Strategic Delta gives me multiple paths, and quantum principles help me see multiple possibilities. But how do they work together?"

Avika stopped by a pond where several streams flowed in and out. "See how these streams form a complex system? Strategic Delta is like mapping those visible streams. But quantum thinking recognises that underground currents exist too—possibilities not immediately visible but equally real."

"And the Quantum Delta Method combines both," Jai nodded slowly. "Mapping visible streams while also sensing underground currents."

"Exactly," Avika smiled. "It's creating structured plans that have built-in adaptability to leverage emerging possibilities. Not just planning for what you can see but designing approaches that can capitalise on what might emerge that you can't yet see."

Jai watched a leaf floating where currents converged. "I think I'm starting to get it. But honestly, this all still assumes I can influence outcomes through better methods. What about situations completely beyond my control?"

Avika's expression turned thoughtful. "That's where we reach the limits of Layer 1 approaches—and why we need to explore Layer 2. But let's master this first."

"The best way to predict the future is to create it."
– Peter Drucker

If you've been following along with the previous chapters, you now understand two powerful approaches:

1. The Strategic Delta Method, which provides a structured framework for navigating complex situations.
2. Quantum Principles, which offer insights into creating possibilities beyond linear cause-and-effect thinking.

But what happens when we combine these approaches? That's where the Quantum Delta Method comes in—a synthesis that creates a uniquely powerful system for shaping reality.

Where Strategy Meets Quantum Thinking

Traditional strategic planning assumes a relatively predictable world. You assess the current situation, chart a course to your desired outcome, and execute with discipline. It's like plotting a course on a map—effective in stable conditions.

But what happens when the map itself keeps changing? When new territories appear, familiar landmarks vanish, and the very physics of movement transform?

That's today's reality. Technology, economics, politics, climate—all shifting rapidly in ways that make traditional planning increasingly limited.

Natasha learned this lesson the hard way. A brilliant financial analyst, she had built her career on her ability to predict market trends based on historical patterns. When we first met, she was still reeling from the impact of a financial crisis that had rendered her carefully constructed models obsolete.

"I felt like a physicist whose experiments suddenly started defying the laws of gravity," she told me, her professional confidence visibly shaken. "Everything I thought I knew about how markets behaved seemed to break down. My models had always worked before, and then suddenly... they just didn't."

Natasha's experience isn't unique. We're all navigating increasingly complex, interconnected systems where small changes can cascade into massive, unpredictable outcomes. The butterfly effect isn't just theory anymore—it's daily reality.

This is where quantum thinking becomes essential. Rather than assuming fixed paths between cause and effect, quantum thinking embraces probability fields, multiple possibilities existing simultaneously, and the creative role of observation itself.

The Quantum Delta Method combines strategic structure with quantum flexibility—creating plans that don't just withstand uncertainty but actively leverage it.

The Four Components of Quantum Delta

The Quantum Delta Method builds on the Strategic Delta foundation but transforms each component through quantum principles:

1. Quantum Assessment

Traditional assessment focuses on "what is"—the observable current reality. Quantum assessment expands to include:

- Probability fields (what might be emerging)
- Hidden interconnections between seemingly separate factors.
- Your own role as an observer influencing the system you're observing.

Riya, a product developer I worked with during a corporate innovation project, applied quantum assessment when evaluating market potential for a new device. Rather than just analysing existing consumer behaviour, she identified emerging probability fields—subtle patterns suggesting how behaviour might evolve.

"Most of my colleagues were focused exclusively on current market data," Riya explained during our strategy session. "But

I kept noticing something interesting in how early adopters were using our previous product—they were taking it into contexts we never designed for."

This subtle observation—that users were employing their product in unexpected settings—led Riya to discover a much larger potential market than conventional analysis had identified.

"If I had only looked at the obvious data points, we would have missed our biggest opportunity," she explained. "The real insight came from paying attention to anomalies and patterns that were just beginning to emerge."

When her team launched the product with features designed for these emerging use cases, it outperformed projections by over 300%—capturing markets that conventional assessment would have missed entirely.

Prem, a healthcare administrator, applied quantum assessment during a hospital reorganisation. Beyond analysing obvious factors like department efficiency and patient outcomes, he mapped subtle interconnections between seemingly unrelated systems—how scheduling in one department created cascade effects in others, how physical layout influenced communication patterns, and how his own presence in meetings altered what information emerged.

"I realised I wasn't just observing a fixed system but participating in a dynamic field that responded to observation itself," Prem told me. "By recognising my role as an observer-participant, I could be much more intentional about how I gathered and interpreted information."

This expanded assessment revealed intervention points invisible to conventional analysis, allowing Prem to implement changes that resolved persistent problems conventional approaches had missed for years.

Try This: For a situation you're currently analysing, go beyond obvious data points. List at least three "weak signals"—subtle patterns or anomalies that might indicate emerging possibilities. What might these signals suggest if they represent the beginning of a larger trend?

2. Quantum Outcomes

Traditional outcome definition focuses on specific, fixed end states. Quantum outcomes expand to include:

- Ranges of acceptable results rather than single targets.
- Seemingly contradictory goals that can coexist.
- Outcomes that evolve as you progress toward them.

Vinay, a city planner working on urban redevelopment, applied quantum outcomes to a project that had stalled due to competing interests. When we first discussed the project, Vinay was frustrated by seemingly irreconcilable stakeholder demands.

"The affordable housing advocates, business interests, and environmental groups all have different visions for this district," he explained. "Traditional planning approaches treat these as trade-offs—we can satisfy one group but only at the expense of others."

Rather than forcing stakeholders to agree on a single vision, Vinay defined success as "a district that simultaneously supports affordable housing, local businesses, and environmental sustainability, with the specific balance emerging through the development process itself."

This quantum approach allowed seemingly contradictory goals to coexist in a field of possibilities that could adapt as the project evolved. What had been an either/or conflict became a both/and exploration.

"Instead of trying to predict exactly what the final development would look like, we created a framework that could evolve based on what emerged during implementation," Pranay told me later. "This gave all stakeholders confidence their concerns would be addressed, even though the specific form remained flexible."

The project, previously deadlocked for years, moved forward with unprecedented collaboration. The final development included elements no single stakeholder had initially envisioned—innovative approaches that emerged precisely because the outcome remained adaptive rather than fixed.

Ekta applied quantum outcomes to her career development after finding herself torn between competing professional goals—creative fulfilment, financial security, and work-life balance. Traditional planning treated these as trade-offs requiring sacrifice of at least one priority.

"I used to believe I had to choose—financial security, creative fulfilment, or a balanced life," Ekta explained during our coaching sessions. "This either/or mindset made me feel like I would lose no matter what."

Through quantum outcomes, Ekta redefined success as "a professional identity that allows for financial sufficiency, creative expression, and work-life balance, with the specific form emerging through exploration and iteration." This approach transformed her relationship with career development from anxious choosing to curious exploration.

"By defining success as a field of possibilities rather than a single fixed state, I could pursue multiple aspects simultaneously without feeling I was sacrificing essential priorities," Ekta reflected. The career that ultimately emerged combined elements she couldn't have predicted initially—a portfolio approach that satisfied multiple priorities through complementary activities rather than a single perfect job.

Real-World Application: For an important goal you're pursuing, rewrite your desired outcome to include ranges rather than fixed targets, potentially contradictory elements that could coexist, and language that allows for emergence rather than fixation. How does this expanded definition change your relationship with the goal?

3. Quantum Pathways

Traditional pathway multiplication develops several distinct routes to your goal. Quantum pathways take this further by:

- Creating pathways that can be pursued simultaneously rather than sequentially.
- Establishing positive interference patterns where paths reinforce each other.
- Developing superposition strategies that exist in multiple states until circumstances clarify.

Ekta applied quantum pathways when launching her consulting business by creating offerings that existed in "superposition," able to serve executive coaching or organisational development depending on client needs. Instead of narrowly defining services, she designed them to adapt flexibly. Simultaneously pursuing speaking engagements, writing, and networking, she discovered these efforts didn't just run in parallel—they enhanced each other, generating momentum no single path could achieve alone. "The magic happened at the intersection of these paths," Ekta explained.

Similarly, Swastik used quantum pathways in his nonprofit's fundraising by blending foundation grants, major donors, and community fundraising into adaptable strategies. This flexible approach allowed rapid resource shifts and created synergies—major donors opened foundation opportunities, while community events attracted supporters linked to foundations.

What once seemed competing strategies became an integrated, reinforcing system.

> *Try This:* Instead of viewing your strategic options as separate paths, identify at least two ways your different approaches could interact to create positive interference patterns—where pursuing one actually enhances the effectiveness of another.

4. Quantum Execution

Traditional execution focuses on disciplined plan implementation. Quantum execution adds to this by incorporating:

-Rapid iteration based on real-time feedback

-Deliberate pattern interrupts to challenge restrictive thinking

-Strategic entanglements with complementary partners or systems

Jaimin applied quantum execution while scaling his software company. Instead of following traditional funding rounds, he formed strategic entanglements with key customers, turning them into development partners whose success became intertwined with his product's evolution.

"Rather than treating customers and investors separately, I linked their interests and outcomes," Jaimin explained. This approach transformed competitors into collaborators and customers into innovation partners. He also introduced pattern interrupts by inviting perspectives from diverse industries and replaced quarterly planning with two-week iterative cycles, enabling rapid response to opportunities.

Within eighteen months, his company outperformed better-funded rivals by embracing these quantum execution principles.

Similarly, Sarita applied quantum execution in healthcare improvement projects previously hindered by rigid plans. She combined disciplined management with rapid feedback loops, adjusting direction based on new information rather than fixed milestones.

She introduced pattern interrupts by rotating team members across workstreams and involving patients and non-clinical staff in discussions. Most critically, she fostered strategic entanglements between traditionally siloed departments, turning resistance into collaboration.

"Entangling outcomes across units transformed siloed efforts into system-wide innovation," Sarita reflected. Projects stalled by departmental boundaries gained momentum through these integrated approaches.

> *Real-World Application:* For a project you're implementing, identify one specific way you could: 1) shorten your feedback cycle, 2) introduce a pattern interrupt that challenges conventional thinking, and 3) create strategic entanglement with a complementary person or organisation.

Quantum Delta in Action: Case Studies

To better understand how this method works in practice, let's look at three case studies across different domains:

Career Transformation

Swastik had spent fifteen years in corporate finance when his industry began experiencing major disruption. Rather than pursuing the traditional approach of updating his skills within his current field, he applied Quantum Delta:

Quantum Assessment

Beyond analysing obvious career paths, Swastik identified emerging fields at the intersection of finance and technology.

More importantly, he recognised how his unique combination of experiences created possibilities invisible to conventional career planning.

"I realised I wasn't just observing career options as fixed paths but participating in creating possibilities through what I chose to observe and explore," Swastik explained during our career coaching sessions. "By paying attention to weak signals and emerging patterns rather than just established tracks, I discovered opportunities conventional career planning would have missed."

Quantum Outcomes

Rather than defining a specific job title or role, Swastik created a broader vision of "leveraging financial expertise in evolving technology contexts while maintaining location flexibility and intellectual challenge." This quantum outcome allowed multiple manifestations to emerge.

"Instead of trying to identify the perfect next job, I defined success as a field of possibilities that could take different forms while fulfilling my core priorities," Swastik reflected. "This freed me from the anxiety of making the 'right' choice and transformed my search into curious exploration."

Quantum Pathways

Swastik developed several paths simultaneously: consulting with fintech startups, creating online educational content about financial innovation, and exploring roles within his current company's digital transformation initiative.

Importantly, these weren't separate backup plans—they were designed to create interference patterns. His consulting built credibility for his educational content, which opened doors for internal opportunities.

"These weren't isolated alternatives but complementary aspects of an integrated approach," Swastik explained. "Each path strengthened the others in ways I couldn't have predicted in advance."

Quantum Execution

Swastik broke traditional career development patterns by sharing his journey publicly through content creation, creating two-week "experiments" to test different aspects of his emerging identity, and establishing strategic entanglements with key innovators who became both mentors and door-openers.

"Instead of treating my career transition as a private, linear process, I made it public and non-linear," Swastik told me. "The content creation became both a credential and a networking tool, while the two-week experiments gave me rapid feedback about which directions energised me most."

The result wasn't a single new job but a portfolio career combining elements of all his pathways—consulting, content creation, and innovation leadership—in a configuration that conventional career planning could never have produced.

Relationship Renewal

Sarita and Partha had been married for twelve years when they realised their relationship had fallen into stagnant patterns. Rather than standard couples therapy, they applied Quantum Delta principles:

Quantum Assessment

Beyond identifying obvious issues, they explored emerging patterns in how they connected, subtle signals that indicated untapped possibilities, and how their own observations were influencing the relationship system.

"We realised we weren't just observing our relationship as something separate from us but actually participating in creating its patterns through what we chose to observe and emphasise," Sarita explained during a couples session. "By shifting our attention from problems to emergent possibilities, we began seeing openings we'd previously missed."

Quantum Outcomes

Instead of defining specific relationship goals, they created a field of possibilities: "A partnership that supports both individual growth and deep connection, manifesting in ways that might surprise us."

"Rather than trying to restore some previous version of our relationship or reach some idealised state, we defined success as an evolving field that could take different forms while fulfilling core needs," Partha reflected. "This freed us from rigid expectations while maintaining a clear direction."

Quantum Pathways

They developed multiple approaches concurrently: a structured date night practice, individual personal development projects, and a shared challenge outside their comfort zones (learning Argentine tango).

These pathways were designed to create interference patterns—their individual growth created new energy for their connection, while their shared challenge created contexts for applying new relationship skills.

"We discovered that these pathways weren't separate alternatives but complementary aspects of relationship renewal," Sarita told me. "The dance lessons became a metaphor and laboratory for our communication, while our individual development created fresh energy we brought back to the relationship."

Quantum Execution

They established weekly mini-assessments instead of waiting for major issues to arise, deliberately broke habitual patterns—such as switching who initiated different types of conversations—and created entanglements with other couples pursuing similar relationship renewal.

"The weekly check-ins gave us rapid feedback rather than letting issues accumulate," Partha explained. "The pattern interrupts were particularly powerful—simply changing who initiated certain conversations completely shifted their quality."

The outcome wasn't just an improved version of their old relationship but an entirely new configuration—one with greater flexibility, deeper connection, and unexpected dimensions of partnership neither had initially imagined.

Health Transformation

Robert had received a concerning diagnosis that required significant lifestyle changes. Rather than following the typical restrictive approach to health improvement, he applied Quantum Delta.

Quantum Assessment

Beyond standard health metrics, Robert explored emerging research on the interconnections between different health systems, subtle patterns in how his energy fluctuated, and how his beliefs about health were influencing his physiological responses.

"I realised I wasn't just observing my health as an objective condition but actually influencing it through what I chose to observe and believe," Robert explained during our health coaching sessions. "By paying attention to subtle patterns and interconnections rather than just obvious symptoms, I discovered intervention points conventional approaches had missed."

Quantum Outcomes

Instead of focusing solely on eliminating disease markers, Robert created a broader vision: "A state of authentic vitality that supports my life purpose, manifesting across physical, mental, and energetic dimensions in an integrated system."

"Rather than defining health narrowly as the absence of disease symptoms, I envisioned it as a dynamic field of possibilities that could take different forms while supporting my broader life," Robert reflected. "This transformed health from a constraint to navigate into a foundation to build upon."

Quantum Pathways

He pursued multiple approaches concurrently: nutrition optimisation, movement practices, stress regulation techniques, and purpose-driven activities that generated natural vitality.

These weren't separate health tactics but an integrated system with interference patterns—his movement practices enhanced his nutrition choices, while his purpose-driven activities created motivation for consistent health behaviours.

"I discovered that these aspects of health weren't separate categories but interconnected dimensions of an integrated system," Robert told me. "Changes in one area created ripple effects that enhanced others in ways I couldn't have predicted."

Quantum Execution

Robert established daily micro-measurements rather than waiting for doctor visits, deliberately introduced pattern interrupts in his health routines to prevent adaptation plateaus and created strategic entanglements with health partners who shared complementary goals.

"The daily measurements gave me immediate feedback rather than waiting months between checkups," Robert explained. "The pattern interrupts prevented the diminishing returns that come from adaptation to the same routines, while the health partnerships created accountability and motivation beyond what I could have maintained alone."

Within six months, his health markers had improved beyond his doctor's expectations. More importantly, he had developed a relationship with health that wasn't based on restriction and discipline but on integration and emergence—a sustainable approach that continued to evolve.

Creating Your Own Quantum Delta

Now, how can you apply this method to your own challenges and opportunities? Here's a structured approach:

1. **Identify Your Focus Area:** Select a specific situation where conventional approaches haven't yielded the results you want, or where complexity and uncertainty make traditional planning inadequate.
2. **Apply Quantum Assessment**
   - What's actually happening? (observable reality)
   - What might be emerging? (probability fields)
   - What subtle patterns or anomalies exist? (weak signals)
   - How might you be influencing what you observe? (observer effect)

3. **Develop Quantum Outcomes**
   - What field of possibilities would constitute success?
   - How can you define outcomes that allow for emergence rather than fixation?
   - What seemingly contradictory elements might coexist in your ideal result?
4. **Create Quantum Pathways**
   - What multiple approaches could you pursue simultaneously?
   - How might these approaches create positive interference patterns?
   - What superposition strategies could adapt to emerging circumstances?
5. **Implement Quantum Execution**
   - How can you shorten your feedback cycles?
   - What pattern interrupts could break limiting thinking?
   - What strategic entanglements would create mutual amplification?

When Ekta faced a tough career shift, she used a structured, "Quantum Delta" approach:

Quantum assessment: She explored not just obvious paths but emerging fields that blended her diverse experiences. She identified energising activities and realised her self-image was limiting her options.

Quantum outcomes: Instead of a fixed role, she defined success as work combining creativity, intellectual challenge, and meaningful impact—open to surprising forms but clear in intent.

Quantum pathways: She pursued parallel efforts—freelance work, exploratory conversations, and a personal project—all reinforcing each other rather than acting as separate bets.

Quantum execution: She used two-week experiments to test progress, broke old habits in presenting herself, and built strategic partnerships for mutual growth.

"The approach changed how I relate to uncertainty," Ekta said. "Ambiguity became a space of possibility, turning anxiety into curiosity."

> *Your Turn:* Pick a current challenge and explore it through these five steps. Take your time—insight comes when you go beyond the obvious.

The First Layer of Resilience

The Quantum Delta Method forms a cornerstone of the first layer of becoming unshakeable—Strategic Control. When you can navigate complexity with both structured approach and quantum flexibility, you develop a form of resilience that conventional strategies can't match.

You're no longer limited to single paths that can be blocked by unexpected obstacles. You're no longer dependent on conditions remaining stable. You're no longer constrained by linear thinking in a non-linear world.

Instead, you become adaptable yet focused, structured yet flexible, planful yet responsive—creating purposeful direction amid uncertainty.

As Natasha, the financial analyst we met earlier, discovered: "Once I integrated quantum principles into my strategic thinking, I stopped trying to predict exactly what would happen. Instead, I created systems that could thrive in multiple possible futures. The irony is that by embracing uncertainty, I became much more effective at shaping outcomes."

This is the essence of Layer 1 resilience—not eliminating uncertainty but developing approaches that transform it from threat to asset.

In the next chapter, we'll explore how to master Layer 1 by overcoming common obstacles and measuring your progress as you develop these capabilities.

FIVE

Mastering Layer 1

Common obstacles and how to overcome them. Metrics for measuring your progress. When strategy isn't enough.

"I've been applying these methods for weeks now," Jai said, frustration evident in his voice. "Sometimes they work brilliantly, but other times I still get completely thrown off course."

Avika nodded. "That's normal. What specific obstacles are you encountering?"

"Well, for one thing, I sometimes get stuck analysing options without actually taking action," Jai admitted. "And when I'm under pressure, I tend to abandon the whole strategic approach and just react."

"Classic obstacles," Avika said. "The first is analysis paralysis, and the second is strategic abandonment. Both can be overcome with specific practices."

"But there's something else," Jai continued, his expression more serious. "Last week my mom had a health scare. Nothing in my strategic toolkit seemed relevant. I felt... completely helpless."

Avika's eyes softened. "And that's where we reach the natural limits of Layer 1. No matter how sophisticated our strategic methods, there will always be circumstances beyond our control."

"So, what then?" Jai asked quietly. "Just accept defeat?"

"Not defeat," Avika said. "Transition. When we reach the limits of strategic control, we're ready to explore Layer 2—developing the mental preparedness to navigate uncertainty with equanimity."

Jai looked sceptical. "So basically, when strategies fail, just be zen about it?"

Avika laughed. "It's much more than that. But yes, Layer 2 is about developing a fundamentally different relationship with circumstances you can't control."

"In preparing for battle I have always found that plans are useless, but planning is indispensable."
– Dwight D. Eisenhower

By now, you've explored the core components of Layer 1 resilience—the Strategic Delta Method, Quantum Principles, and the Quantum Delta synthesis. You've seen how these approaches can transform how you navigate complex situations across different areas of life.

But knowledge alone isn't enough. To truly master Layer 1, you need to overcome common obstacles and develop measurable progress indicators that keep you on track. This chapter addresses both challenges, helping you move from understanding to embodiment of these strategic principles.

Common Obstacles and How to Overcome Them

Even with powerful methods at your disposal, several common obstacles can impede your progress toward strategic mastery. Let's explore these challenges and their solutions:

1. Analysis Paralysis

The Obstacle

Getting stuck in endless research and planning without taking action. This often stems from perfectionism or fear of making the wrong decision.

I witnessed this pattern with Sophia, a talented designer who came to me for help launching her freelance practice. Despite her exceptional creative abilities, Sophia had spent months researching business models, pricing strategies, and market positioning without taking a single concrete step toward launching her business.

"I just want to make sure I get it right," she told me during our first session, surrounded by notebooks filled with research and plans. "There's so much to consider, and I don't want to make mistakes that could hurt my business long-term."

While this sounded reasonable on the surface, I noticed that each time Sophia approached the point of action, she discovered a new area requiring research—creating an endless loop of preparation without execution.

"I think what's happening isn't just thorough preparation," I suggested gently. "There might be something deeper keeping you in the planning phase rather than moving into action."

After some reflection, Sophia recognised the truth: "I'm afraid of failing. As long as I'm still planning, I can't fail because I haven't really started. Once I launch, I have to face the possibility that my business might not succeed."

The Solution

Implement the 70% Rule—when you have about 70% of the information you think you need and a plan that seems about 70% solid, take action. The remaining 30% will emerge through implementation.

Together, Sophia and I created a different approach. She set a non-negotiable launch date six weeks from our session. We identified the minimum viable version of her business—the simplest form that would allow her to start working with clients while continuing to refine her approach.

"Instead of trying to figure everything out in advance," I explained, "think of your business as an evolving entity that will be shaped by actual experience rather than theoretical planning. The 70% Rule acknowledges that some things can only be learned through action, not anticipation."

Sophia broke her paralysis by working backward from her launch date, focusing exclusively on the elements required to start working with clients. Within six weeks, she had her first paying clients—and discovered that many of her assumptions required adjustment anyway.

"I spent months trying to anticipate every possible scenario," Sophia told me later, "but within the first few client projects, I encountered situations I never would have predicted. The real learning happened through action, not analysis."

> *Try This:* Identify a project where you might be stuck in analysis paralysis. What would a 70% version look like? Set a specific date to launch this version, making any concerns about "incompleteness" problems to solve after launch, not barriers to beginning.

2. Strategic Abandonment

The Obstacle

Abandoning strategic methods when facing pressure or emotion, reverting to reactive approaches precisely when you most need structure.

Aditya, a sales executive I worked with during a company turnaround, had developed a sophisticated strategic approach to client development. He created detailed account plans, implemented a structured outreach system, and developed multiple pathways for each major prospect.

Yet whenever revenue numbers dropped below targets, a fascinating transformation occurred. Aditya would panic and abandon his methodology, reverting to high-pressure tactics that damaged long-term relationships in pursuit of short-term results.

"I know the right approach," Aditya admitted during a coaching session after one such episode. "But when I see those numbers dropping, something takes over and I throw the strategy out the window. It's like I have two different operating systems—one for normal conditions and another that activates under pressure."

This pattern is remarkably common. The very situations where strategic approaches would be most valuable—periods of heightened pressure or emotional intensity—are precisely when we're most likely to abandon them in favour of reactive responses.

The Solution

Develop implementation triggers and stress protocols that engage and reinforce your strategic approach during challenging times instead of abandoning it.

Aditya developed what he called his "pressure protocol"—a specific sequence of actions triggered by declining numbers. This protocol included intensified focus on his proven strategy rather than abandonment of it. He created physical reminders (including a laminated card in his wallet) to prompt this protocol when emotions threatened to override his strategic thinking.

"The key insight was recognising that my strategic abandonment wasn't a random failure, but a predictable pattern triggered by specific circumstances," Aditya explained. "By preparing for this pattern in advance, I could interrupt it before it took over."

The protocol included immediate steps: a five-minute breathing exercise to regulate his nervous system, reviewing his strategic principles, consulting with a trusted colleague, and then intensifying proven approaches rather than resorting to panic tactics.

"The protocol gave me a structured way to navigate pressure without abandoning strategy," Aditya reflected after several successful implementations. "It acknowledged my emotional response while providing a path back to strategic thinking precisely when I needed it most."

Real-World Application: Identify a situation where stress or pressure typically causes you to abandon strategic thinking. Create a specific protocol—a series of steps you'll follow when this situation arises. Include physical reminders and accountability mechanisms to ensure you maintain your strategic approach precisely when it's most valuable.

3. Confirmation Bias

The Obstacle

Selectively noticing evidence that confirms your existing beliefs while overlooking contradictory information. This undermines accurate situation assessment—the foundation of effective strategy.

Ekta, a product manager with a technology company, was convinced her team's new feature would be a market success despite early user testing showing mixed results. When we reviewed the testing data together, a clear pattern emerged: Ekta emphasised positive feedback while dismissing negative responses as "not understanding the vision."

"These users clearly don't represent our target market," Ekta insisted, referring to participants who had struggled with the new feature. "Once people understand what we're trying to do, they'll love it."

What made this situation particularly interesting was that Ekta was otherwise a data-driven professional who prided herself on objective analysis. Yet in this specific case, her emotional investment in the product concept created a powerful confirmation bias—she literally saw different information in the same user testing sessions than her colleagues observed.

This selective perception led to a costly product launch that ultimately failed, requiring a complete redesign after considerable investment.

"I was so invested in my initial assessment being right that I filtered everything through that lens," Ekta reflected afterward. "I wasn't seeing reality—I was seeing what I wanted to believe."

The Solution

Implement deliberate contradiction seeking—actively look for evidence that challenges your assumptions and give it equal or greater weight than confirming evidence.

After her product failure, Ekta developed a new approach. For every major decision, she now assigns a team member to play "contradiction advocate"—someone responsible for identifying evidence and arguments against the prevailing view. She also instituted "assumption audits" where the team regularly reviews and challenges their core beliefs about their product and market.

"The breakthrough came when I realised confirmation bias isn't a character flaw but a universal human tendency," Ekta explained. "By building contradiction-seeking into our process, we've transformed it from an individual liability to a team strength."

This approach doesn't mean abandoning conviction or passion for your ideas. It means ensuring that your conviction is grounded in reality rather than selective perception.

> *Try This:* For an important project or decision, make a list of your key assumptions. For each assumption, spend five minutes actively searching for evidence that contradicts it. Consider this contradictory evidence carefully before proceeding.

4. Method Rigidity

The Obstacle

Becoming overly attached to specific methods rather than

underlying principles, leading to inappropriate application of tools to situations that require different approaches.

Jaimin had successfully used the Strategic Delta Method to advance his career but encountered problems when applying the same structured approach to his marriage. His attempts to create strategic pathways for relationship issues felt mechanical to his partner and actually damaged their connection.

"I was trying to apply the exact same methodology to our communication issues that I'd used for my career planning," Jaimin explained during couples counselling. "I created spreadsheets tracking our interaction patterns, developed multiple pathways for conflict resolution, and implemented review metrics for our communication."

His partner's response was revealing: "It felt like he was treating our relationship like a business project. I didn't feel seen as a person—I felt like a problem to be solved through his strategic system."

This method rigidity—applying specific techniques without adapting them to different contexts—often emerges when we experience success with particular approaches. Rather than extracting the underlying principles that made the method effective, we try to replicate the exact technique in inappropriate contexts.

"I was so impressed with how well these methods worked professionally that I started seeing everything as a strategic problem to solve," Jaimin admitted. "I missed that different domains require different approaches."

The Solution

Develop methodological flexibility by focusing on core principles rather than specific techniques, adapting your approach to the nature of each situation.

Jaimin shifted his focus from applying specific methods to understanding the underlying principles—structured thinking, multiple options, and deliberate execution. He learned to express these principles differently in personal relationships, emphasising collaborative exploration over strategy implementation.

"I realised the core principles could translate to our relationship, but the specific methodologies needed complete transformation," Jaimin reflected. "Instead of creating strategic pathways for 'us,' we started exploring possibilities together. Instead of tracking metrics, we developed shared reflection practices."

This methodological flexibility allowed Jaimin to maintain strategic principles while adapting them to the relational context in ways that enhanced rather than damaged connection.

> *Real-World Application:* Think about a situation where your usual approach isn't working well. What core principles might still apply, even if the specific method needs adjustment? How could you express these principles in a way that better fits this particular context?

5. False Dichotomy Thinking

The Obstacle

Creating artificial either/or scenarios that limit your strategic options. This binary thinking forces choices between alternatives that might actually be compatible.

Raj, a small business owner I worked with during a growth transition, believed he had to choose between focusing on existing customers or acquiring new ones, as his limited resources couldn't support both. This false dichotomy created oscillating strategies that undermined both customer retention and acquisition.

"I keep swinging between extremes," Raj explained during our consultation. "I'll spend three months focused entirely on retention—deepening relationships with current customers and improving their experience. Then I'll switch completely to acquisition—pursuing new customers through marketing and outreach. Neither approach is working well because I can't maintain consistent momentum in either area."

What made this situation particularly limiting was that Raj had created an artificial choice between options that could potentially complement rather than compete with each other. His binary thinking—retention OR acquisition—prevented him from seeing integrated possibilities.

The Solution

Practice "both/and" thinking by deliberately seeking complementary rather than competing approaches.

Raj broke through this limitation by asking, "How might these objectives support rather than compete with each other?" This question opened possibilities that binary thinking had obscured.

He discovered that certain retention strategies actually enhanced acquisition through referrals, while specific acquisition approaches brought in customers who required less retention effort. By seeking complementary methods, he created an integrated approach that accomplished both goals simultaneously.

"Once I stopped seeing retention and acquisition as competing priorities, I discovered they could actually reinforce each other," Raj reflected. "Happy existing customers became our best acquisition tool through referrals, while carefully targeted acquisition brought in customers who aligned with our strengths, making retention easier."

This both/and thinking transformed what had seemed like an impossible resource allocation problem into a synergistic approach that accomplished multiple objectives simultaneously.

Your Turn: Identify a situation where you might be trapped in either/or thinking. Challenge this assumption by asking, "What would a both/and approach look like?" Generate at least three possibilities that integrate seemingly competing priorities.

Metrics for Measuring Your Progress

Mastering Layer 1 resilience isn't an abstract goal—it's a measurable skill set that develops through deliberate practice. Here are specific indicators to track your progress:

1. The OODA Cycle Time

The OODA loop—Observe, Orient, Decide, Act—is a decision cycle developed by military strategist John Boyd. Your OODA cycle time is how quickly you can move through this process effectively when facing new situations.

As you master Layer 1, this cycle time should decrease, allowing more rapid strategic responses without sacrificing quality. Track how long it takes you to:

- Gather essential information (Observe)
- Place this information in context (Orient)
- Make a clear decision (Decide)
- Implement your choice (Act)

Smita, a consultant working with healthcare organisations, tracked her OODA times when working with new clients. When we first started working together, she noted that her initial client engagements typically took two weeks to move from information gathering to action implementation.

"I prided myself on thoroughness," Smita explained, "but I realised my extended observation and orientation phases were actually creating challenges. By the time I moved to decision and action, circumstances had often changed, requiring rework."

Through deliberate practice, Smita reduced her average cycle from two weeks to three days—dramatically increasing her effectiveness while reducing stress. She achieved this not by cutting corners but by becoming more precise about what information was truly essential versus nice-to-have.

"I developed better filtering mechanisms for observation—knowing exactly what information would meaningfully impact decisions rather than collecting everything possible," Smita told me. "This actually improved my decision quality while dramatically reducing cycle time."

> *Try This:* For your next three challenges, track how long each phase of the OODA cycle takes. Look for patterns in which phase consumes the most time and focus on streamlining that aspect of your process.

2. Option Generation Capacity

Strategic resilience correlates directly with your ability to generate multiple viable options when facing challenges. This capacity can be explicitly measured.

Set a timer for five minutes and generate as many distinct approaches as possible for a specific challenge you're facing. Count only genuinely different strategies, not variations on the same theme.

As you master Layer 1, both the quantity and quality of options should increase during this timed exercise. More importantly, this capacity should become available in real-time situations, not just during deliberate practice.

Pranay, a nonprofit leader navigating funding challenges, tracked his option generation capacity monthly. His initial assessment yielded four options in five minutes—all variations on traditional grant funding approaches. After six months of practice generating alternatives, he consistently produced nine to twelve distinct approaches in the same timeframe—including innovative partnership models, earned income strategies, and community-based funding approaches he wouldn't have previously considered.

"The most valuable aspect wasn't just having more options," Pranay reflected. "It was that these options represented fundamentally different approaches rather than minor variations on the same theme. This diversity created true resilience since obstacles affecting one category of approaches wouldn't impact others."

Equally important, Pranay found this capacity accessible even under pressure—during board meetings or funder discussions—not just in controlled practice environments.

> *Real-World Application:* Conduct a monthly option generation assessment. Set a timer for five minutes and list as many different approaches as possible to a current challenge. Track how this number changes over time as you develop your strategic thinking.

3. Recovery Time From Setbacks

Perhaps the most practical measure of growing resilience is how quickly you recover from unexpected setbacks. Track the time between:

- Initial setback
- Emotional stabilisation
- Strategic reassessment
- Renewed forward movement

As you master Layer 1, this recovery cycle should steadily shorten. Emotional stabilisation happens more quickly, strategic reassessment becomes more automatic, and renewed action occurs with minimal delay.

Ekta began tracking her recovery times after professional disappointments. When we first started working together, a rejected proposal would disrupt her momentum for days—with at least 24 hours of emotional processing before she could begin strategic reassessment, and often another day or two before implementing adjusted approaches.

After six months of deliberate practice, similar setbacks might impact her for hours or even minutes before she re-engaged with adjusted approaches. The emotional component didn't disappear—she still felt disappointment—but it no longer dominated her response or significantly delayed strategic adaptation.

"What changed wasn't that I stopped feeling disappointment," Ekta explained. "It was that the feelings no longer hijacked my strategic thinking. I could process the emotion and engage in strategic reassessment almost simultaneously, rather than sequentially."

This compressed recovery cycle created significant competitive advantage, allowing Ekta to adapt and redirect while others remained stalled by similar setbacks.

> *Your Turn:* After your next setback, track your recovery timeline. Note when you regain emotional balance, when you strategically reassess, and when you resume forward momentum. Use this as a baseline to measure future improvement.

4. Situational Diagnostic Accuracy

Layer 1 mastery includes the ability to accurately diagnose different types of situations and apply appropriate strategies. This can be measured by tracking:

- How often you correctly identify the nature of challenges from the outset.
- How quickly you adjust your diagnosis when initial assessments prove inaccurate.

- The success rate of strategies based on your situational diagnosis.

Partha, a project manager leading complex technology implementations, found his initial diagnostic accuracy was about 60%—meaning that in 40% of cases, he applied approaches that proved unsuited to the actual situation. After several months of deliberately practicing situational assessment, he improved this accuracy to over 80%, with much faster adjustment when his initial diagnosis proved incorrect.

"I developed better pattern recognition," Partha explained. "More importantly, I became much quicker at recognising when my initial assessment was off and adjusting accordingly, rather than persisting with inappropriate approaches."

This improvement came from both broader categorisation systems for different types of situations and increased humility about initial assessments—holding them as working hypotheses rather than definitive judgments.

> *Try This:* For each new challenge you face, write down your initial assessment of the situation type and what strategy would be most effective. Review these assessments after resolution to identify patterns in your diagnostic accuracy and areas for improvement.

When Strategy Isn't Enough

As you master Layer 1 resilience, you'll inevitably encounter its limitations. There are situations where even the most sophisticated strategic approaches prove insufficient—where the complexity, uncertainty, or fundamentally uncontrollable nature of circumstances reveal the boundaries of strategic control.

This recognition isn't failure but evolution. It marks the threshold where Layer 1 approaches naturally lead to Layer 2 development—the cultivation of mental resilience that allows you to navigate uncertainty with equanimity.

Natasha, a colleague, I worked with through a period of profound health challenges, encountered this threshold when her carefully designed system for managing her condition was overwhelmed by unexpected symptoms that defied predictable patterns.

"I had created the perfect strategic approach," Natasha told me during a particularly difficult session. "Multiple medical pathways, lifestyle interventions, contingency plans for different scenarios. I was doing everything right according to Layer 1 principles. And still, my body kept throwing surprises that my strategies couldn't anticipate."

For weeks, Natasha redoubled her strategic efforts—researching more obscure interventions, tracking more variables, creating more elaborate contingency networks. But eventually, she reached a profound realisation.

"I kept thinking if I just found the right strategy, I could control this situation," she recalled. "It took me months to realise that some aspects of my condition were simply beyond strategic management. The complexity was too great, the variables too numerous, the patterns too unpredictable for even the most sophisticated strategic approach to fully address."

This recognition initially felt like defeat—an admission that her strategic abilities had failed. But it actually marked a profound advancement in her journey toward becoming unshakeable.

"When I accepted the limits of strategic control, something unexpected happened," she explained during a later session. "Instead of feeling more vulnerable, I actually felt more stable. I stopped exhausting myself trying to control the uncontrollable and developed a different kind of strength—the ability to remain centered amid uncertainty."

This is the bridge to Layer 2—the recognition that true resilience requires both strategic capability and mental flexibility. As Viktor Frankl observed from the extreme conditions of concentration camps: "When we are no longer able to change a situation, we are challenged to change ourselves."

Jaimin, a business leader navigating industry disruption, described this transition eloquently: "Layer 1 gave me powerful tools for shaping circumstances within my control. But the most valuable lesson came when I encountered its limits—when I recognised that some aspects of reality will always exceed our strategic management. That's not a failure of strategy but simply the nature of complex reality. Acknowledging this opened the door to a different kind of resilience."

This recognition doesn't invalidate the Strategic Delta Method or Quantum Delta approaches we've explored. These remain valuable tools for navigating aspects of life that respond to strategic influence. But they function within a larger context that includes fundamentally uncertain and uncontrollable elements.

True resilience emerges not from perfect strategic control but from the integration of strategic capability with the mental flexibility to navigate what cannot be controlled—the focus of Layer 2.

In the next section of this book, we'll explore this second layer of becoming unshakeable – developing the mental preparedness to navigate uncertainty with equanimity when strategy alone isn't enough.

DANCING IN THE LIGHT ϕ

It had been seven years since I first met Elise after her "Delta" performance. Life had taken me in different directions—university, first job, relationships formed and dissolved. But I had kept her card, and when I found myself back in New Delhi facing a major career decision, something compelled me to seek her out.

Her studio was in an old industrial building converted to artist spaces. When I walked in, Elise was working with a dancer, a young woman struggling with a complex sequence.

"You're thinking too much about the movement," Elise told her. "Your body knows what to do. The problem is in your mind."

She noticed me standing by the door and nodded in recognition. "We'll continue tomorrow, Anaya," she told the dancer, who gathered her things and left with a curious glance in my direction.

"You've returned," Elise said simply. "Seven years later."

"You remember me?"

"The young man who understood Delta. Yes, I remember." She gestured to a bench along the wall. "You're at a crossroads of some kind."

It wasn't a question, but I nodded anyway.

"I've been offered two very different career paths," I explained. "One safe but limiting, one filled with potential but uncertain. I've made pros/cons lists, consulted mentors, analysed market trends. I've done all the strategic delta work, but I still feel... stuck."

"Because delta is only the first dimension of preparation,"

she said, pouring tea from a thermos. "Strategy alone isn't enough."

"What's the second dimension?"

She handed me a cup. "Did you notice what I told my dancer just now?"

"That the problem was in her mind, not her body."

"Precisely. She knows the movements. She's mapped the variables, understood the patterns. But something in her mind creates resistance. This is where we move from delta to psi."

"Another mathematical symbol?"

"Used in psychology and quantum physics," she nodded. "It represents the mind, mental states, the observer effect. In preparation for an uncertain future, psi represents mental resilience."

She sipped her tea thoughtfully.

"The dancer you just saw, Anaya—she reminds me of you. Intelligent, analytical, good at reading patterns. But when the spotlight moves unexpectedly, she freezes. Her mind becomes her greatest obstacle."

"What's the solution?"

"Building a resilience function. Training the mind to process stress and uncertainty differently. Creating mental algorithms that transform how you respond to change."

She stood and walked to the center of the studio.

"Come," she gestured. "Stand here."

I set down my tea and joined her.

"Close your eyes," she instructed. "Now, I want you to imagine a spotlight on you. It's comfortable, steady. You know exactly where to move within it."

I nodded, visualising.

"Now the spotlight begins to move slowly to your right. What happens in your mind?"

"I start calculating where it's going, how fast, whether I should move now or wait."

"Good. That's delta thinking. Now the spotlight suddenly jumps far to your left. What happens?"

"I feel... anxious. Behind. Like I've failed somehow."

"That's the gap between delta and psi," she said. "Your strategic mind knows what's happening, but your emotional mind creates resistance, self-judgment, anxiety."

She touched my shoulder gently.

"Mental resilience isn't about eliminating those responses. It's about creating space between stimulus and response. It's recognising that thoughts are not facts—they're probability waves that exist in multiple states until you collapse them through action."

I opened my eyes to find her watching me with unexpected kindness.

"Your career decision isn't really about which path is objectively better. It's about your relationship with uncertainty. The path that terrifies you might be precisely the one that will develop your psi dimension."

"So, I should take the riskier path?"

She shook her head. "I'm not telling you which choice to make. I'm suggesting that whichever path you choose, the real work is developing the mental resilience to walk it with both effectiveness and peace."

As I prepared to leave, she handed me a small notebook.

"For mapping your mental coordinates," she explained. "The exercises inside will help you build your resilience function."

At the door, I turned back. "Is this it? Delta and psi—strategy and resilience? Is that the complete equation for preparation?"

A mysterious smile crossed her face. "There is a third dimension, but it cannot be taught directly. It emerges naturally when delta and psi work together long enough. Perhaps in another seven years, you'll discover it for yourself."

As I walked out into the cool autumn air, I opened the notebook. On the first page was a single equation:

$$(\Delta + \Psi) \rightarrow ?$$

LAYER 2

STRATEGY ALONE ISN'T ENOUGH

THE DANCER'S MIND

Ψ

The Psi Dimension (Ψ)

Even the most brilliant strategic planning falls apart without the mental resilience to execute it. This is why our equation doesn't stop at delta. As we enter the Psi Dimension, we turn our attention from external strategies to internal landscapes—the territory of mind and meaning.

Psi, used in both psychology and quantum physics, represents mental states and the relationship between observer and observed. In our equation, it encompasses the mental resilience, cognitive flexibility, and emotional intelligence that determine how effectively we respond to change.

While delta helps us prepare for what might happen externally, psi helps us prepare for what will happen internally when we face challenges. It's not enough to have strategic plans—we need minds capable of executing those plans under pressure, uncertainty, and complexity.

In the chapters ahead, we'll map your cognitive landscape, build your resilience function, introduce quantum thinking to break through limitations, calibrate your mental energy allocation, and guide you through the second transformation—from mental mastery to genuine inner peace.

This section bridges the practical and the profound. The tools here are immediately applicable to daily challenges, yet they also begin to open doorways to the third dimension of our equation—a glimpse of something beyond strategy and psychology that emerges when both work in harmony.

SIX

Beyond Strategy

The limits of control. When perfect plans fail. Introduction to mental resilience.

"Jai stared at his phone, a muscle twitching in his jaw. "They cancelled the project. Six months of work, all the strategic planning, multiple pathways developed—and with one email, it's all irrelevant."

"I'm sorry," Avika said, sitting beside him on the park bench. "That's incredibly frustrating."

"Frustrating doesn't begin to cover it," Jai replied. "I did everything right, followed every principle we've discussed. And still... this."

Avika was quiet for a moment. "What does this experience tell you about the limits of strategic approaches?"

Jai looked up, surprised by the question. "That no matter how good my methods are, some factors will always be beyond my control."

"Exactly," Avika nodded. "This isn't a failure of the methods we've explored—it's a recognition of their inherent limitations. No strategy, no matter how brilliant, can control all variables."

"So, what's the point then?" Jai asked, genuine questioning in his voice.

"The point is to develop something beyond strategy," Avika replied. "A capacity to remain centered and effective precisely when your best plans fall apart. That's Layer 2—mental preparedness amid uncertainty."

Jai took a deep breath. "I'm listening."

"Everyone has a plan until they get punched in the mouth."
– Mike Tyson

Throughout the first section of this book, we've explored the power of strategic methods to actively shape your circumstances. The Strategic Delta Method, Quantum Principles, and Quantum Delta approach provide powerful tools for navigating complexity and creating the outcomes you desire.

But if you've been applying these methods, you've likely encountered a fundamental truth: strategy alone isn't enough. Despite our best planning, preparation, and strategic thinking, life has a way of delivering situations that defy our attempts at control.

This isn't a failure of the methods we've discussed. It's a recognition of the inherent limitations of any approach based primarily on shaping external circumstances. No matter how sophisticated your strategies, there will always be factors beyond your influence—market shifts, others' decisions, health challenges, natural events, and countless other variables that can disrupt even the most brilliant plans.

This realisation brings us to a critical threshold in becoming truly unshakeable: the transition from Layer 1 to Layer 2.

The Limits of Control

Jaimin discovered these limits through painful experience. A brilliant strategic thinker, he had built a successful consulting practice by applying the precise methods we've discussed in previous chapters. His ability to develop comprehensive strategies and contingency plans had served him well for years.

Then his son was diagnosed with a serious medical condition.

When Jaimin first called me after receiving the diagnosis, the shock in his voice was palpable. "I don't know what to do," he said, his usual confident tone replaced by vulnerability. "This isn't something I can solve with a strategic plan."

Over the following weeks, Jaimin experienced a profound reckoning with the limits of control. Despite consulting top specialists, researching treatment options, and leveraging every resource available, he couldn't control his son's health trajectory. The uncertainty was excruciating precisely because his usual tools for managing complexity seemed inadequate.

"For the first time in my adult life, I feel truly helpless," Jaimin told me during one of our conversations. "I realised how much of my identity and security had been built around the illusion that I could control outcomes if I was just strategic enough."

This reckoning with the limits of control isn't unique to extreme situations like health crises. It emerges in countless domains:

- The perfect career strategy disrupted by industry transformation.
- The carefully cultivated relationship ended by a partner's unpredictable choice.
- The meticulously planned event derailed by weather or other circumstances.
- The financial strategy undermined by market forces beyond prediction.

Sarita, a financial advisor, faced this reality during a market crash that devastated portfolios she had constructed with the utmost strategic care. When we met shortly after the crash, she was questioning her entire professional approach.

"I had done everything 'right' according to the best available methods," she explained, her frustration evident. "I diversified across asset classes, built in safeguards, created contingencies. But suddenly that wasn't enough. I realised that no matter how sophisticated my strategies, some factors would always remain beyond my control."

This recognition can be profoundly unsettling, especially if you've invested heavily in developing strategic capabilities. It can feel like discovering that the tools you've relied on have fundamental limitations you never fully appreciated.

But this threshold—this recognition of the limits of control—is not a dead end. It's a doorway to the second layer of becoming unshakeable, where new capacities emerge that complement rather than replace your strategic abilities.

> *Try This:* Identify a situation in your life where your best strategic thinking hasn't created the outcomes you wanted. Rather than immediately looking for better strategies, sit with the recognition that some elements may be inherently beyond your control. Notice any resistance to this acknowledgment and what might lie beyond that resistance.

When Perfect Plans Fail

Even the most carefully constructed plans can fail when they encounter reality. This isn't because planning is worthless—as we've seen, strategic approaches create tremendous value. But plans operate within complex systems where countless variables interact in ways we cannot fully predict or control.

Ekta experienced this when launching her carefully planned product. An experienced entrepreneur, she had approached this launch with meticulous attention to detail. When we first discussed her plans, I was impressed by her comprehensive approach.

"I've done everything by the book," Ekta explained, walking me through her detailed launch strategy. "Market research, prototype testing, strategic pricing, comprehensive marketing. I've accounted for multiple contingencies and created backup plans for all the potential obstacles I could identify."

Her plan seemed robust against foreseeable challenges. But

three days before launch, an unexpected competitor entered the market with a similar product at a price point her model couldn't match. Within a week, her perfect plan—the result of months of strategic development—needed complete reconsideration.

When we spoke again, Ekta's frustration was evident. "How could I have missed this? I thought I'd considered every possibility."

"The issue isn't that you missed something," I suggested. "It's that some possibilities are inherently unpredictable. Your planning was excellent for what could be foreseen, but reality includes elements that simply cannot be anticipated, no matter how thorough your approach."

This recognition doesn't invalidate Strategic Delta or other methods we've explored. Instead, it places them in a broader context—as valuable tools that work within inherent limitations. When we understand these limitations, we can develop complementary capacities that create resilience even when our best plans fail.

As Ekta reflected later: "It wasn't just that I needed a new plan. It was that I needed a fundamentally different relationship with planning itself. I had to recognise that no plan, no matter how thorough, could anticipate every possibility."

This shift—from seeking perfect plans to developing resilience amid inevitable uncertainty—marks the threshold of Layer 2 resilience. It's about maintaining effectiveness precisely when strategies reach their limits.

The key insight of Layer 2 is that true resilience comes not just from better planning but from how we relate to the inevitable failures and limitations of any plan. It's about developing the mental flexibility to navigate uncertainty with equanimity—to remain centered and effective precisely when strategies reach their limits.

Real-World Application: Think about a time when your carefully constructed plan failed. Beyond creating a better plan, how might you have approached the situation differently if you had recognised from the beginning that no plan could anticipate everything? What capacities beyond strategic thinking might have been valuable in that moment?

Introduction to Mental Resilience

Mental resilience is the capacity to maintain equilibrium, clarity, and effective action amid uncertainty and challenge. It's not about being unaffected by difficulty but about how quickly and completely you can restore balance when disruption occurs.

Promesh, a business leader I worked with during a major organisational crisis, discovered the importance of this capacity when his company faced unexpected regulatory changes that threatened their core business model. Despite his sophisticated strategic capabilities, the situation contained too many unknowns for pure strategy to resolve.

"My team wasn't just looking to me for strategic direction," Promesh explained during a coaching session at the height of the crisis. "They were looking for emotional stability and centered presence amid chaos. I realised the most important thing I could offer wasn't a perfect plan but a grounded example of how to function effectively amid uncertainty."

Promesh's insight points to a fundamental truth: people follow leaders who demonstrate mental resilience during turbulence. You can have brilliant strategies, but if you collapse emotionally when those strategies meet unexpected obstacles, your effectiveness as a leader—and your personal wellbeing—will suffer dramatically.

This mental resilience doesn't replace strategic thinking—it creates the conditions where strategic thinking can function optimally despite disruption. It's about maintaining cognitive and emotional balance precisely when circumstances would typically create imbalance.

The qualities that constitute mental resilience include:

Cognitive Flexibility

The ability to adapt thinking patterns when circumstances change, including:

- Revising assumptions based on new information.
- Considering multiple perspectives simultaneously.
- Thinking in systems rather than linear chains.
- Embracing paradox and apparent contradiction.

Smita, a healthcare executive navigating a complex merger, demonstrated this flexibility when initial integration plans encountered unexpected resistance. Rather than doubling down on the original approach, she quickly shifted frameworks—moving from a structural merger model to a cultural integration approach when it became clear that organisational culture was the primary obstacle.

"I had to completely reframe how I was thinking about the challenge," Smita explained. "My initial mental model wasn't working, and continuing to apply it would have created more resistance rather than progress."

This cognitive flexibility—the ability to shift mental models when reality doesn't conform to your initial framework—creates adaptability that rigid thinking cannot match.

Emotional Regulation

The capacity to manage emotional responses to challenging situations, including:

- Acknowledging feelings without being controlled by them.

- Maintaining access to your full capabilities despite stress.
- Recovering quickly from emotional disruption.
- Using emotions as information rather than drivers of action.

Partha, a financial advisor guiding clients through market volatility, described how emotional regulation transformed his effectiveness: "I used to become emotionally entangled in market downturns, which actually impaired my strategic thinking precisely when clients needed it most. Learning to acknowledge my anxiety without being defined by it allowed me to maintain rational analysis even during high-stress periods."

This regulation doesn't mean suppressing emotions—it means developing a different relationship with them. Rather than being controlled by emotional reactions, you learn to experience them while maintaining access to your full cognitive capabilities.

Uncertainty Tolerance

The ability to function effectively without complete information or guarantees, including:

- Making appropriately scaled decisions despite unknowns.
- Maintaining direction amid ambiguity.
- Finding peace within unresolved situations.
- Extracting value from uncertainty itself.

Ekta, a technology entrepreneur, developed this tolerance through multiple product launches in rapidly changing markets. "I realised complete certainty was never going to be available, no matter how much research or planning I did," she reflected. "The question became not how to eliminate uncertainty but how to function effectively within it—how to make good decisions with the best available information while recognising its inherent limitations."

This tolerance doesn't mean embracing uncertainty for its own sake or abandoning the pursuit of clear information. It means developing the capacity to move forward effectively even when perfect clarity isn't available—which is most of the time in complex situations.

These capacities don't emerge from strategic methods alone. They develop through deliberate practices that cultivate a different relationship with uncertainty, challenge, and change—practices we'll explore throughout this section of the book.

> *Try This:* On a scale of 1-10, rate your current capacity in each aspect of mental resilience described above. Which dimension seems most developed for you? Which could benefit from focused attention? What patterns do you notice across these self-assessments?

The Bridge Between Layers

Layer 2 resilience doesn't replace Layer 1—it complements and enhances it. Think of it as a bridge that allows your strategic capabilities to function even when conditions would normally disrupt them.

Menka, a product manager navigating complex technology development, described this integration after developing both strategic methods and mental resilience: "My strategic thinking actually improved when I developed mental flexibility. I could see possibilities I would have missed before, adapt more quickly to changing conditions, and maintain strategic clarity even amid stress."

This integration creates a powerful synergy:

- Strategic methods provide structure and direction for navigating complexity.
- Mental resilience ensures these methods remain available despite disruption.

- Together, they create a capability greater than either alone could provide.

The journey from Layer 1 to Layer 2 isn't about abandoning what you've already developed but about adding vital capacities that address the inherent limitations of strategic approaches alone.

"It's like learning to sail instead of just rowing," explained Jaimin, whom we met earlier. "When I was focused solely on strategic control, I was essentially rowing—using force and direction to move forward. Developing mental resilience added sails to my boat—the ability to work with forces I couldn't control, finding power in what previously seemed like obstacles."

While Jaimin couldn't control his son's medical condition, he discovered that he could control his response to it. By developing mental resilience alongside his strategic capabilities, he created a foundation that allowed him to navigate the uncertainty of the health journey with both practical effectiveness and emotional stability.

"I still used strategic thinking to research treatment options, coordinate medical care, and create support systems," Jaimin reflected. "But mental resilience allowed me to do this without being overwhelmed by the aspects I couldn't control. Both capacities were essential—neither alone would have been sufficient."

Real-World Application: Consider a situation where you're primarily applying Layer 1 approaches (strategic methods). How might developing Layer 2 capacities (mental resilience) enhance your effectiveness in this situation? What specific aspects of mental flexibility would be most valuable given the particular challenges you're facing?

The Path Forward

In the chapters ahead, we'll explore specific aspects of Layer 2 resilience, including:

- How to approach uncertainty as opportunity rather than threat.
- Practices for developing genuine acceptance without resignation.
- Methods for maintaining equilibrium amid chaotic circumstances.
- Approaches for finding freedom within rather than from challenging situations.

Each of these explorations will include practical applications and exercises to develop these capacities in your daily life.

The journey through Layer 2 doesn't require abandoning your strategic capabilities. Rather, it expands your repertoire of responses to include approaches that work precisely when strategy reaches its limits.

As we proceed, remember that becoming unshakeable isn't about eliminating challenges from your life. It's about developing the capacity to navigate any circumstance with presence, clarity, and effectiveness—whether through strategic shaping or mental resilience, and ideally through the powerful integration of both.

Ekta, who eventually rebounded from her disrupted product launch, perhaps expressed this integration most eloquently: "Strategy gives me direction when circumstances allow for influence. Mental resilience gives me stability when circumstances exceed my control. Together, they allow me to navigate the full spectrum of situations life presents—maintaining effectiveness regardless of whether I can shape events or must adapt to them."

In the next chapter, we'll explore how the metaphor of "drawing lines on water" reveals both the limitations of rigid planning and the possibilities that emerge when we develop a more fluid relationship with reality.

SEVEN

Drawing Lines on Water

From fighting against reality's flowing nature to developing the capacity to work with it.

They sat by the river, watching ripples form and dissolve on the surface.

"Try it," Avika suggested, handing Jai a stick.

With a sceptical expression, Jai dipped the stick into the water and drew a line. It disappeared almost instantly.

"Again," Avika encouraged.

Jai drew another line, more forcefully this time. Again, the water's surface returned to its natural state within seconds.

"This is exactly how I've been feeling," Jai admitted. "Like I'm trying to create lasting patterns in circumstances that won't hold them."

"Most of us spend our lives doing exactly this," Avika said. "Drawing lines on water and then getting frustrated when they don't stay put."

"So, what's the alternative?" Jai asked. "Just give up on attempting to create any order at all?"

"Not at all," Avika replied. "The alternative is learning to work with the water's nature rather than against it. Instead of trying to make the river conform to your patterns, you learn to navigate its natural flow."

Jai placed a leaf on the water's surface, watching as it began a journey downstream. "Like this?"

"Exactly like that," Avika smiled. "You're not controlling the river, but you're still engaged with it. That's the essence of Layer 2—not abandoning intentions but holding them in a way that works with reality's fluid nature rather than fighting against it."

When my son was five years old, we were sitting by a river when he decided to conduct an experiment. With intense concentration, he took a stick and drew lines on the water's surface.

"Look, Dad!" he called excitedly. But by the time I looked, the lines had already disappeared.

He tried again and again, growing increasingly frustrated as each attempt to create lasting patterns on the flowing water failed. Finally, he threw the stick down and declared, "This river is broken!"

I couldn't help but laugh, but as I thought about it more, I realised how perfectly his experiment illustrated what most of us do throughout our lives. We try to impose fixed patterns on a reality that is constantly flowing and changing.

We create rigid five-year plans in careers that might be transformed by technology next year. We establish inflexible expectations in relationships with complex, evolving humans. We build certainty around health in bodies that change every day.

We're all drawing lines on water and getting frustrated when they don't stay put.

The Illusion of Fixed Patterns

In Layer 1, we focused on strategic methods for directing your spotlight—tools like Strategic Delta and Quantum Delta that help you actively shape your circumstances. These approaches remain valuable, but they have limitations.

Ekta discovered these limitations the hard way. A brilliant strategic planner, she had mapped out every aspect of her company's growth using the best methods available. Her plans were comprehensive, considering multiple variables and contingencies.

Then the pandemic hit.

Overnight, her carefully crafted strategic map became obsolete. Supply chains collapsed, consumer behaviour transformed, and the market landscape shifted dramatically. All those lines she had drawn so carefully were washed away by a river that suddenly changed course.

"I felt like a failure," she told me. "I had prided myself on my ability to plan for every contingency, but I hadn't planned for a complete paradigm shift in how business operated."

Ekta's story isn't unusual. Whether it's a global event like a pandemic, or personal disruptions like unexpected health issues, relationship changes, or career shifts, life has a way of reminding us that our lines drawn on water are temporary at best.

This isn't because we're doing something wrong. It's because reality itself is more fluid than our minds want to admit. We crave certainty and stability, so we create mental models that suggest more permanence than actually exists. When reality doesn't conform to these models, we often blame reality rather than recognising the limitations of our expectations.

Martin, a software developer, described his realisation of this pattern: "For years, I'd get frustrated when projects didn't follow the roadmaps we created. I'd think, 'Why can't people just stick to the plan?' Then one day it clicked—the plans weren't reflecting reality; they were reflecting our wishes about reality. The territory never perfectly matches the map."

This recognition—that reality is inherently fluid rather than fixed—forms the foundation of **Layer 2 resilience**. It's not about abandoning plans or strategic approaches, but about holding them differently — recognising them as provisional sketches rather than permanent structures.

Flow States and Adaptability

The alternative to rigid pattern-seeking isn't giving up on planning altogether. It's learning to plan like water.

Water doesn't fight against obstacles; it flows around them. It doesn't resist gravity; it harnesses it for momentum. It doesn't break when frozen; it simply changes form and waits.

Leo, a tech entrepreneur, embodied this approach during a major product launch failure. Instead of clinging to his original vision, he paid attention to how users were actually interacting with his product—in ways he hadn't anticipated.

"I realised I was trying to force users to follow the path I'd envisioned rather than observing the paths they naturally wanted to create," he explained. "When I stopped fighting against that current and started flowing with it, we discovered a much better product direction."

Leo's team pivoted and developed a completely different feature set based on actual user behaviour rather than predicted patterns. The company not only survived but thrived, eventually being acquired for a sum that exceeded his original goals.

This is adaptability in action—the capacity to maintain your core purpose while shifting your approach based on changing conditions. It's not abandoning intention but allowing the form that intention takes to evolve in response to reality's feedback.

The morning I watched my son drawing lines on water, I noticed something interesting later that day. After giving up on his frustrating experiment, he discovered a new way to interact with the river. He began placing leaves on the water and watching them navigate the currents. He became fascinated with their journey—how they sped up in narrow passages, got temporarily caught in eddies, and sometimes took unexpected paths.

"Look, Dad!" he exclaimed. "The river is playing with the leaves!"

He had shifted from fighting the river's nature to engaging with it—from frustration to fascination. This simple shift mirrors what happens when we develop Layer 2 resilience: we move from resisting reality's fluid nature to working with it creatively.

Practical Approaches to Adaptability

How do you develop this water-like adaptability in your own life? It begins with recognising the difference between elements you can control and those you can't—and developing different relationships with each.

Distinguish Between Outcomes and Methods

One of the most powerful shifts in developing adaptability is learning to separate desired outcomes from specific methods for achieving them.

Outcome: What you ultimately want to achieve

Method: The specific path to get there

Most of us conflate these, becoming attached to particular methods rather than focusing on the desired outcome. When your method gets disrupted, reconnect with your core outcome and ask, "What other paths might lead there?"

Sarita, a marketing director, discovered the power of this distinction when her carefully planned campaign was derailed by a competitor's unexpected product launch. Rather than trying to force her original approach, she returned to the fundamental outcome she wanted: increasing brand awareness among a specific demographic.

"By separating the outcome from the method, I freed myself to consider completely different approaches," she explained. "Instead of viewing the competitor's launch as an obstacle to our plan, I started seeing it as a river current we could potentially use to our advantage."

Sarita's team developed a responsive campaign that cleverly referenced the competitor's launch while highlighting their own unique value proposition. The approach generated significantly more engagement than their original plan likely would have, precisely because it worked with the actual market conditions rather than an imagined scenario.

This approach doesn't mean abandoning strategic thinking. In fact, it makes your strategic thinking more robust by creating flexibility around how goals are achieved. You maintain clear vision about destinations while remaining adaptable about routes.

Consider how this might apply in your own life. Think about an important goal you're currently pursuing. Can you clearly distinguish between the outcome you want and the specific method you're using to pursue it? What alternative methods might achieve the same outcome if your current approach became unviable?

Create Feedback Loops

Adaptability requires current information. Rather than executing plans in isolation, build regular feedback mechanisms into your process.

Leila, a marketing director, transformed her department's effectiveness with one simple change: decreasing planning cycles from quarterly to bi-weekly. This allowed her team to respond to market changes almost in real-time, making smaller, more frequent adjustments rather than major corrections.

"We used to create elaborate quarterly plans that would be partially obsolete within weeks," she explained. "Now we set broad quarterly objectives but plan specific tactics in two-week sprints. We're constantly getting feedback and adjusting course."

This approach created what Leila called "responsive resilience"—the capacity to adapt quickly to changing conditions without losing overall direction. By decreasing the time between plan and feedback, her team could evolve their approach based on actual results rather than projected outcomes.

The key insight here is that adaptability isn't random responsiveness; it's structured evolution based on real-time information. By building intentional feedback loops into your processes, you create systematic ways to detect when your lines on water are already dissolving and adjust accordingly.

ow might you shorten feedback cycles in areas that matter to you? Could you get weekly instead of monthly feedback on a project? Daily instead of weekly data on your health habits? Immediate rather than delayed responses to relationship concerns?

Practice Provisional Planning

Instead of creating definitive plans, develop provisional ones—plans explicitly designed to evolve as new information emerges.

This shift begins with how you frame your planning language. Start sentences with:

- "Based on what we currently know..."
- "Our provisional approach is..."
- "Our initial direction will be..."

This subtle linguistic shift creates psychological space for adaptation when conditions change.

Pranay, a project manager, implemented this approach when leading a complex software implementation that had previously failed under traditional project management. Instead of presenting the team with a definitive roadmap, he introduced what he called a "living plan" that everyone understood would evolve.

"The psychological impact was remarkable," Pranay noted. "When we encountered unexpected obstacles—which happen in every complex project—the team didn't experience them as failures or deviations. They were simply new information that informed our evolving approach."

By explicitly framing the plan as provisional from the outset, Pranay created a context where adaptation was expected rather than exceptional. This didn't mean abandoning structure or accountability; it meant building evolution into the structure itself.

This approach applies far beyond work contexts. Think about areas in your life where you might benefit from more provisional planning. How would your relationship with uncertainty change if you explicitly designed your approaches to evolve rather than trying to create fixed paths through flowing waters?

Cultivate Beginner's Mind

The Zen concept of shoshin or "beginner's mind" refers to approaching situations without preconceptions, regardless of your experience level.

Aditya, a veteran financial advisor with 30 years of experience, credits his continued success to deliberately questioning his own expertise regularly. "The moment I think I know exactly how markets work is the moment I become vulnerable to being blindsided," he says. "I start each day asking what assumptions I might be making that could be wrong."

This practice of beginner's mind doesn't mean disregarding experience or expertise. Rather, it means holding that expertise lightly — recognising that patterns from the past may not apply to present circumstances in straightforward ways.

Sarita, a therapist, described how this approach transformed her work with clients: "Early in my career, I'd quickly pattern-match client issues to theoretical frameworks I'd learned. Now I deliberately suspend that categorisation to really hear each person's unique experience. Paradoxically, this 'not knowing' approach actually makes my expertise more useful because it's applied contextually rather than automatically."

Cultivating beginner's mind creates adaptability by keeping your perception fresh. When you approach situations with genuine curiosity rather than presumed knowledge, you're more likely to notice subtle shifts and emerging patterns that might otherwise be filtered out by existing mental models.

In what areas of your life might you benefit from more beginner's mind? Where have established patterns of thinking potentially limited your perception of what's possible? How might deliberately suspending "knowing" create space for fresh seeing?

Embracing the River's Natural Course

The shift from drawing lines on water to flowing with the river doesn't happen overnight. It requires practice and often feels uncomfortable at first. We're conditioned to seek certainty and resist change.

What makes this shift particularly challenging is that it doesn't just involve learning new skills; it requires unlearning established patterns of relating to uncertainty. Many of us have been taught—explicitly or implicitly—that uncertainty is a problem to be eliminated rather than a natural condition to be navigated.

Smita, a healthcare executive, described her journey: "I was raised to believe that proper planning eliminated uncertainty. When uncertainty persisted despite my best efforts, I'd feel like I was doing something wrong. Learning to see uncertainty as inherent rather than problematic was actually a relief—it meant I could stop blaming myself for not achieving the impossible."

This shift in perspective—from seeing uncertainty as a problem to recognising it as a natural feature of reality—creates the foundation for genuine adaptability. It's not about lowering standards or abandoning intentions; it's about aligning your approach with reality's actual nature rather than fighting against it.

Remember my son by the river? His frustration wasn't caused by the water; it was caused by his expectation that water should hold the lines he drew. When he shifted to working with the water's nature rather than against it, his frustration transformed into delight.

This is the essence of Layer 2 resilience. When you stop expecting life to conform to your patterns and start appreciating its natural flow, you discover a different kind of resilience—not the rigid strength of resistance, but the flexible strength of adaptation.

The paradox is that by surrendering the illusion of fixed patterns, you actually become more effective at navigating life's currents. By accepting the water's flowing nature, you can work with it rather than exhausting yourself fighting against it.

As the ancient Taoist philosopher Lao Tzu observed: "Water is fluid, soft, and yielding. But water will wear away rock, which is rigid and cannot yield. As a rule, whatever is fluid, soft, and yielding will overcome whatever is rigid and hard. This is another paradox: what is soft is strong."

In the next chapter, we'll explore how quantum uncertainty can become a source of strength rather than anxiety, further developing your capacity to thrive amid the ever-changing river of life.

EIGHT

Quantum Uncertainty as a Strength

The unpredictable nature of life that strategic approaches try to minimise might actually be the soil from which your greatest opportunities grow.

"I used to think uncertainty was always a problem to solve," Jai said as they looked at the job boards. "Something to be eliminated through better information or clearer plans."

Avika pointed to the various postings. "If your future was completely certain—if you knew exactly which job you'd end up with—how would you feel right now?"

Jai considered this. "I guess... it would depend on whether I liked the predetermined outcome or not."

"Exactly," Avika nodded. "But here's a different perspective: uncertainty isn't just something to tolerate until you reach certainty. It's actually the soil from which new possibilities grow."

"How so?" Jai asked.

"If your path was completely certain, only one future would be possible," Avika explained. "Uncertainty means multiple potential futures exist simultaneously including ones better than you could currently imagine."

Jai's expression shifted as he considered this. "So, uncertainty isn't just a lack of information..."

"It's a field of possibilities," Avika finished. "The quantum perspective isn't about eliminating uncertainty but learning to navigate it skilfully—even finding freedom within it."

"Chaos isn't a pit. Chaos is a ladder."
– Littlefinger, Game of Thrones

Most of us have been conditioned to view uncertainty as a problem to be solved or a threat to be eliminated. We create schedules, plans, and routines in an attempt to make life predictable. We seek guarantees, warranties, and assurances to minimise risk. We crave the security of knowing what comes next.

But what if this approach is fundamentally misaligned with reality? What if uncertainty isn't just an unavoidable aspect of life but potentially its most valuable feature?

That's the counterintuitive insight at the heart of quantum physics—and the foundation for developing Layer 2 resilience.

How Uncertainty Creates Possibility

I remember sitting with Priya in a café shortly after she'd been unexpectedly laid off from her "secure" corporate job. Her hands trembled slightly as she stirred her untouched coffee. "Everything's falling apart," she said. "I had the next five years mapped out—career progression, mortgage payments, even when we'd start trying for a second child. Now it's all... uncertain."

The word "uncertain" came out like something bitter on her tongue.

Priya's response was entirely natural. Most of us experience uncertainty as threatening rather than generative. We've been taught—through education, organisational structures, and cultural messaging—that success comes through careful planning and systematic execution. Uncertainty appears as the enemy of this approach, a fog that obscures the path forward.

But this perspective misses something profound about how reality actually operates. In quantum mechanics, particles exist in states of possibility called "superposition" until they're observed or measured. This uncertainty isn't a bug in the system—it's an essential feature that creates the foundation for everything that exists.

The same principle applies to your life, though in a less literal way. Uncertainty isn't just something to tolerate—it's the very soil from which new possibilities grow.

Three months after our coffee shop conversation, Priya called me with excitement in her voice. While attending a networking event, she had met someone who needed exactly her expertise for a project-based opportunity—something she would never have considered while safely employed.

"It's strange," she told me. "If I hadn't lost my job, I would have been too busy following my five-year plan to even notice this opportunity. And honestly, I wouldn't have been open to it—it didn't fit my idea of career progression."

That project led to another, then another. Within a year, Priya had established a consulting practice that provided more income, flexibility, and fulfilment than her corporate role ever had.

"Looking back," she reflected during a hike together, "what seemed like devastating uncertainty was actually the opening of a field of possibilities I couldn't see before. My supposedly 'secure' job had actually been limiting what could emerge in my life."

Priya's story illustrates a paradox many of us encounter: what feels like disruptive uncertainty often creates space for possibilities that couldn't have emerged otherwise. The very thing we resist—the dissolution of fixed plans—can become the gateway to opportunities we couldn't have imagined.

This isn't coincidence or just "making the best of a bad situation"—it's a fundamental principle about how reality operates. Certainty, while psychologically comforting, narrows possibility. Uncertainty, while initially uncomfortable, expands it.

Think about significant positive developments in your own life. How many were the direct result of executing predetermined plans, and how many emerged from unexpected shifts, "lucky" encounters, or apparent disruptions to your intended path? For most people, the most meaningful aspects of life—relationships, career opportunities, personal discoveries—emerged in ways they couldn't have orchestrated through planning alone.

This doesn't mean planning has no value. Rather, it suggests that our relationship with uncertainty might be fundamentally misaligned with how possibility actually emerges in our lives.

The Paradox of Planning Without Attachment

This perspective raises an important question: If uncertainty creates possibility, should we abandon planning altogether? Should we just drift through life without direction, waiting to see what happens?

Absolutely not. The most effective approach isn't planning versus no planning—it's planning without attachment. This paradoxical stance maintains clear intention while remaining open to emergent possibilities.

I witnessed this approach in action while advising a technology startup facing a major strategic decision. The company's CEO, Pranay, had developed a detailed expansion plan with specific targets and timelines. Then an unexpected opportunity emerged that didn't align with the original strategy but offered potentially greater returns.

The leadership team divided into two camps: those who argued for sticking with the established plan and those who advocated abandoning it entirely for the new opportunity. Pranay surprised everyone by taking a different approach.

"We're going to hold our strategic plan as a valuable framework while recognising it's not sacred," he announced. "We'll explore this new opportunity with genuine curiosity, not presupposing either that it's a distraction or that it's superior to our current direction."

What followed was a systematic exploration that neither clung to the original plan nor abandoned strategic thinking. The team gathered information, conducted small experiments, and evaluated results against both existing goals and emerging possibilities.

"I plan thoroughly but hold those plans lightly," Pranay explained to me later. "The plan gives me direction, but attachment to the plan would blind me to opportunities I couldn't have anticipated."

This approach paid off when it became clear that elements of the unexpected opportunity could actually enhance their original direction in ways they hadn't imagined. While competitors were still operating in either/or mode—either rigidly executing existing strategies or chasing every new possibility—Pranay's company integrated the best aspects of both approaches.

"Paradoxically, this dual approach made me more effective, not less," Pranay noted. "Because I wasn't desperately needing a specific outcome, I could remain flexible and responsive. I had direction without attachment, intention without desperation."

This harmony manifests in several practical ways that you can apply in your own life.

When Sarita launched her design business, she created what she called "anchored exploration"—establishing clear baseline goals while deliberately allocating time and resources to explore unexpected directions. Her business plan included both structured milestones and what she called "possibility spaces"—

periods specifically dedicated to pursuing whatever emerged as interesting without immediate pressure to produce results.

"Those possibility spaces ended up generating most of our breakthrough work," Sarita told me. "But they were only possible because the anchored aspects of our business provided the stability to explore. It wasn't structure versus freedom—it was structure enabling freedom."

This approach applies beyond business contexts. Jaimin and Ekta used similar principles when navigating a relationship challenge. Rather than either rigidly enforcing expectations or abandoning them entirely, they created what Jaimin called "directed openness"—clear expressions of needs and boundaries coupled with genuine curiosity about unexpected ways those needs might be met.

"We discovered solutions neither of us could have imagined if we'd been either completely rigid or completely unstructured in our approach," Ekta explained. "The combination of clear intention and openness to unexpected paths created something better than either of us originally envisioned."

This paradoxical stance—planning without attachment, direction without rigidity—creates a resilience that neither rigid structure nor complete flexibility alone can provide. It acknowledges the value of intentional direction while recognising that the path that actually unfolds may be more complex and potentially more rewarding than anything we could have planned in advance.

Finding Freedom in the Unknown

Beyond its practical advantages, embracing uncertainty offers something even more valuable: psychological freedom.

When you build your sense of security on conditions being

certain and predictable, you become vulnerable to inevitable disruption. Your wellbeing becomes hostage to circumstances remaining as expected—something the universe consistently refuses to guarantee.

I was reminded of this during a conversation with Swastik, a highly successful entrepreneur who had built and sold multiple companies. Despite his material success, he described persistent anxiety throughout most of his career.

"I was constantly trying to create certainty in an inherently uncertain environment," he explained. "Each achievement just led to more pressure to maintain control and predict outcomes. The more successful I became, the more I had to lose, and the more threatening uncertainty felt."

The turning point came unexpectedly during a hurricane that destroyed Swastik's home. In the aftermath, as he sorted through the few possessions that remained, something shifted in his relationship with uncertainty.

"Standing there with almost everything gone, I realised I was still fundamentally okay," he told me. "Not because I could control circumstances—obviously I couldn't—but because something in me remained intact regardless of external conditions. It was a strange freedom I'd never experienced before."

This insight transformed Swastik's approach to both business and life. He continued making plans and executing strategies, but without the psychological burden of needing circumstances to unfold exactly as anticipated. His effectiveness actually increased as his desperation decreased.

Leila experienced a similar shift through a very different situation. After meticulously planning her wedding for over a year, controlling every detail from the specific flowers to the exact timing of each moment, disaster struck. Two weeks before the ceremony, the venue called—they had experienced severe water damage and could not host the event.

"It felt like my world was collapsing," Leila recalled. "I had invested so much in this specific vision that any deviation seemed catastrophic."

With limited time and options, Leila was forced to embrace uncertainty. The replacement venue was entirely different from her original choice. Many carefully planned details had to be abandoned or reimagined. Nothing would be quite as she had envisioned.

But something unexpected emerged from this forced flexibility. As Leila loosened her grip on how things "should" be, she reconnected with what actually mattered—celebrating her commitment with loved ones, regardless of the setting or details.

"The wedding was nothing like I'd planned, but it was perfect in a way I couldn't have engineered," she reflected. "There were beautiful moments that only happened because of the last-minute changes—things I would have missed if everything had gone 'perfectly' according to plan."

More importantly, this experience changed Leila's relationship with uncertainty going forward. She discovered that her happiness didn't actually depend on circumstances matching her expectations. This realisation created a profound psychological freedom—the ability to hold intentions without making her wellbeing dependent on specific outcomes.

This freedom doesn't come from abandoning preferences or desires. You can still have clear intentions and work toward specific outcomes. The shift is in recognising that your fundamental wellbeing isn't dependent on circumstances matching your preferences—that something essential in you remains intact regardless of how events unfold.

This is perhaps the deepest aspect of Layer 2 resilience—not just developing strategies for navigating uncertainty but discovering a relationship with uncertainty that creates psychological freedom rather than dependence on specific outcomes.

Quantum Decision-Making: Deciding Without Closing Doors

A practical application of embracing uncertainty is what I call "quantum decision-making"—an approach that keeps possibilities open even as you make specific choices.

Traditional decision-making assumes an either/or paradigm: choose A or B, but not both. This approach prematurely collapses possibilities that might remain viable with a different framework.

Quantum decision-making looks for the both/and possibility—ways to pursue a specific direction while maintaining connection to alternative paths.

I watched this approach transform Menka's career trajectory as she faced a difficult choice between two compelling job offers. One was with an established corporation offering stability and clear advancement paths. The other was with an early-stage startup with greater risk but potentially more significant growth and impact.

Traditional advice suggested she needed to commit fully to one path and close the door on the other. Instead, Menka found a creative alternative.

She accepted the corporate position that offered stability but negotiated a four-day workweek. On her fifth day, she pursued independent projects related to the startup space she was also interested in. She maintained relationships with both professional networks, developing skills relevant to both paths.

"Everyone told me I needed to choose," Menka explained. "But I kept wondering—what if the either/or framework itself is limited? What if there's a both/and possibility I'm not seeing?"

Eighteen months later, this quantum approach paid off. The startup space had evolved in a direction that aligned perfectly with the corporate experience Menka had gained. She was able to transition into a leadership role that combined both worlds—something that wouldn't have been possible had she made an exclusive either/or choice earlier.

"By keeping multiple paths alive rather than fully committing to just one, I ended up somewhere better than either original option," Menka reflected. "And the journey was less stressful because I wasn't constantly worried about whether I'd made the 'right' choice—I was actively exploring multiple possibilities."

This approach doesn't mean avoiding decisions or maintaining uncommitted relationships with everything. It means making decisions in ways that preserve rather than eliminate optionality wherever possible.

Alex applied similar thinking when considering whether to purchase a home or continue renting. Rather than viewing this as a binary choice, he explored options that preserved elements of both paths—including rent-to-own arrangements, purchasing a property with rental potential, and negotiating flexible terms that wouldn't lock him into a single scenario.

"The conventional wisdom was that I needed to decide between the security of ownership and the flexibility of renting," Alex explained. "But when I questioned that frame, I discovered approaches that could potentially provide both."

Quantum decision-making doesn't guarantee perfect outcomes, but it creates resilience by maintaining connection to multiple possibilities rather than committing exclusively to a single path.

It recognises that in complex, uncertain environments, preserving optionality often creates more value than premature certainty.

Practical Tools for Navigating Uncertainty

Beyond these conceptual approaches, several practical tools can help you navigate uncertainty more effectively in your daily life. These aren't about eliminating uncertainty—an impossible goal—but developing a more productive relationship with it.

Probabilistic Rather Than Binary Thinking

Most of us naturally drift toward binary thinking—something will either happen or it won't, a decision will be either right or wrong, a path will either succeed or fail. This mental habit creates unnecessary anxiety about uncertainty because it magnifies the consequences of any single outcome.

Developing probabilistic thinking means replacing these binary assessments with ranges of possibility and likelihood. Instead of "Will this project succeed or fail?" you might ask, "What's the range of possible outcomes here, and which seem most likely based on current information?"

Ekta, a healthcare administrator, transformed her team's relationship with uncertainty by introducing this approach to their planning process. Instead of classifying outcomes as either certain or uncertain, they developed the habit of assigning probability ranges.

"Rather than saying we'll either get this contract or we won't, we started saying there's roughly a 70% chance of securing it, with significant uncertainty around the timeline," Ekta explained. "This created a completely different psychological relationship with the situation. We could plan appropriately without either assuming guaranteed success or becoming paralysed by fear of failure."

This shift seems subtle but profoundly changes how you relate to uncertain situations. It prevents both false certainty and unnecessary anxiety about the unknown.

Try applying this approach to a situation you're currently facing. Instead of framing outcomes in binary terms, assign probability ranges based on available information. Notice how this creates a more nuanced relationship with what might unfold.

Scenario Planning

Rather than trying to predict exactly what will happen, develop multiple scenarios representing different ways the future might unfold. For each scenario, identify early indicators that would suggest this path is emerging, initial responses you would implement, and assets or capabilities that would be valuable across multiple scenarios.

This approach transforms uncertainty from a paralysis-inducing threat to a navigable landscape of possibilities.

Aditya used scenario planning when his industry faced significant regulatory changes with unclear outcomes. Rather than either assuming the worst or hoping for the best, his team developed four distinct scenarios representing different ways the regulatory environment might evolve.

"For each scenario, we identified early signals that would indicate which way things were trending," Aditya explained. "More importantly, we focused on identifying capabilities and positions that would be valuable regardless of which scenario emerged—what we called 'no-regret moves' that made sense across multiple possible futures."

This approach allowed Aditya's company to take meaningful action amid uncertainty rather than waiting for clarity before moving forward. When the regulatory situation finally resolved, they were already positioned to respond effectively because they had been systematically preparing for multiple possibilities.

Consider how you might apply scenario planning to an area of uncertainty in your own life. What are three or four distinctly different ways the situation might unfold? What early indicators would suggest which path is emerging? Most importantly, what actions or preparations would serve you well across multiple possible futures?

Small Experiments

Instead of making major commitments amid uncertainty, design small experiments that generate information without requiring irreversible decisions.

Jaimin used this approach when considering a career change from engineering to design. Rather than immediately quitting his job and pursuing a design degree, he created a series of small experiments:

- Taking a single evening design course
- Volunteering his emerging skills on a small project
- Shadowing a working designer for a day
- Attempting a small client project on weekends

"Each experiment provided valuable information with minimal risk," Jaimin told me. "But more importantly, the results were often surprising—nothing unfolded quite as I had anticipated, either positively or negatively. If I had relied on mental predictions alone, I would have been operating on several false assumptions."

This experimental approach allows you to navigate uncertainty through direct experience rather than abstract deliberation. It recognises that our mental projections about how things might unfold are often inaccurate in both positive and negative directions.

Sarita applied similar thinking when exploring a potential relocation. Rather than making a binary yes/no decision based on limited information, she designed experiments that would generate meaningful data:

- Renting an Airbnb in the target neighbourhood for two weeks while working remotely
- Interviewing several people who had made similar moves
- Exploring specific communities and activities she might join
- Testing her commute during actual work hours

"These experiments revealed aspects of the situation I never would have anticipated," Sarita explained. "Some concerns I had turned out to be non-issues, while unexpected challenges emerged that I hadn't considered. The experiential knowledge was completely different from my mental projections."

What area of uncertainty in your life might benefit from small experiments? How could you design low-risk tests that generate valuable information about possible paths forward?

Optionality Creation

Deliberately cultivate choices and capabilities that maintain flexibility amid changing circumstances. This includes developing transferable skills valued across multiple domains, building diverse professional and personal networks, maintaining financial reserves that allow for transitions, and creating systems with built-in adaptation mechanisms.

Lena applied this principle in her freelance business by developing expertise in three complementary but distinct service areas. When demand in one area decreased due to market changes, she could shift focus to areas with increasing opportunity—maintaining stability through diversity rather than specialisation.

"Many colleagues defined themselves narrowly—'I'm a WordPress developer' or 'I'm a UX designer,'" Lena explained. "I deliberately cultivated multiple professional identities and skill sets. This felt inefficient sometimes, as I was dividing my learning across different domains. But when market conditions changed, this apparent inefficiency became my greatest strength."

This approach creates resilience not by predicting specific changes but by developing the capacity to respond to whatever emerges. It's about creating a personal or organisational structure that can adapt to multiple possible futures rather than optimising for a single anticipated scenario.

How might you increase optionality in your own life? What skills, relationships, or resources would give you more flexibility to respond to unexpected changes or opportunities?

The Quantum Nature of Growth

Perhaps the most profound aspect of embracing uncertainty is recognising that personal growth itself follows quantum rather than linear patterns. Just as quantum particles make discrete jumps between energy states rather than sliding gradually between them, human development often proceeds through discontinuous leaps rather than smooth progression.

These growth leaps frequently emerge from periods of greatest uncertainty—times when familiar patterns have dissolved but new structures haven't yet formed. This liminal space, while uncomfortable, contains extraordinary creative potential.

Ekta experienced this during a period of career upheaval. After leaving a toxic workplace without a clear next step, she entered a phase of profound uncertainty. Her professional identity, daily structure, and social connections had all been disrupted simultaneously.

"It was terrifying at first," she recalled. "I felt like I was floating without anchors, with no clear direction for the first time in my adult life."

But within this uncertainty, something unexpected began to emerge. Without the constraints of her previous role and others' expectations, Ekta reconnected with creative interests she had abandoned years earlier. She experimented with different projects, following curiosity rather than strategic calculation.

This exploration eventually crystallised into an entirely new career direction that combined her professional expertise with her creative passions—something she couldn't have designed from within her previous framework.

"Looking back, I can see that the uncertainty wasn't just something to endure until I found the next certain thing," Ekta reflected. "It was an essential space that allowed a quantum leap in my development—a jump to a different level that couldn't have happened through incremental steps."

This quantum perspective on growth offers profound reassurance during periods of disorientation. What feels like being lost may actually be the necessary condition for finding something beyond your previous horizon of possibility.

Uncertainty as the Path to Layer 2 Resilience

Embracing uncertainty rather than merely tolerating it forms a cornerstone of Layer 2 resilience. This isn't about abandoning strategic approaches from Layer 1, but about developing a complementary capacity—the ability to remain centered and effective precisely when the future is least predictable.

As you develop this capacity, you'll find that uncertainty transforms from threat to asset. Rather than needing specific conditions to feel secure, you develop security within yourself—a confidence in your ability to adapt and thrive regardless of what emerges.

This is the paradoxical strength that quantum uncertainty offers: the less you depend on knowing exactly what comes next, the more capable you become of handling whatever arrives.

The journey toward embracing uncertainty isn't always comfortable. Our minds naturally crave certainty and predictability. But as you practice the approaches we've explored—planning without attachment, finding freedom in the unknown, quantum decision-making, and practical tools for navigating uncertainty—you'll discover a profound shift in your relationship with life's inherent unpredictability.

In the next chapter, we'll explore how this quantum perspective on uncertainty combines with radical acceptance to create genuine resilience through changing circumstances. We'll discover how accepting reality—without resignation—creates the foundation for both peace and effective action amid life's inevitable challenges.

NINE

Resilience Through Acceptance

The transformative power of radical acceptance

"I keep fighting against this reorganisation at work," Jai admitted, frustration evident in his voice. "Writing proposals for alternative approaches, building cases against it, trying to rally support for different models."

"And how's that working out?" Avika asked gently.

Jai sighed. "Exhausting and largely ineffective. The changes are happening regardless of my resistance."

"What if you accepted that this reorganisation is happening?" Avika suggested. "Not resigning yourself to negative outcomes, but simply acknowledging current reality."

"That feels like giving up," Jai frowned.

"There's a profound difference between acceptance and resignation," Avika pointed out. "Resignation says: 'This is happening, so I might as well give up.' Acceptance says: 'This is happening, so I can now respond most effectively to actual reality rather than fighting against it.'"

Jai was quiet for a moment. "I'm spending so much energy resisting what's already occurring that I have little left for navigating it effectively."

"Exactly," Avika nodded. "Acceptance isn't about liking what's happening or abandoning influence. It's about stopping the exhausting fight against reality so you can redirect that energy toward effective response."

"Accepting what is," Jai said slowly, "without adding the story that it shouldn't be this way."

"That's the essence of Layer 2 resilience," Avika smiled. "Not because circumstances deserve acceptance, but because you deserve freedom from the suffering that resistance creates."

"Between stimulus and response there is a space. In that space is our power to choose our response. In our response lies our growth and our freedom."
– Viktor Frankl

There's a fundamental truth that most of us resist: we cannot control much of what happens to us. Market crashes, natural disasters, other people's decisions, aging, illness—these and countless other factors are largely beyond our command.

What makes this truth so difficult to accept? Why do we exhaust ourselves fighting against reality rather than working with it?

The answer lies in a critical distinction that forms the heart of Layer 2 resilience: the difference between acceptance and resignation.

Radical Acceptance vs. Resignation

I first understood this distinction through Aditya's story. A successful retailer for fifteen years, Aditya had built a thriving business serving his local community. Then an online competitor entered his market, offering similar products at prices he couldn't match without losing money on every sale.

His initial response was fierce resistance. He tried competing on price, despite the damage to his margins. He launched a "support local business" campaign highlighting the competitor's distant corporate ownership. He even joined industry associations lobbying for regulations that would level the playing field.

For nearly two years, Aditya exhausted himself battling reality rather than adapting to it. His business suffered, his health declined, and his family felt the strain of his constant stress and anger.

"I kept telling myself I was fighting for my business," Aditya told me over coffee, the exhaustion evident in his eyes. "But looking back, I was really fighting against reality itself—against the fact that the market had fundamentally changed."

When I suggested that perhaps accepting this new reality might create space for more effective responses, Aditya bristled.

"Accept it? That feels like surrendering—like letting them win."

This reaction reveals the misunderstanding that keeps many of us trapped in exhausting, ineffective resistance. We confuse acceptance with resignation, believing that acknowledging reality as it is means giving up on improvement or change.

Nothing could be further from the truth.

Resignation says: "This is how it is, so I might as well give up."

Radical acceptance says: "This is how it is, so I can now respond most effectively."

The turning point for Aditya came during a weekend retreat where he encountered this distinction. He realised he'd been spending enormous energy resisting the simple fact that the market had changed— energy that could have been directed toward adapting his business to the new reality.

"It was like I'd been swimming against a powerful current, insisting it shouldn't be flowing that way," he explained during our follow-up conversation. "Acceptance wasn't about giving up swimming—it was about acknowledging the current's direction so I could navigate it more effectively."

With this shift in perspective, Aditya stopped competing on price and instead focused on elements the online competitor couldn't match: personalised service, community events, and an immersive in-store experience. He even integrated online elements into his business model rather than fighting against them.

Within a year, his business had rebounded stronger than before—not by denying reality but by fully accepting and working with it.

Aditya's story illustrates the transformative power of radical acceptance. By stopping the exhausting fight against what is, he freed up energy and attention for creative, effective response to his actual circumstances rather than the circumstances he wished existed.

This distinction—between resignation and acceptance—is perhaps the most important understanding in developing Layer 2 resilience. It's the difference between passive surrender and active engagement with reality as it actually is.

Separating Reality from Interpretation

A crucial aspect of radical acceptance involves distinguishing between objective events and our interpretations of them.

Consider this formula:
Event + Interpretation = Experience

We can't always control events, but we have tremendous power over our interpretations. By separating these elements, we create space for more effective responses.

I witnessed this process transform Leila's experience after a major presentation went sideways. As a marketing executive, Leila had spent weeks preparing for a pitch to the company's biggest potential client. Despite her thorough preparation, technical problems disrupted her presentation, and the client seemed disengaged throughout the meeting.

When we met for lunch the following day, Leila was devastated.

"My career is over," she said, staring into her untouched salad. "Everyone saw me fail completely. I'll never recover from this."

"Let's separate what actually happened from your interpretation," I suggested. "What are the objective, observable facts—what would a camera have recorded?"

Leila thought for a moment. "The projector malfunctioned for the first ten minutes. Two key decision-makers were on their phones during parts of my presentation. The client asked fewer questions than expected. They said they'd get back to us next week instead of giving immediate feedback."

"And what interpretations have you added to those events?"

"That I've ruined my reputation. That the client hated our proposal. That my team has lost respect for me. That this failure will follow me for years."

Just naming these interpretations as separate from the events created a visible shift in Leila's demeanour. She sat up straighter and took a deep breath.

"I can see I've been treating my catastrophic interpretations as if they're established facts," she said. "But they're really just one possible story about what happened."

This separation—between objective events and subjective interpretation—is a cornerstone of radical acceptance. It allows us to acknowledge what has actually occurred without automatically attaching destructive meanings to those events.

"What other interpretations might be equally or more valid?" I asked.

Leila considered this. "Maybe the decision-makers were checking their phones because they were getting input from their team. Maybe they need time to consider our proposal carefully, which could be a good sign. Maybe my team actually respects how I handled the technical problems."

As Leila developed alternative interpretations, her emotional state shifted dramatically. She wasn't denying the disappointing aspects of the presentation, but she was recognising that her experience of the event came largely from her interpretations rather than the event itself.

Two weeks later, Leila called with surprising news: the client had signed a contract for a pilot project. One of the decision-makers specifically mentioned being impressed with how she handled the technical difficulties with grace and adaptability.

"The events didn't change," Leila reflected. "But by separating my interpretations from reality, I stopped suffering from a story I was telling myself. Even if the client had decided not to move forward, I would have been able to respond more effectively without the weight of catastrophic interpretations."

This practice—separating events from interpretations—creates the foundation for genuine acceptance. It allows us to acknowledge reality without adding unnecessary layers of meaning that intensify suffering and limit our response options.

Try this yourself with a challenging situation you're currently facing. Draw a line down the middle of a page. On the left, list only the objective, observable facts—what a camera would record. On the right, list your interpretations, assumptions, and stories about what those facts mean. Notice how much of your distress comes from the right column, which you have the power to revise.

Finding Peace with "What IS"

Radical acceptance creates a foundation for peace even amid challenging circumstances. This doesn't mean you stop working to improve situations—it means you stop fighting against the reality that exists in this moment.

The paradox is that accepting "what is" often creates more favourable conditions for change than resistance does. When you're not wasting energy denying reality, you have more resources available for constructive action.

Jaimin discovered this when facing a serious health diagnosis. As an active, independent person who prided himself on physical capability, the news was devastating. His initial response was to fight against the reality—denying symptoms, refusing to discuss his condition, and rejecting lifestyle changes that acknowledged his new limitations.

"I was determined not to let this disease define me," he explained during one of our walks, now taken at a slower pace than before his diagnosis. "But by fighting so hard against the reality of my condition, I was actually giving it more power over my life."

Jaimin's resistance wasn't just psychological—it had practical consequences. By refusing to acknowledge his changing energy levels, he would push beyond his body's new limits, resulting in prolonged recovery periods. By rejecting medications that could help manage symptoms (because taking them would mean accepting he had a condition), he experienced unnecessary suffering. By hiding his diagnosis from friends, he denied himself potential support.

The shift came when Jaimin learned to accept his condition without surrendering to it. He acknowledged his reality while separating it from his interpretations about what it meant for his identity and future.

"Once I accepted what was actually happening in my body, without all the catastrophic meanings I'd attached to it, I could respond more effectively," he told me. "Ironically, by accepting my limitations, I discovered new possibilities I couldn't see before."

Jaimin developed daily practices for cultivating this acceptance:

Each morning, he would acknowledge specific realities without judgment: "My energy is limited. Certain activities cause pain. My condition is chronic."

After noting these realities, he would identify and question his interpretations: "Does limited energy mean a limited life? Not necessarily. Does having a chronic condition mean I can't find joy and purpose? No."

With reality acknowledged and interpretations examined, he would consciously choose his response: "Given these realities, how can I best use my available energy today? What possibilities remain open to me?"

These practices transformed his experience—not by changing his medical condition, but by changing his relationship with it. He found peace not despite his circumstances but within them.

This approach applies far beyond health challenges. Sarita applied similar practices to a difficult work environment she temporarily couldn't leave due to financial constraints. Rather than exhausting herself with resentment about circumstances she couldn't immediately change, she clearly acknowledged the reality: "This environment is toxic in these specific ways. I need this job for approximately eight more months until my financial situation allows a transition."

With this reality accepted rather than resisted, she could focus on developing boundaries, self-care practices, and exit strategies that would serve her effectively—rather than wasting energy on the futile insistence that things should be different right now.

"Accepting my current reality wasn't about approving of it or resigning myself to it forever," Sarita explained. "It was about stopping the energy drain of fighting what is, so I could direct that energy toward creating what could be."

The peace that comes through acceptance isn't passive resignation but active engagement with reality as it is—the foundation for effective response rather than ineffective resistance.

The Paradox of Surrender

There's a powerful paradox at the heart of acceptance: sometimes surrendering control creates more favourable outcomes than maintaining tight grip.

This parallels a principle in martial arts like Aikido, where you blend with your opponent's energy rather than directly opposing it. By accepting and working with the force coming toward you, you can redirect it more effectively than by meeting it with rigid resistance.

Yamini experienced this paradox during a contentious divorce. For months, she fought her ex-husband on every detail, convinced that any compromise represented defeat. Their communication grew increasingly hostile, legal fees mounted, and both became entrenched in positions that harmed their children.

"I viewed every interaction as a battle I had to win," Yamini told me. "If he wanted something, my automatic response was to oppose it—even on matters I didn't actually care about."

The breakthrough came when Yamini realised she was exhausting herself fighting against the reality that her marriage had ended and her ex-husband was who he was—not who she wanted him to be.

"I had been telling myself that accepting any of his terms meant he 'won,'" she explained. "But the reality was that my resistance was creating far more problems than it solved."

Yamini began practicing what she called "strategic surrender"—deliberately letting go in areas that weren't truly essential while maintaining clear boundaries around what mattered most. She stopped trying to control her ex-husband's narrative about their marriage, his parenting approach when the children were with him, and his financial choices beyond their divorce agreement.

"The moment I truly accepted that I couldn't control him was the moment I regained control of myself," she said. "It wasn't giving up—it was refocusing my energy where it could actually make a difference."

Within weeks, their co-parenting relationship improved significantly. Not because he had changed, but because she had stopped requiring him to change before she could find peace.

This paradox of surrender applies in countless domains. In creative work, Sameer found that accepting his initial draft's limitations—rather than fighting against them with perfectionist resistance—actually created space for more effective revision. In organisational change, Sheela discovered that acknowledging employee resistance rather than trying to overcome it through force created openings for genuine engagement that ultimately accelerated the transformation process.

The key insight across these examples is that acceptance creates flow where resistance creates friction. By surrendering the insistence that reality be different than it is, you actually enhance your ability to influence how it evolves.

Practical Approaches to Cultivating Acceptance

Radical acceptance isn't a one-time decision but a practice developed over time. Here are practical approaches that have helped many people cultivate this capacity:

The Acceptance Pause

When facing a challenging situation, take a deliberate pause before responding. During this pause, say to yourself: "This is what's happening right now. I can accept that this is the reality I'm working with."

Pranay, a project manager, implemented this practice during a particularly challenging implementation phase. Whenever unexpected problems arose—as they inevitably did—he would take three deep breaths and silently acknowledge: "This is the current reality. I can accept this is happening."

"That brief pause prevented my automatic resistance response," Pranay explained. "Instead of wasting energy thinking 'this shouldn't be happening' or immediately looking for someone to blame, I could move directly to problem-solving mode."

This simple practice interrupts the automatic resistance that often creates additional suffering beyond the initial challenge. It creates space between stimulus and response—space that allows for more effective engagement with the actual situation rather than with our resistance to it.

The "And" Perspective

Replace "but" with "and" in how you frame difficult situations:

Instead of: "I'm facing this challenge, but I shouldn't have to deal with this."

Try: "I'm facing this challenge, and this is part of my current reality."

This subtle linguistic shift acknowledges difficulty without added resistance. It creates mental space for both accepting what is and working toward what could be.

Lisa, a team leader navigating organisational restructuring, found this approach transformed her team's response to unwelcome changes. Rather than framing the situation as "We have to implement these new processes, but they create extra work for us," she shifted to "We have to implement these new processes, and they create extra work for us."

"It seems like such a small change," Lisa noted, "but it had a profound effect on our collective mindset. 'But' creates opposition between the first and second parts of the statement, while 'and' allows both to exist together. We stopped wasting energy fighting against the reality and focused on navigating it effectively."

The Reality Testing Question

When you find yourself fighting against circumstances, ask: "Can I change this situation right now through force of will?" If the answer is no, redirect your energy from resistance to adaptation.

Swastik applied this question during a flight delay that was threatening to make him miss an important meeting. His initial response was intense frustration, mentally arguing against the reality of the delay as if his resistance could somehow speed up the process.

"I caught myself in this futile fight against reality," Swastik recalled. "So I asked myself: 'Can I make this plane leave sooner through force of will?' Obviously, the answer was no. That simple question shifted my focus from resistance to adaptation—I immediately began arranging alternatives for the meeting rather than wasting energy on anger about the delay."

This question helps distinguish between situations where effort might change circumstances and those where acceptance is the only viable path forward. It prevents wasting precious energy fighting against immovable realities.

The Serenity Prayer Practice

Even for those who aren't religious, the core wisdom of the Serenity Prayer offers a practical framework:

> Grant me the serenity to accept the things I cannot change, The courage to change the things I can, And the wisdom to know the difference.

Regularly sorting challenges into these categories—what you can change, what you can't change, and what requires discernment—develops the musculation of acceptance in daily life.

Shalini, an executive coach, uses this framework with clients facing complex challenges. "We literally create three columns on a page," she explained. "Things they can directly control, things they can influence but not control, and things they can only respond to. This simple sorting process prevents the waste of energy on futile resistance while focusing attention on effective action."

The Body Acceptance Scan

Tension in the body often signals resistance to reality. Practice a body scan where you identify areas of tension and consciously relax them while thinking, "I accept what is happening right now." This physical release often facilitates mental acceptance.

Jaimin incorporated this practice into his daily routine after noticing how much physical tension he carried during challenging work situations. "I discovered that my body was often resisting reality even when my mind thought it was accepting things," he told me. "By consciously releasing physical tension while affirming acceptance, I created a much deeper shift than through mental approaches alone."

This practice recognises that acceptance isn't just an intellectual position but a whole-body experience. Our physical response to situations often reveals resistance that our conscious mind might not recognise.

Acceptance as a Pathway to Effective Action

Perhaps most importantly, acceptance isn't an endpoint but a gateway to more effective action. By stopping the exhausting fight against reality, you free up energy and attention for constructive response.

Pranay, a project manager, discovered this when dealing with a significant budget cut midway through a critical initiative. His initial reaction was outrage and resistance—arguing with executives, trying to find loopholes, and maintaining the original scope despite reduced resources.

This resistance created additional problems: team morale suffered, relationships with stakeholders deteriorated, and the project fell further behind as Pranay focused on fighting the budget reality rather than adapting to it.

The turning point came when Pranay fully accepted the budget constraint as his new working reality. With this acceptance, he stopped wasting energy on resistance and redirected it toward creative adaptation.

He gathered his team for a "reality-based innovation" session where they started with the firm premise: "This is our budget. How can we deliver maximum value within this constraint?"

This acceptance-based approach unleashed creativity that hadn't been available when they were focused on resistance. They identified non-essential features that could be eliminated, discovered efficiencies that actually improved the product, and renegotiated timelines in a way that actually enhanced stakeholder trust.

The project not only succeeded despite the reduced budget but became a case study in adaptive management that advanced Pranay's career. As he explained it: "Acceptance wasn't surrendering to failure—it was surrendering to reality so we could succeed within it."

This pattern appears consistently across domains—from health challenges to relationship conflicts, from career setbacks to organisational change. When we stop exhausting ourselves by fighting against what is, we can redirect that energy toward influencing what might be.

The formula is simple but profound:

1. Accept the current reality fully.
2. Separate facts from interpretations.
3. Release resistance that drains energy.
4. Redirect that energy toward constructive response.

Menka applied this approach when her startup lost a major investor just weeks before a planned expansion. Rather than dwelling in resistance ("This shouldn't be happening," "It's not fair," "We deserve better"), she immediately accepted the new financial reality and redirected her team's energy toward creative alternatives.

"By accepting our situation quickly rather than fighting against it, we had time to develop an entirely different approach," Menka explained. "While our competitors might have spent weeks in denial or resentment, we were already implementing creative solutions."

This is the practical power of acceptance—not as passive resignation but as the foundation for timely, effective action based on reality as it is rather than as we wish it were.

The Layer 2 Perspective

This capacity for radical acceptance forms a cornerstone of Layer 2 resilience. While Layer 1 focuses on strategic methods to shape circumstances, Layer 2 acknowledges the inherent limits of control and develops resilience within uncertainty.

The paradox is that by accepting what you cannot control, you gain tremendous power over what you can—your own responses, interpretations, and choices.

As Maya Angelou wisely observed: "You may not control all the events that happen to you, but you can decide not to be reduced by them."

This is the essence of Layer 2 resilience—not an absence of challenges but a transformed relationship with them. Not immunity from life's difficulties but resilience within them.

In the next chapter, we'll explore how to master Layer 2 by developing true mental flexibility—the capacity to navigate life's inevitable uncertainties with both acceptance and purposeful direction. We'll discover how these Layer 2 capacities eventually open the door to Layer 3, where even deeper questions about the nature of self and reality create the foundation for the most profound levels of resilience.

TEN

Mastering Layer 2

A harmonious integration emerges between strategic action and radical acceptance—between the capacity to shape circumstances and the wisdom to work with what cannot be controlled.

"I've noticed something interesting," Jai said as they hiked up the trail. "When I maintain strategic approaches while also practicing acceptance, something different emerges—a kind of harmony between the two."

Avika smiled. "You're discovering the integration that makes Layer 2 so powerful. Planning without rigid attachment. Direction without desperation. Action without the friction of resistance."

"It's like breathing," Jai realised. "Strategic thinking is the inhalation—gathering and directing energy. Acceptance is the exhalation—releasing what can't be controlled. Neither works well without the other."

"That's a beautiful way to describe it," Avika nodded. "Have you noticed any other shifts in your experience?"

Jai paused on the trail, considering. "Yes, actually. Situations that would have completely thrown me off balance a few months ago now move through more quickly. And I'm less attached to being right about everything—more curious about what's actually happening."

"Those are signs you're developing true mental flexibility," Avika said. "And they might also be indications you're ready to explore Layer 3—where questions about the nature of identity itself come into focus."

Jai raised an eyebrow. "Identity? I thought we were talking about handling challenges effectively."

"We are," Avika replied. "But the deepest resilience emerges when you question who exactly is experiencing these challenges in the first place."

"The oak fought the wind and was broken, the willow bent when it must and survived."
– Robert Jordan

Throughout this section of the book, we've explored the components of Layer 2 resilience—drawing lines on water, embracing quantum uncertainty, and cultivating resilience through acceptance. Now it's time to integrate these elements into a cohesive approach to life's challenges.

Mastering Layer 2 isn't about perfecting individual techniques but developing true mental flexibility—the capacity to adapt your response to whatever circumstances arise. It's about cultivating a harmony between strategic action and radical acceptance that allows you to navigate uncertainty with grace and effectiveness.

Developing True Mental Flexibility

Mental flexibility isn't a singular skill but a constellation of capacities that work together to create resilience amid change and challenge. These capacities include cognitive adaptability, emotional fluidity, and response diversity—all of which can be developed through deliberate practice.

I first recognised the profound impact of these capacities while working with Smita, an executive facing a corporate reorganisation that threatened her position and the team she had carefully built over five years.

When we first met, Smita was oscillating between two ineffective responses: rigid resistance (fighting against the reorganisation through political manoeuvring and formal protests) and helpless resignation (updating her resume while mentally checking out from her current role). Neither approach was serving her well.

"I feel stuck between fighting a battle I probably can't win and giving up entirely," she told me. "There doesn't seem to be a middle option."

This either/or thinking—either resist completely or surrender completely—is a common pattern that limits mental flexibility. Over the following weeks, Smita developed a more nuanced approach that integrated multiple perspectives and responses.

Rather than viewing the reorganisation through a single lens (primarily as a threat), she deliberately practiced what I call "cognitive adaptability"—the ability to shift thinking patterns based on changing circumstances rather than clinging to familiar frameworks even when they no longer serve.

"I realised I could choose which lens to view the situation through," she explained during a follow-up session. "Some days I'd look at it as a potential opportunity for growth, other days as a natural evolution of the company, and yes, sometimes still as a challenge to navigate. Each perspective revealed different aspects of reality and suggested different responses."

This capacity to hold multiple perspectives simultaneously—rather than getting locked into a single interpretation—created psychological space for more effective responses. Instead of being limited to either fight or flight, Smita developed a nuanced approach that combined strategic positioning, relationship building, creative proposal development, and personal preparation for multiple outcomes.

The flexibility to shift between these viewpoints gave her options she wouldn't have seen from any single perspective. This wasn't indecision or inconsistency but a deliberate practice of mental agility that allowed her to navigate complexity more effectively.

Along with cognitive adaptability, Smita developed what she called "emotional porousness"—the capacity to experience the full range of emotions without becoming stuck in any particular state, allowing feelings to flow through her rather than defining her.

"I stopped treating emotions as problems to solve," she reflected. "Instead, I approached them as weather patterns moving through the sky of awareness—sometimes intense, sometimes gentle, but always in motion rather than fixed."

This emotional fluidity didn't mean suppressing legitimate feelings about the challenging situation. Smita still experienced frustration, anxiety, and concern about the reorganisation. But she developed the capacity to experience these emotions without being controlled by them—to acknowledge them as information rather than imperatives for action.

Perhaps most importantly, Smita expanded her "response diversity"—having multiple possible responses available rather than defaulting to the same reactions regardless of circumstance.

"Before, I was like a pianist who could only play two notes," she explained. "Fight against what I didn't like, or withdraw when fighting seemed futile. Now I have access to a full keyboard of possible responses, each appropriate to different situations."

This expanded repertoire included:

- Strategic influence (identifying key decision-makers and tailoring communications to their concerns)
- Creative problem-solving (developing proposals that addressed organisational needs while preserving her team's core work)
- Alliance building (finding common ground with others affected by the changes)
- Selective acceptance (distinguishing between aspects of the situation she could potentially influence and those that required adaptation)
- Personal development (using the uncertainty as a catalyst for expanding her own capabilities)

The result wasn't simply a better outcome in this particular situation (though Smita did successfully navigate the reorganisation with most of her team intact). More importantly, she developed capacities that would serve her across countless future challenges—the ability to adapt cognitively, regulate emotionally, and respond diversely to whatever circumstances arose.

This constellation of capacities forms the core of mental flexibility. Like a tree that can bend in strong winds rather than breaking, this flexibility allows you to maintain integrity amid changing conditions rather than either rigidly resisting them or being uprooted by them.

The Harmony of Planning and Acceptance

One of the most powerful aspects of Layer 2 mastery is developing harmony between strategic planning and radical acceptance—approaches that might initially seem contradictory but actually complement each other beautifully.

Think of this harmony as similar to breathing—planning is like the inhalation where you actively shape your approach, while acceptance is like the exhalation where you release attachment to particular outcomes. Just as breathing requires both inhalation and exhalation, effective navigation of complexity requires both strategic intention and radical acceptance.

I witnessed this harmony transform Naveen's approach to a high-stakes business negotiation that had been stalled for months. As the CEO of a growing technology company, Naveen had been trying to secure a partnership with a much larger corporation—a deal that could potentially double his company's revenue and market reach.

His initial approach had been characterised by what he called "desperate preparation"—exhaustive planning coupled with intense attachment to a specific outcome. He had spreadsheets analysing every possible scenario, rehearsed responses to anticipated objections, and detailed fallback positions if his primary proposals were rejected.

Yet despite this thorough preparation, each negotiation session ended in frustration. The more Naveen pushed for his desired outcome, the more resistance he encountered from the potential partner.

"I was doing everything the business books recommend," Naveen told me during our consultation. "Thorough preparation, clear objectives, systematic approach. But something wasn't working, and I couldn't figure out what."

The missing element became clear as we explored his relationship with the negotiation process. While his strategic preparation was excellent, Naveen was approaching each session with a subtle desperation—an attachment to outcomes that created pressure the other party could sense and resist.

"What if you prepared just as thoroughly but held the outcome more lightly?" I suggested. "What if you combined strategic planning with genuine acceptance that the other party might choose paths you can't control?"

This paradoxical approach—planning thoroughly while accepting completely—transformed Naveen's experience of the negotiation process. He still developed clear objectives and multiple approaches (the planning aspect). Simultaneously, he cultivated complete acceptance that the other party might choose not to agree, recognising this possibility was beyond his control (the acceptance aspect).

"Paradoxically, this dual approach made me more effective, not less," Naveen noted after successfully closing the deal. "Because I wasn't desperately needing a specific outcome, I could remain flexible and responsive during the negotiation. I had direction without attachment, intention without desperation."

This harmony manifests in several practical ways that you can develop in your own approach to complex situations:

Planning with Provisional Holding

Develop clear strategies while holding them provisionally rather than rigidly, recognising they are working hypotheses rather than guaranteed paths.

Ankita, a product development leader, implemented this approach when launching a new service line. Rather than creating a fixed roadmap that her team had to follow precisely, she developed what she called a "living strategy"—a clear direction with built-in adaptation points.

"We plan thoroughly but hold those plans lightly," Ankita explained. "Each milestone includes both clear targets and explicit review processes where we assess whether our original approach still makes sense given what we've learned."

This provisional holding doesn't mean vague or half-hearted planning. Ankita's team developed detailed projections, specific action steps, and clear success metrics. The difference was in how they related to these plans—as valuable tools rather than sacred commitments, as maps to be updated rather than territories to be defended.

This approach creates both the benefits of strategic planning (direction, coordination, resource optimisation) and the advantages of acceptance (flexibility, learning orientation, reduced resistance to change). It's not planning versus acceptance but planning with acceptance.

Directed Openness

Maintain clear intention while remaining open to unexpected developments that might lead to even better outcomes than you initially envisioned.

Kunal embodied this approach when expanding his consulting practice into new markets. He had a defined strategy for growth but remained deliberately receptive to opportunities that didn't fit his original plan.

"I think of it as having a destination in mind while staying alert to interesting side paths," Kunal explained. "I'm not aimlessly wandering—I have a clear direction. But I'm also not so fixated on my predetermined route that I miss unexpected opportunities along the way."

This directed openness led Kunal to discover his most successful service offering—one that wasn't part of his original growth plan but emerged through a chance conversation with a client who mentioned an unmet need. Because Kunal combined clear direction with openness to the unexpected, he could recognise and develop this opportunity when it arose.

The key distinction is between openness with direction versus either rigid planning or aimless wandering. Directed openness creates a context where both intention and receptivity can coexist, complementing rather than conflicting with each other.

Active Surrender

Do everything within your control while completely accepting elements beyond your influence, without conflating these categories.

Suchita applied this approach during a challenging health journey with her child. After thorough research and consultation with specialists, she implemented all recommended treatments and lifestyle adjustments within her control. Simultaneously, she practiced complete acceptance of elements beyond her influence—her child's underlying condition, the inherent uncertainties of medical treatment, and the ultimate outcomes that no parent can guarantee.

"Active surrender doesn't mean passive resignation," Suchita emphasised. "I'm doing everything possible within my sphere of influence. But I'm also accepting completely what lies beyond that sphere, rather than exhausting myself fighting against reality."

This combination—active engagement coupled with genuine acceptance—created a sustainable approach to a challenging situation that might otherwise have led to burnout. Suchita could maintain her effectiveness as an advocate for her child precisely because she wasn't wasting energy resisting aspects of reality she couldn't change.

The harmony between planning and acceptance doesn't develop overnight. It requires ongoing practice and frequent course correction when you notice yourself drifting toward either rigid planning without acceptance or passive acceptance without direction. But as you develop this harmony, you'll discover a resilience that neither approach alone can create—the capacity to move purposefully through an uncertain world without requiring certainty to feel secure.

The Dance of Awareness and Action

Another key aspect of Layer 2 mastery is developing a fluid dance between awareness and action—between being and doing. This dance allows you to move seamlessly between receptive observation and decisive engagement based on what each moment requires.

Reena, a creative director, described this dance in her design process: "I've learned to alternate between phases of open reception—where I'm simply observing possibilities without trying to direct them—and focused action where I'm actively shaping what emerges. The rhythm between these modes creates results I couldn't achieve with either approach alone."

Most of us naturally favour one mode over the other—either leaning toward constant action (doing) or toward continuous observation (being). Layer 2 mastery involves developing both capacities and the wisdom to shift between them based on what each situation requires.

Deepak, a technology executive leading a major product redesign, discovered the power of this dance after months of frustration with his team's progress. Their initial approach had been characterised by relentless action—defining requirements, creating specifications, building prototypes, testing features—all executed with admirable efficiency but yielding disappointing results.

"We were so busy doing that we had no space for seeing," Deepak explained during our work together. "We were solving problems and implementing solutions at a remarkable pace, but we weren't stepping back to question whether we were addressing the right problems in the first place."

This insight led Deepak to redesign the process, deliberately alternating between modes of receptive awareness and focused action. He instituted what the team called "observation days"—periods dedicated to noticing patterns, gathering insights, and questioning assumptions without immediate pressure to execute solutions.

These observation phases were followed by focused implementation periods where the team applied insights from their awareness practice to specific, targeted actions. The rhythm between these modes prevented both the paralysis of endless consideration and the limitation of premature action.

"The key insight was that these modes aren't in competition," Deepak explained. "They're complementary aspects of an integrated approach, each valuable in its proper timing and proportion."

This dance requires developing:

Mode Recognition

The ability to clearly discern whether a situation calls primarily for receptive awareness or decisive action in any given moment.

Saniya, a therapist, described how this recognition transformed her work with clients: "I used to feel I always needed to be doing something—offering insights, suggesting techniques, guiding the conversation. Now I can recognise when what's needed is simply holding space with awareness, allowing the client's own process to unfold without my intervention."

This recognition isn't based on rigid rules but on attuned perception of what each unique situation requires. Sometimes the most effective action is non-action—maintaining aware presence rather than adding more doing to the equation.

Mode Shifting

The capacity to transition smoothly between these modes without the friction that typically occurs when changing cognitive and emotional states.

Amrit, an emergency physician, developed this capacity through deliberate practice: "In crisis situations, I need to shift instantly from assessment mode to action mode. I've trained myself to make this transition without hesitation, but also without losing the awareness that informs effective action."

This capacity for smooth transition—like shifting gears in a well-tuned vehicle—allows you to respond fluidly to changing circumstances rather than getting stuck in habitual patterns of either excessive observation without action or impulsive action without sufficient awareness.

Mode Integration

Eventually developing the ability to maintain qualities of both awareness and action simultaneously, with each informing and enhancing the other.

Aashna described this integration in her leadership approach: "I've developed what I call 'active awareness'—taking decisive action while maintaining a wider perspective that keeps me attuned to emerging patterns and potential adjustments. It's not switching back and forth but a blended state, where doing and seeing happen simultaneously."

This integration represents mastery of the dance—not merely alternating between modes but allowing them to inform each other in real-time, creating responses that embody both the clarity of awareness and the effectiveness of focused action.

As you develop this dance of awareness and action, you'll find yourself less likely to get stuck in either habitual mode—neither lost in endless observation without practical engagement nor trapped in reactive doing without perceptive awareness. This fluid movement between modes creates a responsiveness to life that neither mode alone can achieve.

Signs You're Ready for Layer 3

As you develop mastery of Layer 2 capacities, you may begin to notice certain shifts in your experience that indicate readiness for Layer 3 exploration. These signs include identity fluidity, diminishing reactivity, comfort with paradox, narrative recognition, and a curious detachment.

I first recognised these signs while working with Smita, who had spent several years developing the mental flexibility we've explored in this chapter. During a meet, focused on deepening these capacities, Smita described an unexpected shift in her experience.

"Something has changed in how I relate to challenges," she explained. "It's not just that I have better strategies or greater acceptance. There's a more fundamental question emerging about who exactly is experiencing all this, and whether that 'who' is as solid and separate as I've always assumed."

This inquiry into the nature of identity itself—not as an abstract philosophical question but as a lived exploration—marks the threshold of Layer 3 resilience. Let's explore the signs that might indicate you're approaching this threshold:

Identity Fluidity

You may notice that your sense of self feels more flexible and less fixed than you previously believed—that "who you are" is not a static entity but a dynamic process constantly in evolution.

Priyesh described this shift: "I used to experience myself as a fixed entity with specific characteristics—I am this, I am not that. Now there's a fluidity to that sense of self. I still have preferences, patterns, and tendencies, but they don't seem as definitional or permanent as before. It's more like watching a river—there are recognisable patterns in the flow, but it's the flowing itself that seems most fundamental."

This fluidity doesn't mean losing functional identity or becoming ungrounded. Rather, it's a recognition that the self you've always taken to be solid and separate might be more like a process than a fixed entity—more like a verb than a noun.

Diminishing Reactivity

You may notice that circumstances that previously triggered strong automatic reactions now create space for chosen responses—that the gap between stimulus and response has widened.

Namrata observed this change in her experience of criticism: "Feedback that would have immediately triggered defensiveness now seems to land in a different way. There's a space between hearing the critique and any reaction arising—a space where I can actually consider what's being said without feeling personally diminished by it."

This diminishing reactivity doesn't mean becoming emotionless or detached from life. It's about having more choice in how you respond rather than being driven by automatic reactions. The stimulus still registers, but it doesn't immediately hijack your system in the way it once did.

Paradox Comfort

You may find that apparent contradictions no longer create cognitive dissonance but can be held simultaneously as complementary aspects of a more complex reality.

Kirti described this shift: "I used to need things to be logically consistent in a linear way. Now I'm comfortable with paradox—with insights that seem contradictory from one perspective but complementary from another. The need to resolve everything into a single consistent framework has diminished."

This comfort with paradox allows for a more nuanced relationship with complex realities that don't fit neatly into binary categories or linear logic. It creates space for both/and thinking rather than either/or limitations, expanding your capacity to hold multiple perspectives simultaneously.

Narrative Recognition

You may become increasingly aware of how much of your experience is shaped by the stories you tell about events rather than the events themselves, creating space between perception and interpretation.

Sarita noticed this distinction: "I've become fascinated by how my mind creates stories about events—interpretations that feel so compelling I mistake them for reality itself. Now I can watch this storytelling process happen in real-time, which creates a very different relationship with my own thoughts."

This recognition doesn't mean dismissing all narratives as false or meaningless. Stories remain powerful tools for making sense of experience. The shift is in recognising them as creative processes rather than direct perceptions of objective reality—as maps rather than territories.

Curious Detachment

You may develop the capacity to observe difficult experiences with genuine curiosity rather than immediate immersion—maintaining perspective even amid challenge.

Raj described this quality: "When challenging situations arise, there's a new kind of interested distance—not cold detachment, but a warm curiosity about what's unfolding. Instead of being completely identified with my concern or frustration, I can simultaneously be interested in the experience itself."

This curious detachment doesn't mean bypassing genuine human emotions or dissociating from difficult experiences. Rather, it's about developing the capacity to be with these experiences without being completely subsumed by them—to maintain a wider perspective even amid intensity.

These signs don't mean you've "graduated" from Layer 2. Rather, they indicate that your development of mental flexibility has naturally led to questions about the nature of identity itself—questions that form the foundation of Layer 3 exploration.

Smita described her recognition of these signs: "I noticed I was less attached to being right and more interested in seeing clearly. Challenging situations that would have previously consumed my attention for days now moved through more quickly.

And I became fascinated by how my mind created stories about events, recognising these narratives were creative processes rather than objective perceptions."

If you've noticed some of these signs in your own experience, it may indicate readiness to explore the even deeper dimensions of resilience we'll discover in the next section of this book.

Integration and Practice

Mastering Layer 2 isn't a theoretical achievement, but a practical capacity developed through consistent integration and practice. Let's explore approaches for deepening these capacities in your daily life:

Deliberate Mode Shifting

Intentionally practice transitioning between different cognitive and emotional states throughout your day:

- From analytical to creative thinking
- From focused concentration to open awareness
- From achievement orientation to process appreciation
- From social engagement to reflective solitude

The more fluently you can shift between these modes, the greater your mental flexibility becomes.

Pranay implemented this practice in his role as a team leader: "I created transition rituals between different types of work. Before creative sessions, I would take three minutes to shift from analytical to generative thinking. Before one-on-one meetings, I would briefly center myself to move from task focus to relational presence."

These deliberate transitions prevented the automatic continuation of one mode into contexts where a different mode would be more effective. By consciously shifting states rather than remaining in habitual patterns, Pranay developed greater flexibility and responsiveness to different situations.

Pattern Interruption

Regularly disrupt habitual patterns to maintain cognitive and emotional adaptability:

- Take different routes to familiar destinations
- Engage with perspectives that challenge your assumptions
- Alter routines that have become automatic
- Expose yourself to novel experiences that require fresh responses

These interruptions prevent the calcification of neural and psychological patterns, maintaining the flexibility that characterises Layer 2 mastery.

Sarita applied this approach by creating what she called "pattern interrupt days" each month: "I deliberately break as many habits as possible—taking different routes, changing my morning routine, seeking out unfamiliar experiences, even using my non-dominant hand for simple tasks. These disruptions keep my adaptability muscles exercised rather than atrophying into fixed patterns."

The key insight is that flexibility requires regular exercise, just like physical suppleness. By deliberately introducing novelty and disruption in manageable doses, you develop the capacity to adapt when life introduces these elements without your planning.

Mindful Transitions

Bring heightened awareness to transitions between activities, environments, and roles throughout your day. These transition points are opportunities to practice releasing one context and entering another with fresh presence rather than carrying accumulated momentum.

Ekta implemented this practice between client meetings by taking three mindful breaths and mentally acknowledging: "That meeting is complete. This meeting is new." This simple ritual prevented the psychological carryover from one context to another that often creates unnecessary confusion and stress.

"I realised how often I was bringing the energy and expectations from one interaction into the next, creating a blurred experience where nothing received my full, clear attention," Ekta explained. "These mindful transitions create clean breaks between contexts, allowing me to be fully present with what's actually happening now rather than what happened before."

This practice develops the capacity to release and refresh—to complete one experience before beginning another rather than creating a muddy continuity that does justice to neither.

Reflection Integration

Regularly reflect on challenging experiences to extract learning and develop greater response diversity for future situations:

- What worked well in my approach?
- What other responses might have been effective?
- What triggered automatic reactions rather than chosen responses?
- How might I approach similar situations differently in the future?

These reflections transform experiences into development opportunities rather than merely accumulated history.

Swastik integrated this practice through a weekly review: "Every Sunday evening, I reflect on challenging situations from the past week. I don't just rehash what happened but deliberately explore alternative approaches I might have taken. This expands my repertoire for future situations rather than reinforcing habitual responses."

This reflective practice prevents the common pattern of having the same experience repeatedly rather than learning and evolving from each encounter. It deliberately extracts wisdom from experience rather than merely accumulating experiences.

When Mental Flexibility Isn't Enough

As you develop Layer 2 mastery, you'll inevitably encounter its limitations. There are circumstances where even the most sophisticated mental flexibility reaches the boundary of its effectiveness—situations that point toward the deeper exploration of Layer 3.

Jaimin encountered this boundary during an extended health crisis. Despite applying all the Layer 2 capacities we've discussed—acceptance, uncertainty navigation, planning-acceptance harmony—he still experienced a fundamental vulnerability that these approaches couldn't fully address.

"I had developed remarkable mental flexibility," he explained during a conversation about his experience. "I could adapt to changing circumstances, maintain equanimity amid uncertainty, and harmonise strategic action with radical acceptance. But something was still missing—a deeper question about who exactly was experiencing all this, and whether that 'who' was as solid and separate as I had always assumed."

This recognition marks the threshold of Layer 3—the point where questions about the nature of identity itself become not just philosophical inquiries but pressing practical matters. When even the most sophisticated mental flexibility bumps against the limitations of a separate self-sense, the door to Layer 3 naturally opens.

Layer 2 approaches operate within the framework of a separate self navigating external circumstances. They create tremendous resilience within that framework, but they don't question the framework itself. Layer 3 examines whether that fundamental assumption of separation might itself be part of what makes us vulnerable to being shaken in the first place.

Menka described her recognition of this threshold: "I had become incredibly adaptable and resilient through Layer 2 practices. But I started noticing that even with all this flexibility, there was still a subtle anxiety underneath—a sense that 'I' was fundamentally separate from and vulnerable to whatever life might bring. This led me to question whether this separate 'I' was actually as solid as I had assumed."

This questioning isn't abstract philosophy but a practical exploration with profound implications for resilience. If your sense of being a separate self, moving through a potentially threatening world is itself a construction rather than an ultimate reality, then the very foundation of what can "shake you" dissolves.

The Bridge to Layer 3

As you master Layer 2 capacities, you're building a bridge to Layer 3 exploration. The mental flexibility developed in Layer

2 creates precisely the conditions needed for the more profound inquiry of Layer 3 to be fruitful.

Without Layer 2 development, Layer 3 exploration often remains abstract and intellectual rather than transformative. The stability, adaptability, and equanimity cultivated through Layer 2 practices create the foundation for deeper investigation.

Pranay described this progression: "Layer 2 gave me the mental and emotional stability to ask more fundamental questions without becoming destabilised by them. Without that foundation, exploring the nature of self and reality would have been disorienting. With it, these explorations became the natural next step in developing even deeper resilience."

The harmony of planning and acceptance, the dance of awareness and action, and the development of true mental flexibility aren't just valuable ends in themselves. They're also the preparation for the most profound dimension of becoming unshakeable—the Layer 3 recognition that transcends the very notion of a separate self that needs protection from life's circumstances.

In the next section of this book, we'll explore Layer 3—the understanding that your fundamental nature as consciousness itself transcends the apparent boundaries of identity that seem to make you vulnerable to life's challenges.

This exploration isn't abstract philosophy but practical wisdom with profound implications for how you experience everything life brings your way. Just as Layer 2 doesn't replace but enhances Layer 1, Layer 3 doesn't replace but transforms both previous layers—creating an integrated approach to life that operates across all dimensions of becoming truly unshakeable.

THE DANCE OF CONSCIOUSNESS

∞

The rooftop garden of Elise's apartment building offered a panoramic view of the city. Seven years had passed since our conversation about psi, fourteen since our first meeting about delta. She was nearing eighty now, but her posture remained impeccable, her mind sharp.

"I knew you would return," she said as we sat watching the sunset. "The equation demanded it."

I smiled. The equation. It had become a framework for my life in ways I couldn't have imagined when I first heard about delta after that dance performance so many years ago.

"I've been thinking about our conversations," I said. "How they always happened at seven-year intervals. Is there significance to that?"

"Time is just another variable," she replied. "But cycles matter. What brings you here today?"

"Curiosity," I admitted. "And gratitude. The delta strategies helped me anticipate changes in my industry before others saw them coming. The psi techniques helped me maintain perspective through challenges that broke many of my colleagues. I wanted to thank you."

"And?" she prompted, knowing there was more.

"And... something has been happening that I can't quite explain. Moments where strategy and resilience seem to dissolve into something else entirely."

Her eyes brightened. "Tell me about these moments."

"It's like... I'll be in the middle of navigating a complex situation, using everything I've learned about delta and psi, and suddenly there's this shift in perspective. The boundary between me and the situation disappears. I'm no longer trying to control or even respond to change—I'm participating in it, as if I'm part of the same movement."

"The third dimension," she nodded. "Infinity."

"I thought that might just be a metaphor."

"It is, and it isn't," she said. "Infinity in our equation represents something that cannot be achieved directly through effort. It emerges naturally when delta strategic methods and psi mental resilience work together long enough."

She gestured toward the horizon, where the setting sun cast golden light across the cityscape.

"Consider the dancer one last time," she said. "After years of technical training (delta) and mental preparation (psi), there comes a moment when the dancer no longer sees themselves as separate from the spotlight. They don't dance within the light—they become the dance itself, an expression of something larger."

"That's what those moments feel like," I acknowledged. "But I can't maintain that state. It comes and goes."

"Because we're still human, still individual waves in the ocean," she smiled. "The arrow in our equation—from delta plus psi toward infinity—reminds us that infinity is an approach, not an achievement. We don't conquer it; we recognise our connection to it in moments of clarity."

The sun dipped below the horizon, painting the sky in deepening shades of purple and blue.

"So, the complete equation is $(\Delta + \Psi) \rightarrow \infty$?" I asked.

"Yes. We begin with strategic methods to navigate change. We develop mental resilience to implement those methods effectively. And eventually, we glimpse infinity—the recognition that we are not separate from the change we're trying to navigate. We are waves in an infinite ocean, temporarily expressing as individual forms."

"Is that the end of the journey?" I asked.

She laughed; a sound full of genuine joy. "There is no end to infinity, dear one. Only continued exploration. The equation doesn't solve life—it provides a framework for living it more fully."

As darkness fell over the city, lights began to appear, countless tiny spotlights illuminating the urban landscape.

"Look," she said, gesturing toward the view. "Every light you see represents a spotlight moving across someone's stage. Most people spend their lives fighting against delta, trapped in mental patterns that create suffering. But you—you've learned to read the patterns of change, to build mental resilience, and now you're beginning to glimpse the third dimension."

"Thanks to you," I said.

"No," she shook her head firmly. "I only pointed toward the equation. You've been doing the work, solving it in your own life."

She reached into her pocket and handed me a small object—a pendant with the equation elegantly engraved: $(\Delta + \Psi) \rightarrow \infty$

"For the journey ahead," she said. "A reminder that preparation isn't about controlling outcomes—it's about developing a relationship with reality that allows you to move through change with both power and peace."

As we sat in comfortable silence watching the city lights, I felt a familiar shift in perspective—that boundary between observer and observed thinning, dissolving. For a moment, I wasn't watching the lights; I was the awareness in which both lights and observer appeared. Not a dancer in the spotlight, but the dance itself.

Another glimpse of infinity—another step in the unending odyssey of becoming fully human in a constantly changing world.

LAYER 3

APPROACHING INFINITY, BECOMING THE DANCE

THE WAVE DOESN'T NEED PROTECTION FROM THE OCEAN

∞

Approaching Infinity

∞

There comes a point in the journey where effort alone can take us no further. When strategic methods (delta) and mental resilience (psi) have been developed to a certain threshold, something unexpected begins to emerge—a quality of being that cannot be achieved directly but arises naturally from the integration of the first two dimensions.

This is infinity in our equation—not a destination to reach but a reality to recognise. The symbol ∞ represents the boundless and unlimited, and in our context, it points to seeing ourselves as waves in an infinite ocean, connected to something larger than our individual identities and concerns.

The chapters in this section guide you through this subtle territory. Unlike the clear strategic frameworks of delta or the practical mental techniques of psi, infinity operates through metaphor, perspective shifts, and moments of recognition that transcend conventional thinking.

Here we explore wave patterns, the horizon effect, oceanic perspective, the integration of effort and surrender, and ultimately, the final transformation—becoming the wave rather than merely riding it.

This section may challenge your fundamental assumptions about preparation, control, and success. But it also offers something precious: the recognition that true preparation isn't about controlling outcomes but about developing a relationship with reality that allows you to move through change with both power and peace.

The arrow in our equation (→) reminds us that infinity isn't something we achieve through force of will. It's something we approach naturally when delta and psi work together in harmony. As we conclude our journey through The Odyssey Equation, this recognition becomes not just an intellectual understanding but a lived experience.

ELEVEN

The Nature of Consciousness

Who are you, really?

They sat in silence as the sun rose, early morning light gradually illuminating the landscape around them.
"What are you noticing right now?" Avika asked softly.
"Colours appearing as light increases," Jai replied. "Birds beginning to sing. A slight chill in the air."
"And who is noticing these things?" Avika asked.
Jai gave her a quizzical look. "Me, obviously."
"Look more closely," Avika suggested. "There are sensations, sounds, visual perceptions, thoughts about those perceptions... and there's the awareness in which all these experiences are appearing. Which of these is the 'me' you're referring to?"
Jai was silent for a long moment. "I've never thought about it that way. I've always just assumed I am this body and mind experiencing the world around me."
"That's the conventional understanding," Avika nodded. "But what if your fundamental nature isn't a separate self experiencing the world, but the awareness in which both 'self' and 'world' appear?"
"That sounds very philosophical," Jai said sceptically. "What does it have to do with becoming unshakeable?"
"Everything," Avika replied. "Because most of what can 'shake you' depends on believing you are a separate self vulnerable to circumstances. What if that separate self is less solid than it appears?"

"The universe is not only stranger than we imagine; it is stranger than we can imagine."
– Sir Arthur Eddington, astrophysicist

Let me ask you something: Who are you, really?

If you're like most people, your answer probably includes elements of your identity—your name, job, relationships, accomplishments, beliefs, and experiences. These are all part of your story, the narrative you've constructed about who you are.

But what if I told you that you are not your story? What if the "you" that you've been protecting, promoting, and worrying about is actually just a temporary configuration—a wave that mistakenly believes itself separate from the ocean?

This is where our journey takes a profound turn. In Layer 1, we explored strategic methods for directing your spotlight. In Layer 2, we expanded to recognise the whole stage beyond your spotlight's beam. Now, in Layer 3, we explore the possibility that you are the light itself.

The Observer and the Observed

I met Smita at a professional conference where I'd been speaking about resilience. A successful entrepreneur who had built her company from scratch into a thriving enterprise, she approached me during the reception afterward, wine glass in hand, eyes bright with curiosity.

"Everything you've said about strategic approaches and mental flexibility makes sense," she said. "But I keep feeling there's something deeper that I'm missing. Despite all my achievements and ability to navigate challenges, I still experience this... I don't know how to describe it... this sense of separation that never quite goes away."

Smita had achieved remarkable success by conventional standards—a thriving business, loving family, beautiful home, and robust health. She had mastered both strategic planning (Layer 1) and adaptive resilience (Layer 2). Yet something still felt missing.

We began working together, exploring the source of this persistent sense of separation. Smita was diligent in applying the methods we'd discussed, but the breakthrough came through an unexpected channel. During a silent meditation retreat, something shifted. The boundary between "Smita" and "everything else" temporarily dissolved.

"It wasn't that I disappeared," she explained during our follow-up session, her voice both excited and reverent. "It was more like I expanded to include everything. I could see that the observer and the observed were not two separate things but aspects of the same reality."

This experience—often called non-dual awareness—is at the heart of Layer 3. It's the recognition that consciousness itself is the foundation of all experience, and you are that consciousness.

Smita's initial encounter with this understanding was brief but transformative. "For days afterward, I kept noticing how automatically I create a sense of separation—how I divide experience into 'me in here' and 'world out there.' But now I could see this division as an activity rather than an inherent truth. Sometimes I could relax that activity, and when I did, the sense of separation would dissolve."

This recognition isn't merely a pleasant altered state or philosophical position. It has profound practical implications for resilience. When you recognise yourself as the consciousness in which all experience arises rather than as a separate entity moving through a potentially threatening world, the very foundation of what can "shake you" is transformed.

Smita noticed this shift in how she related to business challenges: "Before, problems felt like they were happening to me—attacks on my security that I needed to defend against. Now they appear more like movements within consciousness—

patterns arising and dissolving in awareness. I still respond to them, but without the added suffering that comes from feeling personally threatened by their existence."

This shift doesn't happen in a single moment of insight but unfolds gradually through direct investigation of your own experience. It begins with a simple but profound question: Who or what is aware of your current experience?

When you look at these words, who or what is seeing them? When thoughts arise, who or what is aware of those thoughts? When emotions move through, who or what is experiencing them?

The conventional answer is "me" or "I"—but this begs the question. Who or what is this "I" that experiences? Is it your body? Your thoughts? Your memories? Your sense of being a separate self?

When you look closely, you discover something remarkable: while experiences constantly change (sensations, thoughts, emotions, perceptions coming and going), the awareness in which they appear remains unchanged. This awareness—your fundamental nature—is not itself an object or experience but the knowing space in which all objects and experiences arise and dissolve.

Quantum Entanglement and Non-Duality

Interestingly, modern quantum physics offers a scientific parallel to this ancient wisdom. In quantum entanglement, particles that have interacted remain connected regardless of distance. When you measure one particle, you instantly know information about its entangled partner, even if they're on opposite sides of the universe.

Einstein famously called this "spooky action at a distance" because it defied classical physics' understanding of separation and locality. Yet experiments have repeatedly confirmed that at the quantum level, separation is more apparent than real.

This scientific insight points toward a profound truth: the universe is not a collection of separate objects but a unified field of interrelated processes. The apparent boundaries between "things" are more like temporary patterns in this unified field than absolute divisions.

Partha, a former physicist turned entrepreneur, discovered how this understanding could transform his approach to business challenges. We met at a retreat where I'd been teaching about Layer 3 resilience, and he was initially sceptical about connecting quantum physics to practical resilience.

"I've studied quantum mechanics academically," he explained, "but I've always kept that separate from how I navigate everyday challenges. They seem like completely different domains."

Over the following months, however, Partha began experimenting with applying this non-dual perspective to his business difficulties. He described the shift in our follow-up conversation:

"I used to see problems as external forces attacking my business—obstacles I needed to defeat or overcome. Now I see that these 'problems' aren't separate from me or my business; they're patterns within the same field of reality that I'm part of. This shift changes everything about how I respond."

Instead of approaching challenges from a position of separation and potential threat, Partha began seeing them as information arising within the same system he was part of. This fundamentally altered his emotional response—from reactivity to curiosity, from resistance to engagement.

"When my largest client unexpectedly cancelled their contract—something that would have previously thrown me into panic and resentment—I was able to approach it with genuine curiosity: 'This pattern is emerging in the field. What's it telling me about the system as a whole? How might this shift actually be revealing new possibilities I couldn't see before?'"

This perspective doesn't mean passively accepting whatever happens. Partha still took strategic action in response to the client loss. But that action emerged from a different foundation—not from a sense of being under attack but from an understanding of being part of an evolving whole.

The client loss ultimately led Partha to restructure his business model in ways that created greater stability and opportunity than the previous approach—something he might have missed if he'd been focused solely on "fixing the problem" from a position of separation.

Ekta, a healthcare executive, discovered a parallel to quantum entanglement through her relationship with her twin sister. Despite living on different continents with an eight-hour time difference, they frequently experienced synchronised intuitions, identical thoughts, or emotional resonance without any conventional communication.

"There have been times when I'll suddenly feel anxious for no apparent reason, then discover my sister was in a crisis at that exact moment," Ekta explained. "It's as if we operate as a single system despite the apparent separation of space and time."

While Ekta's experience might be dismissed as coincidence, the accumulation of such accounts across human experience suggests something more significant—that our conventional understanding of separate individuals existing in linear time may be an incomplete picture of a deeper reality.

Beyond the Separate Self

At this point, you might be wondering: "This sounds interesting philosophically, but what does it have to do with becoming unshakeable?"

Everything.

Think about it—what makes something capable of shaking you"? It's the belief that you are a separate entity vulnerable to external forces. When you recognise that the apparent boundary between "you" and "everything else" is more like a permeable membrane than a solid wall, the very foundation of vulnerability begins to dissolve.

Lena, a corporate executive, discovered this firsthand when dealing with intense workplace bullying. Despite using every strategic and psychological tool available, she continued to feel deeply affected by her colleague's attacks.

"I was doing everything right according to Layers 1 and 2," she told me during a coaching session. "I had strategic responses planned, set healthy boundaries, practiced resilience techniques... but his words still hurt every time."

The breakthrough came when Lena realised something profound: "He wasn't attacking 'me'—he was attacking an image of me that existed in his mind. And that image had nothing to do with who I really am at my core."

This insight shifted everything. Lena didn't become indifferent to the bullying behaviour (in fact, she still took practical steps to address it), but she no longer experienced it as a threat to her fundamental being.

"It was like watching storm clouds pass across the sky," she explained. "I could observe the patterns without believing they defined me or determined my experience."

This shift wasn't intellectual understanding but direct recognition—Lena could see that her essential nature as awareness remained untouched regardless of what appeared within it, including difficult interactions and others' judgments.

Samuel had a similar revelation through a very different circumstance—receiving unexpected public recognition for his work. While most would consider this a purely positive experience, Samuel noticed something interesting: the praise was just as capable of shaking him as criticism had been.

"When people praised me, I felt temporarily elevated but also anxious about living up to their image of me," he explained. "I realised that both criticism and praise were equally capable of disturbing my peace when I identified with the separate self they were directed toward."

Through this insight, Samuel discovered that true resilience wasn't about becoming immune to negative feedback but about recognising that his fundamental nature transcended both criticism and praise. This didn't make him dismissive of others' perspectives—he still valued constructive feedback—but he no longer derived his sense of identity from these external assessments.

The implications of this understanding extend far beyond how we handle others' opinions. When you recognise that you are the consciousness in which all experience appears rather than a separate entity navigating that experience, everything transforms—from how you relate to emotions to how you approach uncertainty to how you experience challenges.

Pranay, a healthcare provider working in high-stress emergency situations, described how this shift transformed his relationship with intense emotions: "I used to either be overwhelmed by anxiety during crisis situations or try to suppress it completely. Now I can see anxiety arising in awareness—an energetic pattern appearing in consciousness rather than something happening to 'me.' This creates space where there was none before, allowing me to respond to the situation without being hijacked by the emotion."

This isn't emotional bypassing or dissociation. Pranay fully acknowledges the anxiety when it appears. The difference is that he recognises it as an appearance in consciousness rather than a definition of who he is or a threat to his being. This recognition creates freedom to respond effectively even as intense emotions move through.

The Wisdom of Ashtavakra: Ancient Insights for Layer 3 Resilience

> *"You are not earth, water, fire or air. Nor are you empty space. Liberation is to know yourself as Awareness alone—the Witness of these."*
>
> – *Ashtavakra Gita,* 1:3

The journey toward Layer 3 resilience—recognising that your fundamental nature transcends the separate self that seems vulnerable to life's challenges—has been articulated with remarkable clarity in ancient wisdom traditions. Perhaps none expresses this understanding more directly than the *Ashtavakra Gita,* a profound Sanskrit text that distils the essence of non-dual awareness into piercingly direct insights.

While modern psychology and quantum physics have recently arrived at similar understandings, the *Ashtavakra Gita* has pointed toward this recognition for thousands of years. Its teachings offer a roadmap for the deepest level of resilience—freedom that comes not from controlling circumstances or developing mental flexibility, but from recognising your true nature beyond all circumstantial identity.

Beyond the Separate Self: Ashtavakra's Core Insight

The central teaching of the *Ashtavakra Gita* is revolutionary in its simplicity: you are not what you think you are. Your fundamental nature is not a separate self, navigating a threatening world, but pure awareness in which all experience arises.

> *"You are not the body. You are not the mind. You are pure Awareness—the Witness of all things. You are without expectation, free. Wherever you go, be happy."*
>
> – *Ashtavakra Gita,* 1:6

This direct pointing to your nature as awareness itself—rather than as a separate entity moving through time—addresses the very foundation of what can "shake you." When you recognise yourself as the awareness in which all experience appears rather than as a vulnerable entity within that experience, the basis of suffering fundamentally shifts.

Ekta discovered this during a period of intense career uncertainty. Despite applying both strategic approaches (Layer 1) and mental flexibility (Layer 2), she still experienced underlying anxiety about possible outcomes.

"I was doing everything 'right' according to both strategic methods and psychological techniques," Ekta explained. "But beneath it all remained a subtle but persistent fear—that somehow the 'me' I identified with could be fundamentally damaged by certain outcomes."

Through exploring the insights of the *Ashtavakra Gita,* Ekta recognised something profound: the separate self she had been trying to protect wasn't as solid or fundamental as she had assumed.

"The text points to a recognition that was simultaneously simple and revolutionary," she reflected. "My fundamental nature isn't the story of 'Ekta' with her career concerns, accomplishments, and fears, but the awareness in which that entire narrative appears. This wasn't abstract philosophy but direct recognition with immediate practical implications for my relationship with uncertainty."

This recognition didn't invalidate Ekta's strategic planning or mental flexibility but provided a foundation from which these approaches could function without the constriction of believing her fundamental wellbeing depended on particular outcomes.

Practical Freedom: Ashtavakra's Approach to Action

What makes the *Ashtavakra Gita* particularly relevant to Layer 3 resilience is its practical approach to action. Unlike some spiritual traditions that might suggest withdrawal from engagement, Ashtavakra offers insights for remaining fully engaged while free from identification with outcomes.

> *"The wise one is not concerned with the getting or the giving up of anything. Finding the natural joy of his own nature, he plays like a child."*
>
> – *Ashtavakra Gita,* 18:25

This addresses the paradox of doing we explored in Chapter 13—how purposeful action can coexist with the recognition that the doer is itself an appearance within consciousness.

Swastik applied this understanding to his leadership role during organisational change. Rather than approaching leadership either from rigid strategic control or complete detachment, he discovered a middle path based on Ashtavakra's insights.

"I realised I could be fully engaged in directing the change process without being psychologically identified with outcomes," Swastik explained. "This wasn't detachment in the sense of not caring, but freedom from the belief that my fundamental worth or being depended on particular results."

This shift created both greater effectiveness and psychological freedom. Without the constriction of believing his identity was at stake in the change process, Swastik could respond to emerging situations with unusual clarity and creativity.

> *"When you know for certain that everything is the Self, when you've seen all as only the Self, then all your desires dissolve."*
>
> – *Ashtavakra Gita,* 2:13

This dissolution of desire doesn't mean absence of intention or purpose but transformation of how purpose functions—arising from alignment with deeper values rather than from anxious ego needs. This creates a different quality of action—one flowing from freedom rather than compulsion.

Liberation from the Known: Ashtavakra's Approach to Certainty

Another aspect of the *Ashtavakra Gita* that directly addresses Layer 3 resilience is its guidance on moving beyond the security of conceptual knowing toward the freedom of direct recognition.

> *"My child, you can talk about knowledge forever, and it will only burden your mind. But to be free you must let go of knowledge itself."*
>
> – *Ashtavakra Gita,* 16:2

This points to the paradoxical wisdom of "not knowing" we explored in Chapter 14—the recognition that true freedom comes not from perfect knowledge but from releasing attachment to conceptual certainty.

Sarita discovered the practical dimension of this insight during complex business negotiations. Despite extensive preparation and strategic planning, the negotiations reached an impasse where no amount of analysis seemed to reveal a clear path forward.

"I had been approaching the situation as a problem to solve through more knowledge and better analysis," Sarita reflected. "The breakthrough came when I recognised that no amount of information could eliminate the fundamental uncertainty of the situation."

Rather than continuing to seek certainty where it wasn't available, Sarita shifted to a fundamentally different relationship with the unknown—one based on Ashtavakra's insights about releasing attachment to knowing.

"Instead of seeing uncertainty as a problem to solve, I recognised it as the field within which creative possibilities could emerge," she explained. "This wasn't philosophical abstraction but practical recognition that transformed how I engaged with the negotiation process."

From this release into "not knowing," Sarita discovered options that hadn't been visible from her previous position of trying to force clarity where complexity existed. The negotiations progressed through unexpected pathways that conventional analysis couldn't have anticipated.

Integration with Modern Understanding

While expressed in the language of ancient India, the insights of the *Ashtavakra Gita* align remarkably well with contemporary understanding of consciousness and identity. Modern neuroscience, quantum physics, and psychological research increasingly suggest that our conventional sense of being a separate self is more constructed than fundamental—exactly what Ashtavakra pointed toward thousands of years ago.

> *"Bondage is when the mind desires or grieves about anything, rejects or accepts anything, feels happy or angry about anything."*
> – *Ashtavakra Gita*, 8:1

This understanding of how identification with mental states creates psychological bondage parallels modern research on how cognitive fusion—over-identification with thoughts and feelings—underlies many forms of psychological suffering.

The integrated perspective recognises that both ancient wisdom and modern research point toward the same fundamental truth: the separate self that seems vulnerable to life's challenges is not as solid or fundamental as it appears. From this recognition emerges the deepest level of resilience—resilience based not on controlling external circumstances or developing better mental strategies, but on recognising your true nature beyond all that can be threatened.

Practical Applications: Ashtavakra's Guidance

How can we apply these ancient insights in modern life? The Ashtavakra Gita offers surprisingly practical guidance:

Recognise Your True Nature

> *"You are pure Awareness—unchanging, pristine, serene. Don't get caught in the world."*
>
> – *Ashtavakra Gita,* 1:12

This isn't abstract philosophy but direct pointing to what you already are. Several times each day, pause and notice the awareness that is present regardless of what experiences are arising within it. This simple recognition creates space between your fundamental nature and the changing circumstances that previously seemed capable of threatening you.

Release Identification with Outcomes

> *"You are not the doer nor the enjoyer. You have always been free. Go about your business with detachment."*
>
> – *Ashtavakra Gita,* 1:15

This doesn't mean abandoning purpose or responsibility but transforming how you hold them. Engage fully in purposeful action while recognising that your fundamental wellbeing doesn't depend on particular results. This creates both greater effectiveness and psychological freedom.

Embrace the Paradox of Being and Becoming

> *"In me, the boundless ocean, let the waves of the universe rise and fall as they will. I am neither enriched nor impoverished."*
> – *Ashtavakra Gita,* 8:2

This beautiful metaphor captures the essence of Layer 3 resilience—the recognition that the changing circumstances of life (the waves) arise and fall within your fundamental nature (the ocean) without affecting what you essentially are. From this perspective, challenges lose their power to fundamentally disturb you, even as you remain fully engaged with navigating them.

Rest in Natural Awareness

> *"Rest in awareness, with no purpose. The world is a passing show unfolding before you."*
> – *Ashtavakra Gita,* 2:15

This isn't passive withdrawal but recognition of the awareness that is already present prior to any effort. Several times each day, allow yourself to rest as awareness itself rather than as a separate self trying to solve problems. From this natural resting, effective action often emerges spontaneously without the friction of anxious effort.

The Journey of Recognition

The insights of the *Ashtavakra Gita* point not toward acquiring something new but recognising what has always been present—

your fundamental nature as awareness itself. This recognition doesn't replace the strategic methods of Layer 1 or the mental flexibility of Layer 2 but provides the foundation from which these approaches can function without the limitations imposed by identification with a separate self.

As you integrate these ancient insights with modern understanding, remember that this isn't about achieving a permanent state of transcendence but developing increasing familiarity with your fundamental nature beyond all circumstantial identity. Even as you continue to navigate life's practical challenges through strategic methods and mental flexibility, this deeper recognition remains available as the foundation of true resilience.

> *"You are everywhere, forever free. The only bondage is not knowing this. Seeing yourself as separate creates bondage."*
> – *Ashtavakra Gita,* 1:11

This simple yet profound recognition—that separation is more apparent than real—creates a liberation that no external circumstance can threaten. This is the essence of Layer 3 resilience—resilience based not on what you do or how you adapt, but on recognising what you fundamentally are.

Practical Approaches to Layer 3

Layer 3 can sound abstract, but there are practical ways to explore this understanding in your daily life:

The Witnessing Practice

Several times throughout your day, pause and notice that you are aware. Don't just think about being aware—directly experience the awareness that is reading these words right now.

Notice that this awareness is always present, regardless of what's happening in your experience. It remains unchanged whether you're experiencing pleasure or pain, success or failure, praise or criticism.

This unchanging awareness is what you fundamentally are—not the changing contents of consciousness (thoughts, emotions, sensations, perceptions) but consciousness itself.

Jaimin incorporated this practice into his daily life by setting three random alarms on his phone. When each alarm sounded, he would pause and directly notice the awareness that was present, regardless of what he was doing or experiencing at that moment.

"What surprised me most was the consistent quality of awareness itself," Jaimin reflected. "Whether I was in a stressful meeting, enjoying lunch with friends, or focused on a complex problem, the awareness in which these experiences appeared remained unchanged—spacious, clear, and undisturbed by whatever was arising within it."

This simple practice gradually shifted Jaimin's sense of identity from exclusive identification with the changing contents of consciousness to recognition of himself as the awareness in which all contents appear. This didn't make him detached from life but paradoxically allowed him to engage more fully, without the constriction that comes from believing his wellbeing depends on particular experiences.

> *Try This:* Set three random alarms on your phone today. When each alarm sounds, pause and ask: "What is aware of my current experience?" Don't answer conceptually—directly notice the awareness that is present.

The Question of Origin

When thoughts or emotions arise, especially difficult ones, ask: "Where is this coming from? Where does it appear? Where does it go when it passes?"

Jai, a chronic worrier, transformed his relationship with anxiety through this simple practice. "I noticed that thoughts appear from nowhere, exist briefly in awareness, and then disappear back into nowhere," he explained. "Once I saw this clearly, they lost much of their power over me."

This practice helps you recognise that thoughts and emotions are temporary appearances in consciousness rather than solid realities that define you or determine your experience. By tracking their arising and passing, you develop a different relationship with these experiences—more like watching weather patterns move across the sky than being defined by each passing cloud.

Smita applied this approach during a period of significant work stress. Rather than being consumed by anxious thoughts about project deadlines, she began noticing where these thoughts appeared and disappeared.

"I realised I couldn't actually find where thoughts come from or where they go," she told me. "They simply appear in awareness and dissolve again, like waves forming and subsiding in the ocean. This doesn't mean ignoring their content when it's useful, but it creates a fundamentally different relationship with thinking itself."

This practice doesn't suppress or deny thoughts and emotions but transforms your relationship with them through direct investigation of their nature. Rather than being solid realities that define you, they're recognised as temporary patterns appearing in the field of consciousness that you fundamentally are.

The Mirror Perspective

Imagine you're looking in a mirror. The reflection you see appears to be you, but it's actually just an image appearing in the mirror.

Similarly, the "self" you typically identify with (your thoughts, emotions, sensations, and perceptions) is like a reflection appearing in the mirror of consciousness. It's not who you fundamentally are—it's what appears to you.

Ekta used this perspective during a period of professional criticism that had been deeply affecting her sense of self-worth. "When negative feedback came, I would ask myself: 'If I am the mirror rather than the reflection, how would I experience this criticism?' This immediately created space—I could see the critical thoughts and painful emotions as reflections appearing in awareness rather than definitions of who I am."

This shift didn't make Ekta dismissive of feedback or immune to natural human emotion. She still felt the sting of criticism and considered its validity when appropriate. But she no longer experienced it as a threat to her fundamental being, which remained as untouched by criticism as a mirror remains untouched by the images it reflects.

> *Real-World Application:* The next time you feel emotionally triggered, pause and ask: "What would this look like if I were the mirror rather than the reflection? What if I am the awareness in which this emotion appears rather than the emotion itself?"

The Interconnection Contemplation

Take something simple—an apple, for instance. Consider everything that had to occur for this apple to exist: sunlight, soil, water, the seed's genetic code, the farmer's work, transportation systems, economic exchanges, and countless other factors.

In this contemplation, you recognise that nothing exists independently. Everything is the result of innumerable interconnections and interdependencies.

Swastik, a business leader, used this practice to transform his understanding of both success and failure. "I had been taking both credit and blame too personally," he explained, "as if my successes and failures were solely my own creation. This contemplation helped me see how every outcome emerges from countless interconnected factors, many beyond my awareness or control."

This recognition didn't diminish Swastik's sense of responsibility but placed it within a more accurate context—as one factor within a vast web of interconnected conditions rather than as the sole determinant of outcomes. This shift created both greater humility about successes and less personal devastation about setbacks.

> *Your Turn:* Choose something in your immediate environment and trace its existence back through as many connections as you can identify. Notice how this object is not separate from the world but an expression of countless interrelated processes.

Not Spiritual Bypassing

It's important to clarify that Layer 3 is not about denying your human experience or using spiritual concepts to avoid dealing with practical challenges.

You still have a body, emotions, relationships, and responsibilities. You still plan, act, feel, and engage with the world. The difference is that you do so from a broader perspective—one that recognises these experiences are appearing within consciousness rather than defining who you fundamentally are.

Smita, whom we met earlier, explained it this way: "I haven't stopped being human—I've just stopped being exclusively identified with my humanity. It's like I've gone from watching a movie and believing I'm the main character to recognising I'm also the screen on which the whole movie appears."

This broader perspective doesn't make you indifferent to life's experiences; it allows you to engage with them more fully, without the constriction that comes from believing your identity depends on particular outcomes.

Jogi, a therapist working with trauma survivors, found that this understanding enhanced rather than diminished his compassion and effectiveness. "Recognising our shared nature as consciousness doesn't make me less connected to others' suffering," he explained. "Paradoxically, it creates a deeper connection because I can see that the same consciousness experiencing this conversation is the consciousness experiencing my client's pain. The boundaries between us aren't as solid as they appear."

This perspective also doesn't mean bypassing necessary growth or avoiding difficult emotions by prematurely claiming transcendence. Sanjukta, a spiritual teacher, emphasised this point: "Layer 3 understanding includes everything—joy and sorrow, ease and difficulty, success and failure. Nothing is excluded or bypassed. The shift is in recognising that what you fundamentally are includes but transcends all these temporary experiences."

This inclusive recognition creates a unique kind of resilience—not by eliminating challenges or difficult emotions but by transforming your relationship with them. When you recognise that what you fundamentally are is the consciousness in which all experience appears rather than any particular experience itself, you discover a security that doesn't depend on controlling circumstances.

Direct Experience Beyond Concepts

The understanding we're exploring in Layer 3 isn't primarily conceptual but experiential. Reading about these ideas might be interesting and even intellectually compelling, but the real transformation comes through direct recognition in your own experience.

Sarita, a long-time meditator, described the difference: "For years, I understood non-duality intellectually—I could explain it clearly and even teach the concepts to others. But there was a profound difference between understanding it as an idea and directly recognising it in my experience. The former was an interesting philosophy; the latter transformed everything about how I relate to life."

This direct recognition often happens in ordinary moments rather than dramatic spiritual experiences. Swastik was washing dishes when he suddenly noticed that the boundary between "him" and "the experience of washing dishes" wasn't as solid as he had always assumed. "There was still the activity of washing dishes, but the sense of a separate 'me' doing it momentarily fell away. There was just washing happening, without a washer separate from the washing."

These glimpses of non-dual awareness typically come and go, especially initially. They aren't about achieving a permanent state but about increasingly recognising your fundamental nature even as you continue to function in the conventional world of apparent separation.

Ekta described her experience: "At first, these recognitions were brief and infrequent—moments when the sense of separation would dissolve, followed by the return of habitual patterns of identification with a separate self. Over time, these moments became more frequent and extended, but even now, I move between clear seeing and habitual patterns. The difference is that I can now recognise the habitual patterns as just that—patterns rather than fundamental truths about who I am."

This recognition is available to everyone regardless of spiritual background or belief system. It doesn't require adopting any particular philosophy or religion. It's simply the direct noticing of what is already present but often overlooked—the awareness in which all experience appears.

As you explore the practices we've discussed in this chapter, approach them with genuine curiosity rather than seeking particular experiences or trying to make something happen. The recognition we're pointing toward isn't something new to be achieved but something fundamental to be noticed—your own nature as consciousness itself.

In the next chapter, we'll examine how this Layer 3 understanding transforms your relationship with time itself, further dissolving the foundations of what can "shake you."

TWELVE

Time as an Illusion

What if the linear progression from past to future through the present moment isn't as solid or fundamental as it appears?

"I'm anxious about this deadline," Jai admitted as they walked through the city. "It feels like there's not enough time, and I'm imagining all the negative consequences if I don't finish in time."

"Where do those imagined consequences exist?" Avika asked.

"In the future, obviously," Jai replied.

"But does the future actually exist right now?" Avika pressed. "Or is it appearing as thoughts and images in your present awareness?"

Jai stopped walking. "Well... technically it's just thoughts right now. But those thoughts are about something real that will happen."

"Will happen—or might happen?" Avika asked. "And even when that moment arrives, you'll experience it as the present, not as the future. Have you ever actually experienced the future directly, or only ever the present moment?"

"Only the present," Jai admitted. "But that doesn't make the future irrelevant."

"Not irrelevant," Avika clarified. "But perhaps not as solid or fixed as we typically believe. From the Layer 3 perspective, time as we conventionally experience it—a linear progression from past to future through the present—might be more constructed than fundamental."

"And this helps with deadlines how exactly?" Jai asked with a hint of impatience.

"When you recognise that your anxiety exists only as a present experience about an imagined future, something shifts," Avika explained. "You recognise that the only point of reality and power is this present moment—the only place life is actually experienced."

"Time isn't precious at all, because it is an illusion."
– Eckhart Tolle

Most of us experience time as a fundamental reality—a linear progression from past to future through the present moment. We organise our lives around this conception, creating schedules, setting deadlines, celebrating anniversaries, and measuring progress along this seemingly absolute dimension.

But what if our conventional understanding of time is just a useful fiction? What if, at the deepest level of reality, time as we typically conceive it doesn't actually exist?

This isn't just a philosophical thought experiment. Quantum physics, relativity theory, and ancient wisdom traditions all point toward a radical reconsideration of time—one that has profound implications for becoming truly unshakeable.

The Eternal Now

I first witnessed the transformative power of this understanding while working with Aditya, a high-achieving executive who had built his career on his ability to optimise every minute of every day. When we met, Aditya was experiencing debilitating anxiety despite his considerable success.

"I feel like I'm constantly racing against time," he explained during our initial consultation. "There's never enough of it, and no matter how efficiently I use it, I'm always behind where I think I should be."

Aditya organised his life on an elaborate timeline. His past consisted of accomplishments that never felt quite sufficient. His future loomed as an endless series of goals and deadlines. His present was merely a thin slice of experience, constantly overshadowed by regrets about what hadn't been achieved and anxiety about what might not be accomplished.

"I'm successful by most standards," he admitted, "but I never feel successful in the moment. I'm always comparing current reality to where I planned to be, or worrying about whether I'll reach future targets."

This relationship with time—treating it as an objective reality against which we measure ourselves—creates a particular kind of suffering that no amount of achievement can resolve. As long as we believe we are entities moving along a timeline, we remain vulnerable to regrets about the past and anxieties about the future.

For Aditya, the shift began during a silent meditation retreat. After several days of practice, he had an unexpected experience that changed his entire relationship with time.

"Suddenly, there was only now," he described. "Not as a concept or a fleeting moment between past and future, but as the only reality. I could see that what I called 'past' was actually just present memories arising now, and what I called 'future' was present imagination arising now. Everything was happening in this eternal present moment."

This wasn't a philosophical idea for Aditya but a direct experience. The seemingly solid timeline of his life dissolved into a single point of awareness in which all experience arose. Past regrets and future anxieties, which had dominated his mental landscape, suddenly had no place to stand.

"It was like I'd been living in a film, believing each frame was separate and that I was moving through them," he explained. "Then I realised I was the screen on which all frames appeared simultaneously."

Einstein's theories of relativity had already shattered the Newtonian concept of absolute time a century ago. We now understand that time is relative—it flows at different rates depending on factors like gravity and velocity. Two synchronised clocks will show different times if one is placed on a mountain and another at sea level, or if one remains stationary while the other moves at high speed.

At quantum scales, time becomes even stranger. In certain quantum experiments, effects appear to precede causes. Particles can become "entangled" such that measuring one instantaneously affects another, regardless of the distance between them—what Einstein called "spooky action at a distance."

These scientific insights align remarkably with the perspectives of contemplative traditions that have pointed toward the illusion of time for thousands of years.

"After that retreat, I couldn't go back to my previous relationship with time," Aditya told me during a follow-up session. "I still use calendars and schedules—they're practical tools for coordinating with others. But I no longer experience myself as moving along a timeline where my worth depends on past achievements or future attainments."

This shift transformed Aditya's experience of both work and life. The anxiety that had plagued him for decades diminished dramatically, not because his circumstances changed but because his relationship with time itself transformed. He could engage fully with present activities without the psychological burden of time pressure that had previously dominated his experience.

> *Try This:* For five minutes, notice how everything you experience—memories, anticipations, sensations, thoughts—is actually arising in the present moment. When thoughts of past or future appear, recognise them as present thoughts rather than actual destinations your consciousness travels to.

Spooky Action at a Distance

Quantum entanglement—Einstein's "spooky action at a distance"—demonstrates that at the quantum level, separation in space and time is more apparent than real. When particles become entangled, they form a single system such that measuring one instantaneously affects the other, regardless of the distance between them.

This phenomenon, repeatedly confirmed by experiments, suggests a profound interconnectedness that transcends our conventional understanding of separate objects existing in linear time.

Ekta discovered a parallel to this quantum insight through her relationship with her twin sister. Despite living on different continents with an eight-hour time difference, they frequently experienced synchronised intuitions, identical thoughts, or emotional resonance without any conventional communication.

"There have been times when I'll suddenly feel anxious for no apparent reason, then discover my sister was in a crisis at that exact moment," Ekta explained during one of our conversations. "It's as if we operate as a single system despite the apparent separation of space and time."

While Ekta's experience might be dismissed as coincidence by some, the accumulation of such accounts across human experience suggests something more significant—that our conventional understanding of separate individuals existing in linear time may be an incomplete picture of a deeper reality.

What makes these experiences particularly interesting isn't just their seeming defiance of spatial separation but their challenge to our conventional understanding of time. If Ekta feels her sister's distress simultaneously with the actual event despite being in a different time zone, what does this suggest about the nature of the "present moment"?

These experiences hint at a perspective where the present isn't just a thin slice moving along a timeline but a more expansive dimension in which apparently separate events exist in relationship regardless of their placement in conventional time.

Christopher, a physician who had long been sceptical of such accounts, had his perspective transformed through his own unexpected experience. During a routine day at his medical practice, he suddenly felt an overwhelming urge to call his brother—something so unusual and compelling that he cancelled his next appointment to do so.

His brother, as it turned out, had just been rushed to the emergency room with a cardiac event at precisely the time Christopher felt the urge to call. There was no conventional way Christopher could have known about this emergency; no one had contacted him, and it was happening thousands of miles away.

"As a doctor trained in physical medicine, I had always assumed a clear causal order to events," Christopher told me. "But this experience suggested something different—a connection that didn't rely on conventional cause-effect sequences unfolding in linear time."

These phenomena don't necessarily invalidate our practical use of clocks and calendars. They simply suggest that the reality underlying our everyday experience of time is more complex and interconnected than our conventional understanding allows.

> *Real-World Application:* Pay attention to instances of meaningful synchronicity in your life—events that seem connected despite having no conventional causal relationship. Rather than dismissing these as mere coincidence, consider them potential glimpses of a deeper interconnectedness beyond linear time.

How Quantum Physics Supports Ancient Wisdom

What's particularly striking is how modern physics has arrived at insights that contemplative traditions have pointed toward for millennia. The Buddhist concept of "emptiness," the Hindu understanding of "Maya" (illusion), and the Taoist perspective on non-dual reality all suggest that our conventional perception of separate objects moving through linear time is a limited view of a deeper reality.

Anurag, a physicist turned meditation teacher, bridges these traditions in his work. "What's remarkable isn't that ancient contemplatives somehow anticipated quantum physics," he explains. "It's that when humans directly investigate the nature of reality—whether through advanced mathematics and experimental apparatus or through refined contemplative techniques—they tend to discover similar patterns. The universe reveals consistent truths regardless of the tools used to explore it."

This convergence suggests we're not dealing with mere metaphor or philosophical speculation but with fundamental insights about the nature of reality—insights that have profound implications for how we relate to our lives.

I witnessed this convergence transform Sarita's relationship with chronic illness. After years of struggling against her condition and its limitations, she began exploring both quantum perspectives and meditation practices that pointed toward a different relationship with time.

"I had been living in a story where my illness had taken away my past capabilities and threatened my future possibilities," Sarita explained. "I was constantly comparing present experience with memories of how things used to be or projections of how they 'should' be in the future."

Through both scientific understanding and contemplative practice, Sarita began recognising that this narrative existed only in thought—arising in the present moment rather than extending along an objective timeline.

"When I noticed that both past losses and future fears existed only as present thoughts, something shifted," she told me. "There was just this moment of experience, which included sensations in the body and thoughts about 'past' and 'future,' but all arising now."

This recognition didn't cure Sarita's physical condition, but it transformed her relationship with it. The added suffering that came from constant comparison with an imagined past or projected future began to dissolve, leaving her more capable of responding effectively to her actual present experience.

> *Your Turn:* Explore a contemplative tradition that interests you, paying particular attention to its perspective on time. How might these ancient insights complement modern scientific understanding? What practical implications might this integrated perspective have for your daily experience?

Beyond the Separate Self in Time

The most significant implication of this reconsideration of time is how it transforms our understanding of self. The conventional notion of a separate entity moving through linear time forms the foundation of most human suffering.

When you believe you are a separate self traveling from past to future:

- You carry the burden of past actions as defining who you "are"
- You project current limitations into an imagined future
- You experience anxiety about what might happen to "you" later
- You resist the present moment as insufficient compared to an idealised future

But when you recognise the illusory nature of linear time and the separate self that supposedly travels through it, a profound shift occurs. You realise that:

- The "past" exists only as present memory
- The "future" exists only as present imagination
- Who you are transcends the particular story unfolding in apparent time
- The only point of power and reality is this eternal now

Sara experienced this shift during a period of overwhelming anxiety about her future. After her company announced potential layoffs, she became consumed with fear about what might happen—running endless scenarios about financial hardship, career setbacks, and loss of security.

Through mindfulness practice, Sara began to notice something important: her suffering wasn't coming from any actual experience but from projecting herself into an imagined future. The present moment—the only reality she ever actually experienced—contained no disaster. Even her anxious thoughts and feelings about the future were just present experiences that arose and passed.

"I realised I was creating my own suffering by constantly projecting myself into a future that didn't actually exist," she explained. "When I fully embraced that the only reality was now, a weight lifted. The future remained uncertain, but that uncertainty no longer had the power to disrupt my present peace."

This wasn't a denial of practical reality—Sara still updated her resume and explored options. But she did so from a foundation of present awareness rather than anxious projection into an imagined future.

Swastik, a cancer survivor, discovered this same truth through his health journey. During treatment, he had been consumed with thoughts about his prognosis—constantly projecting himself into potential futures where his condition worsened or improved.

"I was living in imagined futures rather than in my actual life," Swastik reflected. "Then one day during meditation, I noticed something simple but profound: I had never once experienced the future. Every moment of my life had been now. Even when the future I had anticipated actually arrived, I experienced it as now, not as the future."

This recognition created a radical shift in Swastik's relationship with his health situation. Instead of living in fearful anticipation of what might happen, he discovered he could be fully present with whatever was actually occurring in each moment. This didn't eliminate the challenges of his treatment, but it dramatically reduced the added suffering that came from constant projection into imagined futures.

Try This: Notice when you're experiencing stress about the future or regret about the past. Remind yourself: "The only reality is now. Past and future exist only as present thoughts." Feel the immediate shift this recognition creates in your experience.

The Paradox of Doing

This perspective raises an important question: If time is ultimately illusory, what's the point of doing anything? Why set goals, make plans, or work toward change if everything is just happening in an eternal now?

This is where we encounter the paradox of doing—the recognition that purposeful action can coexist with the understanding that time is not fundamental.

Think of it this way: When you watch a movie, you know the entire film exists simultaneously on the reel or digital file. Yet you can still be fully engaged with the unfolding story without believing each frame is a separate reality.

Similarly, recognising the illusory nature of linear time doesn't mean abandoning purposeful action. It means engaging with the apparent timeline of your life from a deeper foundation—one that isn't dependent on particular outcomes or trapped in a limited identity.

Pranay embodies this paradox in his approach to environmental activism. He works with complete dedication toward long-term goals, yet does so from a foundation of present awareness rather than anxious attachment to future outcomes.

"I used to burn out regularly because I believed the future of the planet literally depended on what I did," he explained during a workshop on sustainable activism. "I carried the weight of future generations on my shoulders. Now I still work just as hard, but from a completely different place—not from fear of a catastrophic future but from love of this present moment and all it contains."

Pranay found that this shift actually made him more effective. When he stopped carrying the psychological burden of an imagined future, he had more energy available for present action. When he stopped identifying so strongly with the specific role of "environmental saviour," he became more collaborative and innovative.

"There's a beautiful paradox here," he reflected. "By releasing my attachment to controlling the future, I became more effective at influencing what unfolds. By recognising that time is ultimately illusory, I'm more able to use the apparent timeline skilfully."

Ekta discovered a similar paradox in her creative work as a writer. For years, she had struggled with procrastination and anxiety about her projects, constantly worried about whether future readers would approve of her work and whether she would meet her deadlines.

Through exploring the nature of time through both quantum perspectives and meditation, Ekta had an insight that transformed her relationship with writing: "I realised I had never actually written in the future—every word I had ever put on the page happened in the present moment. My anxiety about future completion was actually preventing me from being fully engaged with the only time I could actually write: now."

With this recognition, Ekta's creative process transformed. She still had deadlines and project timelines, but she held them as practical organising structures rather than psychological pressures. By focusing on full engagement with the present moment of creation rather than anxiety about future outcomes, both her productivity and the quality of her work improved dramatically.

> *Real-World Application:* For an important goal you're pursuing, explore this paradox of doing. How might you maintain full engagement with purposeful action while simultaneously recognising the illusory nature of the timeline in which this action seems to unfold? What shifts in your experience when you hold both perspectives simultaneously?

Freedom from Outcome

Perhaps the most practical application of recognising time as an illusion is the freedom it creates from attachment to specific outcomes. When you understand that:

- The "past" doesn't define who you fundamentally are
- The "future" isn't a real destination your consciousness will inhabit

- Your identity transcends the particular story unfolding in apparent time

You discover a profound liberation—the ability to act with full intention without making your wellbeing dependent on results.

Menka experienced this freedom during her work as an artist. For years, she had tied her identity and worth to the reception of her creations. A successful exhibition would elevate her; a critical review would devastate her. Her emotional wellbeing oscillated wildly based on external validation.

Through meditation practice, Menka began to recognise how she was projecting herself into imagined futures—ones where she was either celebrated or rejected. She noticed how these projections existed only as present thoughts, not as realities she actually experienced.

"I realised I was living for moments that never actually arrived," she explained during an interview about her creative process. "Even when I achieved 'success,' I experienced it only as a present moment that quickly gave way to anxiety about the next achievement. I was never arriving at that imagined future where I finally felt secure."

This recognition gradually shifted her relationship with her art. She continued to create with full dedication and care, but no longer tied her worth to outcomes. She could envision success, work toward it diligently, and remain completely present with the process rather than living in an imagined future.

"The paradox is that my work actually improved," Menka reflected. "When I stopped creating from a place of anxiety about outcomes, a different quality emerged—one that came from connection with the present moment rather than projection into an imagined future."

Jaimin experienced similar freedom in his athletic pursuits. A competitive cyclist, he had structured his identity around achievements and rankings. Each race became a statement about his worth, with results determining whether he would feel fulfilled or disappointed.

"I was constantly comparing present performance with past results or future expectations," Jaimin explained. "I was never just riding—I was always measuring myself against who I had been or who I thought I should become."

Through exploring non-dual perspectives on time and identity, Jaimin discovered a different relationship with his sport. He still trained diligently and competed wholeheartedly, but he no longer experienced his value as contingent on outcomes.

"Now when I ride, there's just riding," he told me. "There's full engagement with the present activity without the psychological burden of comparing it to past or future performances. Paradoxically, this liberation from outcome-attachment has improved my results because I'm fully present with the actual riding rather than divided between physical activity and mental time-travel."

This freedom from outcome doesn't mean abandoning preferences or desires. You can still have clear intentions and work toward specific outcomes. The shift is in recognising that your fundamental wellbeing isn't dependent on circumstances matching your preferences—that something essential in you remains intact regardless of how events unfold.

> *Try This:* For an important goal you're pursuing, practice full engagement with the process while consciously releasing attachment to outcome. Notice how this affects both your present experience and, paradoxically, your effectiveness. What qualities emerge in your action when you're not psychologically projected into an imagined future?

The Complete Liberation

This understanding of time as ultimately illusory creates perhaps the most profound aspect of becoming unshakeable. When you recognise that:

- Your fundamental identity isn't a separate entity moving through linear time
- The only reality you ever experience is the present moment
- Past and future exist only as present thoughts and images

You discover that what can "shake you" is dramatically reduced. The regrets, resentments, and remorse that seem to come from the past are revealed as present thoughts about memory. The anxieties, fears, and attachments that seem to be about the future are exposed as present thoughts about imagination.

When your identity is no longer tied to a particular story unfolding in linear time, what remains to be disturbed? What external circumstance can threaten who you fundamentally are?

Jaimin expressed this understanding after navigating a period of profound loss—including the end of his marriage and a serious health diagnosis within the same year.

"Before, I would have experienced these events as devastating blows to my life story," he reflected. "But from this perspective, I could see them simply as experiences arising in awareness—challenging and painful, yes, but not threatening to who I fundamentally am. The awareness in which these experiences appear remains unchanged, just as the sky remains unchanged by passing storms."

This isn't spiritual bypassing or denial of human experience. Jaimin still felt grief, fear, and other natural emotions. But these feelings moved through him rather than defining him. He could be with them fully without being overwhelmed by them—

precisely because he recognised they were temporary appearances in consciousness rather than threats to his fundamental being.

Ekta discovered similar freedom in her relationship with professional setbacks. After her company downsised her department, eliminating her carefully cultivated role and team, she found herself navigating circumstances that would have previously triggered identity crisis and anxiety.

"There was still disappointment and practical concerns about finding new work," Ekta explained. "But I could see that these were experiences arising in the present moment rather than devastation of my past achievements or threat to my future security. My identity wasn't actually contained in the timeline of my career—that was just a story appearing in present awareness."

This recognition allowed Ekta to respond to her situation with remarkable clarity and effectiveness. Without the added burden of existential threat that comes from identifying with a timeline-based self, she could address practical concerns directly while remaining open to possibilities that didn't fit her previous narrative.

Beyond Logic: Direct Experience

It's important to acknowledge that this perspective on time transcends logical understanding. You can comprehend it intellectually while still experiencing life primarily through the conventional lens of linear time and separate selfhood.

The shift from intellectual understanding to lived experience typically happens through direct investigation—practices that allow you to explore the nature of time and identity firsthand rather than merely thinking about them.

These practices might include:

- Mindfulness meditation, particularly approaches that investigate the arising and passing of experience in awareness
- Self-inquiry that directly questions the nature of the "self" that supposedly travels through time
- Flow states that naturally dissolve the sense of separate selfhood and linear time
- Contemplative traditions that offer specific methods for recognising the illusory nature of conventional time

The key insight across these approaches is that time as we typically experience it is conceptual rather than fundamental. The only direct experience we ever have is of the present moment—the eternal now in which all appearances arise.

Swastik described his journey from intellectual understanding to direct recognition: "I had read about non-dual perspectives on time for years and found them fascinating philosophically. But there was a vast difference between understanding these ideas conceptually and directly recognising them in my own experience. The former was interesting; the latter was transformative."

The shift often happens in ordinary moments rather than dramatic spiritual experiences. Sarita was washing dishes when she suddenly noticed that past, present, and future existed only as concepts arising in her current awareness rather than as objective realities she moved between.

"It wasn't a mystical revelation with angels and light," she laughed. "I was just washing a pot, and suddenly I could see that the 'past' where the pot got dirty and the 'future' where it would be used again existed only as thoughts arising now. There was just this washing happening in the eternal present."

These recognitions typically come and go, especially initially. What matters isn't having a permanent experience of timelessness but increasingly seeing through the illusion of time-bound identity even as you continue to function in the conventional world of schedules and deadlines.

Your Turn: Experiment with a daily practice that helps you directly investigate the nature of time and identity. This might be formal meditation, self-inquiry, or simply regular moments of noticing that everything you experience—including thoughts about past and future—is actually arising now. Pay attention to how this investigation affects your relationship with challenges that previously could "shake you."

The Bridge to Layer 3 Resilience

Understanding the illusory nature of time forms a cornerstone of **Layer 3 resilience**. While Layer 1 focuses on strategic methods and Layer 2 develops mental preparedness, Layer 3 transcends the very foundation from which disturbance arises—the belief in a separate self moving through linear time.

From this perspective, challenges that previously seemed personally threatening are recognised as impersonal appearances in consciousness. The question shifts from "How can I protect myself from what might happen?" to "Who is this 'self' that seems threatened by appearances in awareness?"

This represents the most profound level of becoming unshakeable—not through strengthening a separate self against potential threats, but through recognising that the separate self is itself an appearance within something more fundamental: consciousness itself.

In the next chapter, we'll explore this paradox of doing—how purposeful action can coexist with the recognition that the doer is itself an appearance rather than an ultimate reality.

THIRTEEN

The Paradox of Doing

If the separate self is more appearance than ultimate reality, and if time as we experience it is largely constructed, what does this mean for action in the world? Why do anything at all?

"I'm confused," Jai admitted as they sat in the garden. "If the separate self is an appearance in consciousness, and if time is ultimately illusory, then what's the point of doing anything? Why set goals or make efforts if it's all just consciousness playing with itself?"

Avika smiled. "That's the paradox of doing—perhaps the most practical aspect of Layer 3. Action continues, often more effectively, but without the psychological burden of a separate doer anxious about results."

"I'm not sure I understand," Jai frowned.

"Think about when you're completely absorbed in an activity you love," Avika suggested. "Playing music, engaged in sports, deep in creative flow. Haven't you experienced moments where self-consciousness falls away, yet action continues naturally?"

Jai nodded slowly. "Yes... some of my best work happens in those states. It feels like the activity is happening through me rather than by me."

"That's a glimpse of action without an actor," Avika explained. "Not inaction or passivity, but action freed from the constriction of an anxious controller. The paradox is that when the sense of being a separate doer relaxes, action often flows more effectively."

"So Layer 3 isn't about stopping activity," Jai realised.

"Quite the opposite," Avika replied. "It's about engaging fully in life from a different foundation—one where purpose and care remain while the psychological burden of separate authorship dissolves."

"Action with inaction. Work with non-work."
– Lao Tzu

We've arrived at a fascinating threshold in our exploration of becoming unshakeable. The previous chapters have revealed that time as we typically experience it, may be more illusion than fundamental reality, and that our conventional sense of being a separate self, moving through linear time is a limited perspective rather than an ultimate truth.

This raises an important question: If the separate self is not as solid as it appears, and if time is not as linear as we experience it, what does this mean for action? Why do anything at all? What's the point of goals, plans, or purposeful effort if the doer is itself an appearance rather than an ultimate reality?

This is the paradox of doing—perhaps the most practical and profound aspect of Layer 3 understanding. Let's explore how purposeful action can coexist with the recognition that the actor is itself an appearance within consciousness.

Action Without an Actor

The conventional view of action presumes a distinct entity (you) performing actions that affect separate objects or other entities. Within this framework, you are the doer—the author of your actions and the one responsible for their results.

This perspective isn't wrong—it's functionally useful in many contexts. But it's incomplete. From the Layer 3 perspective, both the apparent doer and the apparent action are manifestations of a single reality—consciousness expressing itself in form.

I witnessed this understanding transform Prabhat's relationship with performance anxiety that had plagued him for years. As a senior executive regularly required to give high-stakes presentations, Prabhat had developed elaborate coping strategies to manage his fear of public speaking. Despite his outward success, each presentation brought intense stress as he worried about how he would perform and how others would judge him.

"I was always preparing, rehearsing, and worrying," Prabhat told me during one of our coaching sessions. "I saw myself as this separate entity who had to perform well or risk negative consequences. The anxiety sometimes became almost unbearable."

The breakthrough came unexpectedly during a particularly important presentation to the company's board of directors. Midway through his carefully prepared remarks, something shifted.

"There was still speaking happening, gestures occurring, and responses to questions arising—but without the sense that 'I' was doing any of it," he explained, struggling to put the experience into words. "It was as if the presentation was giving itself through this body and mind, without a separate controller."

Far from undermining his effectiveness, this shift enhanced it. Without the anxious self-monitoring and performance concerns that came with his usual sense of separate self-hood, the presentation flowed with unusual clarity, presence, and impact.

"It was both the easiest and most effective presentation I've ever given," Prabhat reflected. "Without the burden of self-consciousness, there was just the natural unfolding of what the moment required."

This experience of "action without an actor" or "doing without a doer" appears across diverse traditions:

- In Taoism, it's called "wu-wei" or "non-doing"—action that arises naturally without forced effort
- In Hindu traditions, it's "nishkama karma"—action without attachment to results
- In Buddhist psychology, it's recognised as the natural functioning that continues when the illusion of a separate self temporarily dissolves

- In flow psychology, it's described as the merging of actor and action where self-consciousness disappears

What these perspectives share is the recognition that our most effective and effortless action often emerges precisely when the sense of being a separate doer relaxes or temporarily dissolves.

Anoushka, a concert pianist, described a similar experience during performances: "My best playing happens when 'I' get out of the way. There's still technique, interpretation, and expression, but they're happening naturally without a separate controller directing each element. It's paradoxical—my most powerful performances occur when the sense of performing disappears."

This isn't just about peak experiences or special states. It points toward a different relationship with everyday action—one where doing arises naturally from being rather than from a sense of separate self, trying to make things happen.

> *Try This:* Recall a time when you were so absorbed in an activity that you temporarily lost self-consciousness—perhaps while playing music, engaged in sports, deep in creative work, or in conversation. Notice how in these moments, the usual sense of being a separate actor diminishes, yet action continues and often flows more naturally. This offers a glimpse of action without an actor.

The Dance of Consciousness

If the separate self is not the ultimate author of action, then what is? From the Layer 3 perspective, what we call "your" actions are actually movements of the total field of consciousness playing through the particular form you appear to be.

Think of it as a dance. In conventional understanding, you are a dancer performing movements. In the Layer 3 perspective, you are dance itself—consciousness in motion. The particular form you call "me" is one expression of this universal dance.

This shift in perspective transforms how you relate to action and its results. Rather than seeing yourself as the sole author of what happens, you recognise your participation in a much larger unfolding—one where "your" contributions and those of the "external world" are not ultimately separate.

Ekta experienced this understanding during a period of creative collaboration on a community project. For years, she had struggled with both control issues and credit concerns—either trying to direct everything herself or feeling unrecognised for her contributions.

"Something shifted when I began experiencing the project as a dance of consciousness rather than my personal creation," she explained during a group reflection session. "I could still contribute fully, but without the psychological burden of ownership. Ideas would arise that I might voice, but they didn't feel like 'my' ideas—more like possibilities emerging through this particular node in a creative network."

This perspective didn't diminish Ekta's engagement—if anything, it enhanced it. Without the psychological friction of ego investment, her contributions flowed more naturally and synergised more effectively with others. The project became not a collection of individual efforts but a unified creative emergence.

"The paradox is that by releasing the need to control or own the process, I actually had more impact," she reflected. "Without the separate self constantly monitoring for credit or control, there was more energy available for the work itself."

Mrinal, a therapist, discovered how this understanding transformed his clinical work with clients. For years, he had approached therapy with a strong sense of being the helper—a separate self, using skills and knowledge to assist others in need.

"I noticed how much energy I was investing in maintaining this identity," Mrinal told me during a professional supervision session. "There was constant evaluation: 'Am I saying the right things? Am I being effective? Am I missing something important?' This self-consciousness created a subtle barrier between myself and my clients."

Through mindfulness practice, Mrinal began experiencing therapy sessions differently. There was still listening, reflecting, questioning, and guiding happening, but without the same sense of a separate self, performing these actions.

"Now there's just the therapeutic conversation unfolding naturally," he explained. "Questions arise that I wouldn't have thought to ask from my separate perspective. Insights emerge that seem to come from the field of the relationship rather than from 'me' or 'them' as distinct entities. The whole process feels more alive and effective."

This shift doesn't make Mrinal passive or absent. The training, knowledge, and compassion that inform his work remain fully active. The difference is that they operate without the constriction of a separate controller evaluating and directing each moment.

> *Real-World Application:* In a current project or activity, experiment with this perspective. Instead of seeing yourself as the sole author of your contributions, view them as possibilities emerging through the particular form you are—consciousness dancing in this specific pattern. Notice how this shift affects your relationship with both the process and outcomes.

Freedom from Outcome

One of the most liberating aspects of this understanding is the freedom it creates from attachment to specific outcomes. When you recognise that:

- The separate self is not the ultimate author of action
- Action arises from the total field of consciousness
- Both "you" and "your results" are appearances within this larger field

You discover a profound release from the psychological burden of outcome attachment. You can care deeply about results without making your identity or worth dependent on them.

Jaimin experienced this freedom during a career transition after his company downsised. Despite applying the most effective strategies and maintaining mental flexibility, he faced repeated rejection in a challenging job market.

"Initially, each rejection felt like a personal failure," he explained during one of our conversations. "Even with all my Layer 1 and Layer 2 skills, I still suffered because my sense of worth was tied to outcomes I couldn't fully control."

The breakthrough came when Jaimin recognised that both his efforts and their results were movements in a larger dance—neither entirely personal achievements nor personal failures. This didn't make him passive or fatalistic. He continued applying strategic approaches and maintaining mental flexibility, but without the psychological burden of believing these outcomes defined him.

"I discovered I could care deeply about results without suffering when they didn't match my preferences," he reflected. "This wasn't detachment in the sense of not caring, but a profound shift in how I related to the entire process of action and outcome."

This freedom from outcome doesn't replace strategy or diminish dedication—it transforms your relationship with the entire process of acting in the world. You can pursue goals with complete commitment while recognising that both the pursuer and the goal exist within the same field of consciousness.

Menka experienced this transformation through her work as an artist. For years, she had tied her identity and worth to the reception of her creations. A successful exhibition would elevate her; a critical review would devastate her. Her emotional wellbeing oscillated wildly based on external validation.

Through meditation practice, Menka began to recognise how she was projecting herself into imagined futures—ones where she was either celebrated or rejected. She noticed how these projections existed only as present thoughts, not as realities she actually experienced.

"I realised I was living for moments that never actually arrived," she explained. "Even when I achieved 'success,' I experienced it only as a present moment that quickly gave way to anxiety about the next achievement. I was never arriving at that imagined future where I finally felt secure."

This recognition gradually shifted her relationship with her art. She continued to create with full dedication and care, but no longer tied her worth to outcomes. She could envision success, work toward it diligently, and remain completely present with the process rather than living in an imagined future.

"The paradox is that my work actually improved," Menka reflected. "When I stopped creating from a place of anxiety about outcomes, a different quality emerged—one that came from connection with the present moment rather than projection into an imagined future."

> *Your Turn:* Identify a situation where you're strongly attached to a specific outcome. How would your experience change if you recognised both your efforts and their results as movements within a unified field rather than personal achievements or failures? What quality might emerge in your action if it were freed from the psychological weight of outcome attachment?

The Flow of Purpose

This perspective raises another important question: If the separate self isn't the ultimate author of action, what about purpose and intention? Do these still have meaning within the Layer 3 understanding?

Absolutely—but their source and nature are understood differently. Rather than seeing purpose as something generated by a separate self, it's recognised as an organising principle within consciousness itself—a direction of creative flow that expresses through the particular form you appear to be.

Think of a river. From one perspective, it appears to have purpose and direction—moving purposefully toward the ocean. Yet this purpose doesn't require a separate decision-maker within the river. It emerges from the total configuration of the landscape, gravity, and water's nature.

Similarly, purpose in human life doesn't require a separate self, generating intentions. It can be understood as the natural expression of consciousness through your particular form, influenced by the total configuration of capacities, circumstances, and underlying patterns.

Smita discovered this understanding during a period of purpose exploration after achieving long-sought career goals that ultimately left her feeling empty. Despite extensive self-analysis and purpose exercises, she couldn't seem to manufacture meaningful direction.

The breakthrough came when she shifted from trying to generate purpose to allowing it to reveal itself. She began noticing what naturally energised her, what she found herself doing when not obligated, and where her attention spontaneously flowed.

"I realised I'd been approaching purpose backward," she explained during one of our sessions. "I was trying to manufacture it from a sense of separate self, when actually it was already present as a natural flow waiting to be recognised. My job wasn't to create purpose but to attune to what was already emerging through this particular expression of consciousness."

This didn't lead to passive drifting. Smita still made choices, set goals, and took strategic action. But these emerged from alignment with an underlying flow rather than from a separate self trying to impose direction on life.

Bimal described a similar shift in his understanding of his environmental work. For years, he had approached his activism from a place of separate selfhood—seeing himself as an individual fighting against destructive forces to protect the planet.

"I was constantly exhausted and often discouraged," Bimal told me. "I felt personally responsible for outcomes I couldn't fully control, and each setback became a source of demoralisation."

Through both contemplative practice and scientific understanding of ecosystems, Bimal began recognising himself as an expression of the living system he was trying to protect rather than a separate saviour acting upon it.

"Now I experience my environmental work as the ecosystem becoming aware of itself and taking action for its own healing," he explained. "I'm not a separate hero fighting external forces but a particular node where the living system is expressing its own intelligence and regenerative capacity."

This perspective didn't make Bimal any less committed or strategic in his approach. He still organised campaigns, engaged with policymakers, and developed innovative solutions. But these actions now flowed from a different understanding—not from the burden of a separate self, trying to save something external, but from consciousness expressing its natural tendency toward balance and wholeness through this particular form.

Try This: For one week, approach purpose as something to discover rather than create. Pay attention to what naturally energises you, where your attention spontaneously flows, and what you find yourself doing when not externally obligated. Look for patterns in these observations without immediately trying to formulate them into a fixed purpose statement.

The Paradox in Daily Life

How does this paradoxical understanding—action without an actor—translate to ordinary daily living? It's not about abandoning conventional functioning but about holding it within a broader perspective that transforms your relationship with doing.

Practically speaking, this manifests as:

Effortless Effort

Action that emerges naturally without the friction of an anxious controller trying to make things happen.

This doesn't mean passivity but a different quality of engagement—one flowing from alignment rather than forcing.

Sarita described this quality in her work as a teacher: "Before, I approached each class with a sense of having to make learning happen—forcing content into students through sheer will. Now teaching feels more like participating in a natural process already unfolding. I still prepare thoroughly and engage fully, but without the friction of trying to control every aspect of the learning process."

This effortless effort is not about doing less or abandoning rigor. Sarita continued to create detailed lesson plans, provide thoughtful feedback, and maintain high standards. The difference was in how these actions emerged—from alignment with a natural process rather than from the strain of a separate controller trying to force particular outcomes.

Responsive Rather Than Reactive

Choices emerging from clear seeing of what the situation calls for rather than from the needs and fears of a separate self.

This creates more effective action precisely because it's not filtered through the distorting lens of egoic concerns.

Madhur noticed this shift in his leadership role at a nonprofit organisation: "I used to make decisions based on a complex mix of what the situation required and what would make me look good, feel secure, or validate my identity as a leader. Now decisions emerge more cleanly from seeing what the organisation actually needs in this moment, without that overlay of personal concern."

This responsiveness doesn't mean abandoning personal perspective or becoming a passive conduit for external demands. Madhur still brought his unique capacities, experience, and values to each decision. But these informed his choices rather than being conflated with a separate self, needing validation or protection.

Natural Responsibility

Caring for outcomes without the psychological burden of ownership.

This paradoxically creates more effective action because energy that would be consumed by self-concern becomes available for the task itself.

Aashna applied this understanding in her role managing complex product launches: "I still create timelines, coordinate teams, and track metrics. But now I do this without the psychological weight of believing my worth depends on perfect execution. I care deeply about results without making my identity contingent on them."

This natural responsibility doesn't mean diminished accountability. Aashna continued to hold herself and her team to high standards and addressed issues directly when they arose. The difference was that she did so without the added suffering that comes from entangling outcomes with identity.

Madhur applies this understanding in his leadership role: "I still create strategies, make decisions, and hold people accountable. But these actions emerge from a different place—not from a separate self with something to prove, but from clarity about what the situation requires. It's a subtle but profound shift that others sense even if they wouldn't articulate it this way."

This understanding doesn't replace practical skills or strategic thinking. You still learn, develop capabilities, and apply appropriate methods to situations. But these occur within a different context—one where "your" skills and "your" thinking are recognised as patterns within consciousness rather than possessions of a separate self.

> *Real-World Application:* In everyday tasks over the next week, experiment with this perspective. When engaged in ordinary activities—whether working, conversing, or performing household tasks—notice the habitual sense of being a separate doer. Then allow this sense to relax (without trying to eliminate it) and observe how action continues naturally, often with greater ease and effectiveness.

The Ultimate Resilience

This paradox of doing—action without an actor—represents perhaps the ultimate dimension of becoming unshakeable. When you recognise that:

- The separate self that seems vulnerable to life's challenges is itself an appearance within consciousness
- Action emerges naturally from the total field rather than from a separate controller
- Both doer and doing are expressions of the same underlying reality

You discover a freedom more profound than any strategic method or mental flexibility could create alone. The very foundation of what can "shake you" is revealed as less solid than it appears.

This doesn't mean transcending humanity or floating above life's challenges. Pain still hurts, loss still brings grief, challenges still require response. But these experiences unfold within a different context—one where they're recognised as movements in consciousness rather than threats to a separate self.

As Menka described her experience: "Difficulties still arise, but they're not happening to 'me' in the same way. They're more like weather patterns moving through awareness—sometimes intense, sometimes gentle, but not defining or threatening who I fundamentally am."

This understanding creates a unique kind of resilience—not by strengthening a separate self against potential threats, but by recognising that what you fundamentally are was never threatened in the first place. The dance of consciousness continues through all circumstances, with challenge and ease as different aspects of the same unfolding.

Jaimin expressed this understanding after navigating a period of profound loss—including the end of his marriage and a serious health diagnosis within the same year.

"Before, I would have experienced these events as devastating blows to my life story," he reflected. "But from this perspective, I could see them simply as experiences arising in awareness—

challenging and painful, yes, but not threatening to who I fundamentally am. The awareness in which these experiences appear remains unchanged, just as the sky remains unchanged by passing storms."

This isn't spiritual bypassing or denial of human experience. Jaimin still felt grief, fear, and other natural emotions. But these feelings moved through him rather than defining him. He could be with them fully without being overwhelmed by them—precisely because he recognised they were temporary appearances in consciousness rather than threats to his fundamental being.

Living the Paradox

The paradox of doing invites you into a new relationship with action—one that maintains full engagement while releasing the psychological burden of separate authorship. This isn't about abandoning purpose or responsibility but transforming how you hold them.

As you explore this understanding, you may find that action becomes simultaneously more effective and less effortful. Without the friction of an anxious controller monitoring for credit or blame, more energy becomes available for the action itself. Without the psychological weight of outcome attachment, your responses become more fluid and adaptive.

This paradoxical perspective doesn't replace the strategic methods of Layer 1 or the mental flexibility of Layer 2. Rather, it provides the context within which these approaches function optimally – freed from the limitations that come when they're deployed by a separate self, anxious about results.

In the next chapter, we'll explore how these three layers integrate to create true resilience—not as a fixed achievement but as an ever-deepening capacity to meet life's full spectrum with presence, clarity, and effective response.

FOURTEEN

True Resilience

The journey through all three layers culminates not in perfect knowledge or invulnerability but in a fundamentally different relationship with life itself.

They sat beneath a massive oak tree, watching how its branches moved flexibly with the wind while its trunk remained stable.

"I've been reflecting on this journey," Jai said. "When we started, I thought becoming unshakeable meant developing better strategies and mental techniques. But it's evolved into something much deeper."

"How would you describe that evolution?" Avika asked.

"It's like I started seeking tools to strengthen a separate self against potential threats," Jai replied. "But gradually discovered that the most profound resilience comes from recognising that what I fundamentally am was never threatened in the first place."

"That's a beautiful articulation of the journey through all three layers," Avika nodded. "Strategic methods provide practical tools, mental flexibility creates adaptability amid uncertainty, and philosophical recognition transforms the very foundation of what can 'shake you.'"

"But these shifts don't happen smoothly or continuously," Jai observed. "They come as quantum jumps—sudden recognitions that change everything."

"Exactly," Avika smiled. "Personal development follows quantum patterns rather than linear progression. You can't force these shifts through effort alone, but you can create conditions where they're more likely to occur."

"And paradoxically," Jai added with a laugh, "the journey culminates not in perfect knowledge but in comfortable not-knowing—a recognition that reality transcends all our models and maps."

"The real voyage of discovery consists not in seeking new landscapes, but in having new eyes."
– Marcel Proust

Throughout this book, we've explored three distinct layers of becoming unshakeable:

Layer 1: Strategic Control – Methods for actively shaping your circumstances through approaches like Strategic Delta and Quantum Delta.

Layer 2: Mental Preparedness – Capacities for navigating uncertainty with equanimity when strategy reaches its limits.

Layer 3: Philosophical Transcendence – The recognition that your fundamental nature as consciousness itself, transcends the separate self that appears vulnerable to life's challenges.

Each layer offers valuable tools and perspectives for navigating life's complexities. But true resilience emerges not from any single layer but from their integration—creating a resilience that works across all dimensions of human experience.

In this chapter, we'll explore how these layers come together, the quantum nature of growing through them, and the paradoxical wisdom of embracing "not knowing" as the culmination of the journey.

The Quantum Nature of Personal Growth

Personal development doesn't unfold as a smooth, continuous progression but through discrete shifts in consciousness—quantum jumps from one state of understanding to another. Just as electrons don't slide gradually between energy levels but make instantaneous leaps, human development often proceeds through discontinuous shifts rather than incremental changes.

I witnessed this quantum pattern in Menka's journey through the three layers. A successful entrepreneur who had initially approached resilience purely through strategic methods, Menka had spent years developing increasingly sophisticated approaches to navigating business challenges.

"I was the queen of strategic planning," she told me during a leadership retreat. "I had systems for everything—risk management, contingency planning, opportunity analysis. I believed if my strategies were complex enough, I could control any situation."

This Layer 1 approach served Menka well in many contexts but eventually revealed its limitations during a period of unexpected market disruption that defied her most sophisticated contingency plans. This led her to explore Layer 2 approaches—developing mental flexibility, practicing acceptance, and cultivating comfort with uncertainty.

For months, Menka diligently applied these practices, gradually developing greater equanimity amid changing circumstances. But the shift to Layer 3 understanding didn't happen through this gradual progression.

"For months, I understood the Layer 3 perspective intellectually," Menka described. "I could articulate it clearly and even explain it to others. But it remained a concept rather than a lived reality."

Then suddenly, during an ordinary moment of frustration about work, something shifted.

"It wasn't that I learned new information," Menka explained, struggling to find words for the experience. "It was as if the same understanding suddenly dropped from my head to my cells. The separate self that had seemed so solid was recognised as an appearance within something more fundamental."

This quantum shift shared several important characteristics that I've observed across many people's developmental journeys:

It Cannot Be Forced

Unlike skills that develop through deliberate practice, quantum shifts in consciousness can't be directly manufactured through effort. They emerge when conditions are right rather than when you demand them.

Mridul, a physician who had spent years studying contemplative traditions alongside his medical practice, described his frustration with trying to force a shift in understanding: "I approached it like medical training—thinking that if I just put in enough hours of meditation and study, I would 'achieve' enlightenment. But that very attitude of striving and achieving prevented the very recognition I was seeking."

The shift happened not through intensified effort but when Mridul temporarily abandoned his spiritual seeking during a period of family illness. While caring for his sick child with no agenda beyond being present, the recognition he had been striving for emerged naturally.

"It was like I had been trying to force a fist to grasp itself," he reflected. "Only when I stopped trying did the recognition become possible."

It Often Occurs Unexpectedly

While preparation creates the conditions for shifts to occur, the actual transitions frequently happen during ordinary moments rather than in dramatic circumstances or formal practice settings.

Ekta had imagined her spiritual awakening would happen during a silent retreat or peak experience in nature. Instead, the shift occurred while she was standing in line at the grocery store, irritated about the wait.

"I was mentally complaining about the slow cashier when suddenly something shifted in how I was experiencing the situation," Ektaa recalled. "There was still irritation arising, but it was no longer happening to 'me'—it was just an experience appearing in awareness, like everything else in that moment.

The boundary between 'inner' and 'outer' temporarily dissolved, and everything was recognised as appearances in consciousness."

These unexpected moments of recognition often happen precisely when you've temporarily stopped seeking them—when the agenda of a separate self, trying to "get somewhere" has momentarily relaxed.

They Transform Your Relationship With Experience

These shifts don't just add new information but fundamentally alter how you relate to all experience, including previously acquired knowledge and capabilities.

Bimal described how his shift transformed his relationship with strategic planning: "I still use strategic methods, but they function differently now. Before, they were tools wielded by a separate self, trying to control circumstances for its own security. Now they're expressions of intelligence flowing through this particular form, without the psychological burden of a controller who needs certain outcomes."

This transformed relationship with experience doesn't make previously developed capacities irrelevant. Rather, it places them in a different context—one where they can function without the limitations imposed by identification with a separate self.

They Are Irreversible in Important Ways

Once a shift in understanding occurs, you can't genuinely return to your previous perspective. You might temporarily lose access to the new understanding during stress, but you can't truly unsee what has been recognised.

A therapist who experienced a profound shift during a period of personal crisis, described this quality: "Even when I get caught in old patterns of reactivity or self-concern, there's an underlying recognition that these patterns aren't who I fundamentally am. I might temporarily identify with the separate self and its concerns, but I can't completely believe in that identification the way I once did."

This irreversibility doesn't mean permanent perfection or completion. Most people continue to move between clear recognition and habitual patterns of identification with a separate self. But even when identification returns, it's recognised as a pattern rather than an ultimate truth about who you are.

> *Try This:* Reflect on significant shifts in your own understanding—moments when your perspective fundamentally changed rather than merely adding new information. What characterised these transitions? Were they gradual developments or more sudden recognitions? How did they affect your relationship with experience beyond the specific content of the insight?

Crossing Thresholds of Consciousness

While quantum shifts can't be forced through direct effort, you can create conditions that make them more likely to occur. Understanding these conditions helps you cooperate with rather than obstruct the natural evolution of your understanding.

Threshold Energy

Quantum particles require specific energy thresholds to jump to higher states. Similarly, consciousness shifts require a certain quality of attention and awareness—a threshold energy that builds through various practices and experiences.

Ekta described this energy threshold in her development: "For years, I engaged with spiritual teachings and psychological work that pointed toward Layer 3 understanding. This created a kind of potential energy in my system—an accumulated readiness for a shift that hadn't yet occurred. When the shift finally happened, it felt less like learning something new and more like recognising what had been quietly accumulating beneath my conscious awareness."

This threshold energy develops through various channels:

Contemplative Practice

Regular meditation, self-inquiry, or other approaches that cultivate awareness of awareness itself—the capacity to notice not just the contents of consciousness but consciousness itself.

Jaimin incorporated a simple practice into his daily routine: three times each day, he would pause and directly notice the awareness that was present, regardless of what experiences were arising within it. "I wasn't trying to change anything or achieve a particular state," he explained. "I was simply recognising what was already here—the awareness in which all experience appears."

Over time, this regular recognition created a familiarity with awareness itself rather than exclusive identification with its changing contents.

Intellectual Understanding

Clear conceptual frameworks that give the mind a context for understanding experiences that might otherwise be dismissed or misinterpreted.

Sarita found that studying both contemplative traditions and quantum physics helped create a conceptual framework for experiences she had occasionally glimpsed but couldn't integrate. "Having language and models for these experiences helped me recognise and validate them when they occurred," she explained.

"Without these frameworks, I might have dismissed these glimpses as meaningless anomalies rather than recognising their significance."

Intellectual understanding alone isn't sufficient for transformation, but it can create important context for direct recognition to occur.

Challenging Experiences

Situations that disrupt habitual patterns and force fresh seeing, whether through crisis, transition, or deliberate pattern interruption.

Mridul's shift occurred during a period of intense professional challenge that disrupted his usual ways of functioning and creating meaning. "The situation was too complex for my existing frameworks to handle," he reflected. "This forced me to let go of approaches that had always worked before, creating space for a fundamentally different way of seeing to emerge."

While crisis isn't necessary for shifts to occur, challenging experiences often create openings by disrupting habitual patterns that might otherwise remain unquestioned.

Transmission Through Relationship

Contact with others who embody deeper understanding, creating a resonance that can catalyse similar recognition in your own experience.

Bimal found that his shift occurred through this relational transmission: "I had done years of individual practice with limited transformation. The breakthrough came during a retreat with a teacher who clearly embodied what they taught. Something in their presence catalysed a recognition that intellectual understanding alone hadn't created."

This transmission doesn't involve giving you something you don't already have but creating conditions where you can recognise what's already present but overlooked.

> *Real-World Application:* Consider which of these channels might best support your own development at this stage. Which seems most accessible or resonant with your current situation? How might you engage with it not as a technique to force change but as a way of creating conducive conditions for natural evolution?

Embracing "Not Knowing"

Perhaps the most counterintuitive aspect of this journey is that it culminates not in perfect knowledge but in the profound recognition of "not knowing"—a wisdom that transcends both ignorance and conceptual understanding.

This isn't the same as the initial not-knowing of ignorance, where you simply lack information. It's a higher-order not-knowing that emerges after exploring the limits of conceptual understanding—a recognition that reality transcends all our models and maps.

Jaimin described his experience of this paradoxical wisdom: "I spent decades accumulating knowledge—degrees, certifications, spiritual teachings, psychological frameworks. I was constructing what I thought was an increasingly accurate map of reality. The profound shift came when I recognised that no map, no matter how sophisticated, could capture the territory itself. This wasn't disappointing—it was liberating. Reality was revealed as far more alive and immediate than any conceptual understanding could contain."

This embrace of not-knowing manifests in several important ways:

Living in the Question Rather Than the Answer

Maintaining an orientation of genuine curiosity rather than conclusion — holding understanding provisionally rather than as fixed truth.

Ekta described how this quality transformed her approach to both life and work: "Before, I was always trying to arrive at final answers—about myself, others, how the world works. Now I'm more interested in living in the questions themselves, allowing them to reveal new dimensions rather than trying to resolve them prematurely."

This orientation doesn't mean abandoning clarity or discernment. Ekta continues to make decisions and take positions when appropriate. But she does so while recognising the provisional nature of all understanding rather than mistaking her conclusions for ultimate truth.

Comfort With Paradox

Recognising that apparent contradictions often point toward dimensions of reality that transcend binary thinking—not needing to resolve tensions that might actually be complementary aspects of a more complex whole.

Mridul described this shift: "I used to need things to be logically consistent in a linear way. Now I'm comfortable with paradox—with insights that seem contradictory from one perspective but complementary from another. The need to resolve everything into a single consistent framework has diminished."

This comfort with paradox allows for a more nuanced relationship with complex realities that don't fit neatly into binary categories or linear logic. It creates space for both/and thinking rather than either/or limitations, expanding your capacity to hold multiple perspectives simultaneously.

Ongoing Openness to Discovery

Approaching each moment as fresh territory rather than filtering experience through accumulated knowledge—allowing reality to reveal itself rather than imposing pre-existing frameworks.

Sarita noticed this quality in how she related to familiar experiences: "I can walk the same path in my neighbourhood that I've walked a thousand times, but now there's a freshness to it—as if I'm seeing it for the first time. Not because I'm trying to see it differently, but because I'm less quick to overlay my previous knowledge on top of direct experience."

This openness doesn't mean discarding useful knowledge or expertise. Sarita still benefits from her familiarity with her neighbourhood. But that knowledge informs rather than replaces direct perception, allowing for discovery even in the midst of the familiar.

Freedom From Authority

Recognising that no external source—whether text, teacher, or tradition—can provide ultimate truth, while remaining open to the guidance and wisdom they offer.

Bimal described how this understanding transformed his relationship with spiritual teachings: "I used to approach teachings as authoritative pronouncements I needed to accept or reject. Now I see them as fingers pointing toward a truth that can only be directly recognised, not transmitted through concepts. This creates a different relationship—neither blind acceptance nor dismissive rejection but engaged exploration."

This freedom doesn't mean dismissing traditions or teachings but relating to them as invitations to direct recognition rather than as definitive statements requiring belief or disbelief.

Menka found this not-knowing to be the most practical aspect of her development: "When I released the need to have life figured out—to have the 'right' understanding or approach—something remarkable happened. I became more responsive to what each situation actually required rather than imposing my pre-existing frameworks. This wasn't vague or uncertain but precisely the opposite—a more direct and unmediated relationship with reality itself."

Your Turn: Notice areas where you might be clinging to the security of "knowing"—having things figured out or settled. How might your experience shift if you allowed yourself to release into not-knowing while maintaining full engagement with life? What qualities might emerge in your responses if they arose from fresh seeing rather than accumulated conclusions?

The Complete Resilience

When these three layers integrate—strategic capability, mental flexibility, and the recognition of your nature as consciousness itself—a unique kind of resilience emerges. This isn't about becoming immune to life's challenges but developing a fundamentally different relationship with them.

This complete resilience manifests as:

Strategic Wisdom Without Attachment

The capacity to use strategic methods effectively while holding them lightly – deploying them from clarity rather than anxiety about outcomes.

Ekta described this integration: "I still use the strategic approaches from Layer 1 and the mental flexibility from Layer

2, but they function differently now. They operate within a broader context where both the strategies and the strategist are recognised as expressions of the same underlying reality. This creates an unusual combination of full engagement without the friction of a separate controller monitoring for success or failure."

This quality doesn't diminish strategic effectiveness but enhances it by removing the psychological friction that comes from a separate self anxiously monitoring for validation or security through results.

Mental Adaptability Without Effort

Flexibility that emerges naturally rather than requiring constant self-management – an ease of adaptation that flows from fundamental security rather than psychological technique.

Mrinal noticed this shift in how he navigated organisational change: "Before, I had to deliberately practice acceptance and consciously manage my responses to uncertainty. Now mental flexibility emerges more naturally, without the sense of a separate self, working hard to maintain equilibrium. There's still adaptation happening, but without the effortful quality it once had."

This effortless adaptability doesn't mean never being challenged by circumstances. Mrinal still experiences the full range of human responses to change. The difference is in how these responses move through rather than defining or overwhelming him.

Transcendent Understanding in Practical Action

The recognition of your deeper nature expressing through ordinary activities rather than being reserved for special states or spiritual contexts.

Prabhat found this integration transforming his everyday experience: "The **Layer 3 understanding** isn't separate from washing dishes, attending meetings, or having difficult conversations. It's the context in which all these activities unfold—the recognition that what I fundamentally am is the awareness in which these experiences arise rather than a separate self, performing them."

This integration doesn't create a division between "spiritual" and "mundane" activities but reveals how even the most ordinary actions can be expressions of your deepest nature.

This integrated resilience doesn't mean perpetual bliss or the absence of challenging emotions. Pain still hurts, loss still brings grief, and uncertainty still requires navigation. But these experiences unfold within a different context—one where they're recognised as movements in consciousness rather than threats to a separate self.

> *Real-World Application:* Consider a current challenge you're facing. How might you approach it differently by integrating all three layers? What strategic methods might be appropriate (Layer 1), what mental flexibility might be required (Layer 2), and how might the recognition of your deeper nature transform your relationship with the entire situation (Layer 3)?

Quantum Jumps in Daily Life

How do these quantum shifts and integrations manifest in ordinary life? Not through perpetual special states or dramatic experiences, but through subtle yet profound changes in how you relate to everyday circumstances.

Prabhat noticed these changes in his relationship with work challenges: "Before, criticism would trigger immediate defensiveness—a visceral sense of being personally diminished. Now there's a natural space between the comment and response—not from applying a technique but from the recognition that who I fundamentally am isn't threatened by any evaluation.

This doesn't make me indifferent to feedback, but it transforms how I receive and work with it."

Smita observed changes in her creative process: "I used to approach creativity as something I had to generate through effort—forcing insights and monitoring progress against standards. Now creation feels more like participation in an unfolding that moves through this particular form. There's still discipline and craft, but they serve something that isn't 'mine' in the way I previously believed."

Jaimin found transformation in his experience of anxiety: "Anxiety still arises, but my relationship with it has fundamentally changed. Rather than being something happening to 'me' that I need to manage or eliminate, it's recognised as a pattern moving through awareness—sometimes intense, sometimes subtle, but not defining or threatening who I fundamentally am."

These examples illustrate how the quantum nature of development expresses not through permanent special states but through ordinary experiences transformed by a different quality of recognition. The circumstances themselves may be unchanged, but your relationship with them shifts at a fundamental level.

> *Try This:* Over the next week, notice moments when your relationship with ordinary experiences differs from habitual patterns. Pay particular attention to situations that would typically trigger reactivity or resistance. Is there a different quality available in how you relate to these experiences, even if subtle or temporary? What characterises this difference when it appears?

Beyond Techniques to Recognition

As you integrate these layers, an important shift occurs from relying on techniques to trusting recognition. While specific methods remain valuable, they increasingly serve rather than create the fundamental resilience that emerges from recognising your deeper nature.

This shift parallels learning to ride a bicycle. Initially, you rely on explicit techniques and conscious monitoring—keep your balance, pedal at this rate, turn the handlebars this way. With integration, these actions become natural expressions of a more fundamental recognition—you know how to ride, and specific adjustments emerge spontaneously from this knowing rather than from applied techniques.

Ekta described this evolution: "I used to rely heavily on specific practices—meditation techniques, cognitive reframing, strategic protocols. These were valuable and still have their place. But increasingly, resilience emerges not from applying methods but from a more fundamental recognition that's always available, with specific responses arising naturally from this ground."

This doesn't mean abandoning practices or methods but holding them differently—as expressions of understanding rather than means to create it. The techniques themselves may be unchanged, but their context and function transform.

> *Real-World Application:* Notice areas where you might be over-relying on techniques rather than allowing responses to emerge from deeper recognition. Are there situations where applying methods has become a form of control rather than natural expression? How might your approach shift if specific practices served rather than substituted for fundamental understanding?

The Ongoing Journey

Becoming truly unshakeable isn't a fixed achievement but an ever-deepening journey. Even profound recognitions continue to permeate more aspects of experience, integrating across different domains of life and challenging circumstances.

This ongoing nature is not a flaw but an inherent quality of development. Just as a tree continues growing throughout its life, consciousness continues unfolding through ever-new expressions and integrations. The quantum leaps we've discussed aren't final destinations but openings to new dimensions of exploration.

Menka described this continuing unfolding: "What I once thought would be a final realisation proved to be just the beginning. The initial recognition continues to deepen, revealing new dimensions in everyday experiences I thought I understood. It's less like reaching a destination and more like discovering that reality itself is bottomless—endlessly revealing new aspects of itself through this particular form."

This ongoing quality doesn't diminish the significance of what's already recognised but places it within a larger context of continuous evolution. The resilience we're exploring isn't a static state but a living, breathing capacity that continues developing throughout life.

> *Your Turn:* Consider your own development not as a path to a final destination but as an ongoing unfolding. How might this perspective shift how you approach growth itself? What qualities emerge when you release the need for final arrival while maintaining full engagement with the journey?

The Beginning, Not the End

As we conclude our exploration of true resilience, we find ourselves not at an endpoint but at a beginning—a doorway opening to ever-new dimensions of discovering what it means to be human.

The three layers we've explored—strategic control, mental preparedness, and philosophical transcendence—aren't separate territories but aspects of an integrated approach to life. The quantum nature of growth through these dimensions isn't a hurdle to overcome but an invitation to cooperate with the natural unfolding of consciousness itself.

And perhaps most importantly, the wisdom of not-knowing that emerges at the furthest reaches of this journey isn't a resignation but a profound opening—a release into the immediate, ever-fresh reality that conceptual understanding can point toward but never capture.

This is the paradox at the heart of becoming truly unshakeable: the greatest resilience comes not from perfect knowledge or impenetrable defence but from the recognition that what you fundamentally are was never at risk in the first place. From this recognition, you can fully engage with life's complete spectrum—its joys and sorrows, challenges and opportunities, certainties and mysteries—without the constriction that comes from believing your fundamental wellbeing depends on particular circumstances.

In the next chapter, we'll explore how to live across all these layers simultaneously – integrating strategic action, mental flexibility, and transcendent understanding into a cohesive approach to daily life. This integration isn't about achieving perfection but about embracing the full richness of human experience from the ground of your deepest nature.

FIFTEEN

Living Across All Layers

True mastery comes from moving fluidly between strategic action, mental flexibility, and philosophical transcendence based on what each situation requires.

"The challenge now," Jai said as they watched people in the busy marketplace, "is integrating all these layers in daily life. I find myself operating primarily from Layer 1 at work, Layer 2 with family challenges, and glimpsing Layer 3 during meditation or in nature."

"That's natural," Avika replied. "Different situations often call for different layers. The mastery comes in moving fluidly between them as circumstances require, rather than being stuck in any single approach."

"I've noticed something interesting," Jai continued. "The more I recognise Layer 3 truths, the more effectively Layers 1 and 2 actually function. Strategic methods work better when they're not deployed by an anxious separate self. Mental flexibility comes more naturally when it's grounded in deeper recognition."

"That's the beauty of integration," Avika nodded. "Each layer enhances rather than replaces the others. Strategy informed by acceptance becomes more effective. Acceptance grounded in deeper understanding becomes more natural."

"So true resilience isn't about transcending ordinary life," Jai realised.

"It's about bringing extraordinary awareness to ordinary circumstances," Avika finished. "Navigating the full spectrum of human experience with presence, clarity, and effectiveness—whether through strategic wisdom, mental flexibility, or the recognition of your deeper nature."

"The oak fought the wind and was broken, the willow bent when it must and survived."
– Robert Jordan

Throughout this book, we've explored three distinct yet complementary layers of becoming unshakeable. Now comes a practical question: How do we integrate these layers in daily life?

The answer isn't about choosing one layer over others or progressing from Layer 1 to Layer 3 and then abandoning the earlier layers. It's about developing the capacity to move fluidly between all three as different situations require.

The Art of Layer Fluidity

Think of these layers like different rooms in the same house. Each serves a purpose, and mastery comes from knowing which room to occupy in various circumstances.

I witnessed this fluid integration in Pranay, a surgeon I worked with during a hospital leadership programme. When performing surgery, Pranay fully embodied Layer 1—employing precise technical skills and strategic thinking to achieve specific outcomes. This focused attention is exactly what's needed in the operating room.

"During surgery, I'm completely engaged with strategic processes," Pranay explained during one of our conversations. "There's a clear goal, specific techniques to apply, and a need for precise execution. This is Layer 1 operating at its best—directed attention focused on shaping specific outcomes."

Yet when unexpected complications arose during operations (as they inevitably do), Pranay would seamlessly shift to Layer 2—maintaining equanimity amid uncertainty, adapting to changing conditions without attachment to his original plan.

"When we encounter unexpected anatomy or complications, there's no time for distress about the disruption to my plans," he told me. "I need to immediately accept the new reality and respond appropriately. This isn't resignation but mental flexibility that allows effective action amid changing circumstances."

And undergirding both these approaches was Pranay's Layer 3 understanding—a recognition that beneath his role as a surgeon, beneath the drama of each operation, he was the awareness in which all these experiences arise. This allowed him to fully engage without being defined by outcomes or others' judgments of his performance.

"Behind both the strategic focus and the adaptive flexibility is a deeper recognition," Pranay reflected. "I am not ultimately defined by success or failure in any particular surgery. I bring my full capabilities to each operation while recognising that my fundamental nature transcends any specific role or outcome."

"I used to believe I had to be in only one state of mind," Pranay told me. "Either focused on strategic control OR accepting of uncertainty OR transcending the ego. Now I see these as complementary aspects of a complete approach to life."

This fluid integration creates a resilience no single layer alone can provide. When strategic approaches reach their limits, mental flexibility allows adaptation without disruption. When mental flexibility encounters existential questions about identity and meaning, philosophical transcendence provides a foundation that isn't dependent on specific conditions.

Recognising Your Default Layer

Most of us habitually operate from one primary layer. Some people live almost exclusively in Layer 1, constantly planning and strategising. Others naturally gravitate toward Layer 2, flowing with circumstances. A few may prefer Layer 3, focusing on philosophical perspectives.

Ekta, a corporate executive who participated in a leadership development programme I facilitated, discovered her strong default orientation toward Layer 1.

"I approach everything as a problem to solve or a situation to optimise," she admitted during a group discussion. "This works brilliantly in many business contexts, but I've realised it creates unnecessary suffering in areas of life where acceptance or deeper perspective would serve better."

Through reflection and practice, Ekta began noticing when her strategic orientation was helping and when it was creating limitations. "Now I ask myself: Is this a situation that requires strategic planning, mental flexibility, or philosophical perspective? This simple question has transformed how I approach both work and life."

Swastik, by contrast, discovered his default was Layer 2—adaptability and going with the flow. "I'm naturally good at accepting circumstances and adjusting accordingly," he explained. "But I've realised this sometimes becomes an excuse for not employing strategic approaches when they would be beneficial. I've been working on strengthening my Layer 1 capabilities while maintaining my natural flexibility."

Sarita found her orientation was primarily toward Layer 3—philosophical perspective and transcendent understanding. "I easily see the big picture and recognise the limited nature of the separate self," she told me. "But I've had to deliberately develop strategic skills and practical approaches for navigating daily challenges. The deeper perspectives are valuable, but they need to be complemented by practical capabilities."

Identifying your default orientation isn't about judging it as right or wrong but recognising both its strengths and limitations. Each layer has contexts where it serves beautifully and others where it creates unnecessary limitations.

Try This: For the next three days, notice which layer you tend to default to in various situations. Don't judge your tendencies—simply observe them with curiosity. When do you automatically turn to strategic approaches? When do you naturally flow with circumstances? When do you spontaneously adopt a more transcendent perspective? Look for patterns in when each approach serves you well and when it might create limitations.

Expanding Your Range

Once you've identified your default approach, deliberately practice operating from the other layers to expand your range of responsiveness.

If you're typically a strategic planner (Layer 1), deliberately practice accepting uncertainty without immediate action plans (Layer 2) or contemplating the nature of consciousness (Layer 3).

Jaimin, a financial advisor with a strong Layer 1 orientation, incorporated deliberate Layer 2 and 3 practices into his weekly routine. "Each Monday, I do what I call 'purposeless sitting'—just being present with whatever arises without trying to optimise or direct it. This Layer 2 practice balances my strategic tendencies. And each Friday, I spend time in self-inquiry, asking 'Who am I beyond my roles and achievements?' This Layer 3 practice keeps my strategic activities in a larger perspective."

These complementary practices didn't diminish Jaimin's strategic capabilities but expanded his overall resilience by developing capacities that balanced his natural tendencies.

If you naturally go with the flow (Layer 2), challenge yourself to create more structured strategic approaches (Layer 1) or explore philosophical questions about the nature of self (Layer 3).

Riya, an artist who thrived in the adaptive flow of Layer 2, discovered how incorporating more Layer 1 structure transformed her creative business. "I was always great at adapting to circumstances but terrible at creating circumstances strategically," she explained. "By developing basic business systems and strategic approaches, I transformed my financial situation without sacrificing my creative freedom."

Simultaneously, Riya explored Layer 3 understanding through meditation and self-inquiry, discovering that her adaptability could be grounded in something deeper than circumstantial flexibility. "Now my adaptability isn't just a personality trait but an expression of recognising that what I fundamentally am isn't dependent on conditions."

If you're philosophically inclined (Layer 3), balance this with practical strategic planning (Layer 1) and the middle path of mental flexibility (Layer 2).

Partha, a meditation teacher with deep Layer 3 insight, recognised he needed to develop Layer 1 capacities to effectively share his understanding with others. "I had profound recognition of non-dual awareness but lacked the strategic skills to create contexts where others could discover this for themselves," he told me during a teaching programme we co-facilitated.

By developing strategic approaches to programme design, marketing, and participant engagement, Partha greatly expanded his impact—not by compromising his deeper understanding but by creating practical structures through which it could be shared.

This expansion beyond default tendencies doesn't happen overnight. It requires deliberate practice and a willingness to experience the discomfort that often comes with operating outside your habitual mode. But with consistent attention, you can develop fluidity between layers that allows you to engage with life's full spectrum more effectively.

> *Real-World Application:* Identify which layer feels least natural or accessible to you currently. Create a simple daily practice that helps develop your capacity in this layer. For example, if Layer 1 is challenging, implement a basic strategic planning routine. If Layer 2 feels difficult, practice deliberate acceptance of a challenging circumstance. If Layer 3 seems inaccessible, incorporate brief periods of self-inquiry into your day.

Layer-Appropriate Responses

Different situations call for different layers. Here's a simple guide for recognising when each layer might be most appropriate:

Layer 1 is optimal when:

- Clear outcomes are needed
- You have substantial control over variables
- Strategic planning can significantly impact results
- Technical expertise is required

Ekta found that business strategy meetings clearly called for Layer 1 approaches. "When we're planning market expansion or product development, strategic thinking is exactly what's needed," she explained. "Trying to operate primarily from Layer 2 or 3 in these contexts would actually be less effective and might even be irresponsible."

Layer 2 works best when:

- Variables are largely outside your control
- Adaptability is more valuable than rigid planning
- Emotional resilience is being tested
- You need to navigate unexpected changes

Swastik recognised that his relationship with his teenager benefited most from Layer 2 approaches. "I tried to strategically plan our interactions and guide his development in a Layer 1 way," Swastik admitted with a laugh. "It was a disaster. What actually works is maintaining adaptability, accepting who he is in each moment, and responding to what is rather than what I think should be."

Layer 3 is powerful when:

- Identity-level challenges arise
- You face existential questions
- Fundamental beliefs are being tested
- You need to access your deepest resources

Savita found that her mother's terminal illness called for Layer 3 understanding. "Strategic approaches couldn't change the fundamental reality we were facing, and even acceptance had its limits," she explained. "What truly helped was recognising that who we fundamentally are transcends the story of birth and death—that consciousness itself isn't threatened by the transitions that appear within it."

Recognising which layer might best serve in different contexts doesn't create rigid rules but develops discernment about how to engage with life's varied situations.

Raj, a business leader, described how he applies this framework: "When setting quarterly objectives, I'm fully in Layer 1. When unexpected market shifts occur, I shift to Layer 2. And when facing criticism that would have previously devastated me, I access Layer 3."

This fluidity between layers doesn't develop through intellectual understanding alone but through practical application across different life circumstances. As you experiment with different approaches, you'll develop an intuitive sense of which layer might best serve in various situations.

Your Turn: Identify three current situations in your life—one that might best be served by Layer 1 approaches, one by Layer 2, and one by Layer 3. For each situation, note what specifically suggests that particular layer might be most effective. Then experiment with consciously engaging from that layer, noting what shifts in your experience and results.

The Foundation Approach

Another way to integrate the layers is to establish Layer 3 as your foundation, Layer 2 as your general approach, and Layer 1 as your specific methodology.

Imagine three concentric circles:

- The outer circle (Layer 1): What you do
- The middle circle (Layer 2): How you adapt
- The inner circle (Layer 3): Who you fundamentally are

This arrangement allows you to engage in strategic planning (Layer 1) with the flexibility of adaptive resilience (Layer 2), all while grounded in the understanding that you are the awareness in which all experience occurs (Layer 3).

Pranay described how this integrated approach transformed his experience of leadership: "At my core is the recognition that I am fundamentally the awareness in which all experience appears (Layer 3). This grounds me in something deeper than circumstantial changes. From this foundation, I maintain adaptability to whatever emerges (Layer 2), which allows me to implement specific strategic approaches (Layer 1) without rigid attachment to them."

This integration creates a unique resilience—the ability to act decisively without being defined by outcomes, to adapt fluidly without losing direction, and to maintain perspective that transcends circumstantial changes.

Ekta implemented this approach during a particularly challenging product launch. "The launch faced unexpected obstacles that no amount of planning could have anticipated," she explained. "My Layer 3 foundation allowed me to recognise that these challenges weren't happening to 'me' in any ultimate sense—they were simply appearances in awareness. This created space for Layer 2 adaptability, adjusting our approach based on emerging realities rather than fighting against them. From this responsive stance, I could implement specific Layer 1 strategies that addressed the actual situation rather than my initial expectations."

The launch ultimately succeeded, though in a form quite different from what Ekta had originally envisioned. "The integration of all three layers allowed both persistence and adaptation—holding our core purpose firmly while letting go of specific methods that weren't serving in the emerging context."

> *Real-World Application:* For an important project or relationship, experiment with this foundation approach. Before strategic planning, ground yourself in Layer 3 recognition of your fundamental nature as awareness. From this foundation, cultivate Layer 2 adaptability to whatever circumstances might emerge. Then engage Layer 1 strategic thinking to develop specific approaches. Notice how this sequence affects both your experience and effectiveness.

Common Integration Challenges

As you work with integrating these layers, several common challenges may arise. Recognising these patterns can help you navigate them more effectively.

Layer Confusion

Sometimes we think we're operating from one layer when we're actually in another. For instance, passive resignation might masquerade as Layer 2 acceptance, or spiritual bypassing might pose as Layer 3 understanding.

Swastik encountered this confusion in his meditation practice: "I thought I was experiencing Layer 3 non-dual awareness, but I eventually realised I was actually in a subtle form of dissociation—disconnecting from experience rather than recognising myself as the awareness in which experience appears. True Layer 3 recognition doesn't avoid or disconnect from anything; it includes the full spectrum of human experience within a larger context."

Regular reality-checking with trusted others who understand these distinctions can help clarify when you might be confusing one layer for another.

Layer Conflict

Sometimes different aspects of your life may call for different layers simultaneously, creating a sense of internal conflict or fragmentation.

Ekta experienced this when facing both strategic business decisions and a family health crisis concurrently: "One part of me needed to be in Layer 1 strategic mode for work, while another part was being called to Layer 2 acceptance with my father's illness. I initially felt torn between these seemingly contradictory approaches."

The resolution came through recognising that these layers could coexist without contradiction. "I realised I didn't need to be in only one layer across all domains. I could engage strategically at work while practicing acceptance with my father's health situation, all grounded in a deeper recognition that transcended both contexts."

Layer Rigidity

Sometimes we correctly identify which layer might best serve but find ourselves unable to shift into it due to habitual patterns or psychological inertia.

Jaimin recognised Layer 2 acceptance would best serve his relationship with his teenage daughter but found himself stuck in Layer 1 strategic approaches: "I intellectually understood that acceptance rather than control was needed, but I couldn't seem to make the shift. My planning mind kept trying to solve what wasn't actually a problem to be solved."

The breakthrough came through deliberate practice of acceptance in less charged contexts, gradually developing the capacity to shift layers more fluidly when it mattered most. "By practicing acceptance with minor irritations, I developed the muscle that eventually allowed me to bring this quality to my relationship with my daughter."

These challenges aren't failures but natural aspects of integrating sophisticated capacities. Each challenge, when navigated consciously, actually strengthens your ability to move fluidly between layers in response to life's varied circumstances.

Case Studies in Integration

Let's explore how this integration of layers manifests in real-world scenarios across different domains:

Professional Leadership

Menka, a technology executive, faced a significant organisational restructuring that created both strategic challenges and emotional turbulence among her team. She described how integrating all three layers transformed her approach:

"From Layer 3, I recognised that while this restructuring was significant, it wasn't happening to 'me' in any ultimate sense—it was an appearance in awareness that I could respond to without being defined by. This created spaciousness that allowed Layer 2 acceptance of the realities we were facing, without resistance that would have depleted my energy and clarity. From this foundation of spaciousness and acceptance, I could engage Layer 1 strategic thinking to develop specific approaches for navigating the transition effectively."

This integrated approach allowed Menka to maintain both clarity and compassion throughout a challenging process—addressing practical concerns while holding them within a larger perspective that created resilience beyond circumstantial changes.

Health Navigation

Pranay faced a serious health diagnosis that required both practical management and deeper perspective. He described how the integration of layers supported this journey:

"Layer 1 strategic approaches were essential for researching treatment options, creating lifestyle modifications, and coordinating medical care. Layer 2 acceptance was crucial for emotional wellbeing amid uncertainty and adapting to changing capabilities. But what truly transformed my experience was **Layer 3 recognition** that who I fundamentally am—consciousness itself—isn't threatened by health changes that appear within it."

This integration didn't deny the reality of physical challenges but placed them in a context that allowed Pranay to respond effectively without being overwhelmed by circumstantial changes.

Relationship Transformation

Ekta and her partner discovered how integrating all three layers transformed a relationship pattern that had created recurring conflict. She explained their approach:

"From Layer 3, we recognised that beneath our specific roles and patterns, we were expressions of the same consciousness—not fundamentally separate selves in conflict. This created space for Layer 2 acceptance of each other exactly as we were, without demanding change before we could experience peace. From this foundation, we could engage Layer 1 strategic approaches to communication and need-fulfilment that addressed practical concerns without the charge of existential threat."

This integration didn't eliminate differences or challenges but transformed how they were experienced and navigated—not as threats to separate selves but as opportunities for consciousness to know itself through relationship.

> *Your Turn:* Consider a complex situation you're currently facing. How might integrating all three layers transform your experience and effectiveness? What specific qualities might each layer contribute to a more complete response?

The Dance of Consciousness

As you develop fluidity between these layers, a beautiful understanding emerges: these apparently distinct approaches are actually expressions of the same underlying reality—consciousness knowing itself through diverse forms.

Strategic methods, adaptive flexibility, and philosophical recognition aren't ultimately separate approaches but varied expressions of consciousness engaging with its own appearances. The capacity to move between them isn't about switching between fundamentally different realities but about allowing consciousness to express through different patterns as circumstances invite.

This understanding transforms the integration from a technique you apply to a dance you participate in—consciousness itself moving between different expressions based on what each moment calls for.

Menka described this experience: "It no longer feels like 'I' am choosing between different approaches. There's a natural intelligence that expresses strategically when appropriate, adapts fluidly when needed, and recognises its own nature when deeper perspective serves. This doesn't happen through control but through allowing consciousness to express naturally through this particular form."

This dance isn't perfect or complete—the expression through human form includes limitations and blind spots that continue to evolve through experience. But there's a grace that emerges when consciousness is allowed to move naturally between these expressions rather than being confined to habitual patterns by a sense of separate self.

Living the Unshakeable Life

As we conclude this exploration of becoming unshakeable, let's return to where we began—with the fundamental question of how to develop resilience that transcends circumstantial changes.

The journey through these three layers reveals that true resilience isn't an achievement or a fixed state but a living process of engaging with life's full spectrum. It's not about becoming immune to challenges but developing a fundamentally different relationship with them—one that includes practical strategy, mental flexibility, and philosophical depth.

This integrated approach doesn't promise perfection or perpetual bliss. You'll still experience the full range of human emotions, face genuine challenges, and navigate complexity and uncertainty. The difference is in how these experiences unfold—not as threats to a separate self but as movements within consciousness that can be engaged with wisdom, flexibility, and strategic intelligence.

Jaimin expressed this understanding after navigating significant professional and personal challenges: "I used to think becoming unshakeable meant reaching a state where nothing could affect me. Now I understand it's about having a complete relationship with whatever arises—responding strategically when appropriate, adapting fluidly when necessary, and recognising my deeper nature throughout. It's not about becoming immune to life but becoming fully available to it, without the constriction of believing my wellbeing depends on particular circumstances."

This availability to life—engaged but not defined by circumstances—is the essence of true resilience. It allows you to participate fully in human experience while remaining grounded in something deeper than its changing patterns.

As you continue integrating these layers in your own life, remember that this isn't a linear journey with a fixed destination but an ever-deepening exploration of what it means to be human. Each challenge, each joy, each ordinary moment offers a fresh opportunity to embody this integrated understanding—to live from the recognition that you are not merely a separate self navigating circumstances but consciousness itself expressing through this particular form.

May this understanding serve you in navigating life's full spectrum with presence, wisdom, and an open heart.

EPILOGUE

The Spotlight and the Dancer

The theater was dark except for a single spotlight illuminating a solitary dancer on the otherwise black stage. Jai and Avika sat in the front row, watching the performance unfold.

"It's beautiful," Jai whispered, "how she moves so precisely within that circle of light."

Avika nodded. "Notice how the audience only sees what's illuminated by the spotlight. Everything else on stage remains invisible."

"Like our attention," Jai realised. "We focus on one small area of experience while missing the larger reality around it."

"Exactly," Avika smiled. "This is the perfect metaphor for our entire journey toward becoming unshakeable."

As the performance continued, Jai observed how the dancer remained aware of the entire stage even while moving within the spotlight's beam.

"In Layer 1," Avika said softly, "we learn to direct our spotlight intentionally rather than letting it wander randomly or be pulled toward whatever shines brightest in the moment. We develop the discipline to focus it where we choose through strategic methods."

The lighting subtly shifted, and while the dancer remained the primary focus, the edges of the stage became faintly visible, revealing hints of set pieces and potential pathways that had been hidden in darkness.

"Layer 2," Jai whispered, recognising the parallel. "We begin to perceive beyond our spotlight's beam. We sense the vastness of the stage that remains in darkness and understand that our illuminated portion is just one small area of a much larger reality."

"Yes," Avika nodded. "We develop the mental flexibility to navigate uncertainty. We acknowledge that our spotlight may suddenly shift to unexpected areas, revealing scenes we hadn't anticipated. Rather than resisting these shifts, we learn to adapt our movements to whatever becomes illuminated."

The performance reached its climax, and in a breathtaking moment, the entire theater was briefly illuminated—revealing that the spotlight, dancer, stage, and audience all existed within the same encompassing space.

"And Layer 3," Jai said with quiet recognition, "is realising that we are not merely directing the spotlight—we are the light itself."

"The profound transformation," Avika added, "occurs when we recognise that there is no spotlight separate from consciousness, no dancer separate from the dance. The entire theater—stage, audience, lighting, music—exists within consciousness, not the other way around."

As the lights came up and the audience applauded, Jai sat in thoughtful silence.

"What are you thinking?" Avika asked as they gathered their things.

"I came looking for techniques to prevent life from affecting me," Jai replied. "Instead, I discovered something much more powerful—that true resilience isn't about strengthening a separate self against potential threats but recognising that what I fundamentally am was never threatened in the first place."

Avika smiled. "And yet this recognition doesn't make you withdraw from life—it allows you to engage more fully, doesn't it?"

"That's the paradox," Jai nodded. "The more I recognise my nature as the light itself, the more freely the dancer can move. Strategic methods still matter. Mental flexibility is still valuable. But they operate within a different context—one where both the spotlight and the dancer are recognised as expressions of the same fundamental reality."

They stepped out of the theater into the bustling street, where life continued in all its complexity and beauty.

"So where does the journey go from here?" Jai asked.

"It doesn't end," Avika replied. "In many ways, it's just beginning. True resilience isn't a destination but an ever-deepening capacity to dance with life exactly as it unfolds, knowing that beneath all appearances, you are the awareness that makes the dance possible."

APPENDICES

Appendix A:

The Three-Layer Assessment

Use this assessment to identify which layer of resilience you're currently operating from in different areas of your life. Circle the number that best reflects your current experience in each domain.

Career/Work

Layer 1: Strategic Control

1. I have multiple viable approaches to achieving my professional goals.
2. I develop contingency plans for potential obstacles rather than being blindsided.
3. I regularly review and adjust my strategies based on emerging information.
4. I use structured approaches to navigate complex work situations.
5. I'm able to develop strategic patience when immediate results aren't possible.

Layer 2: Mental Preparedness

1. I can adapt quickly when professional plans encounter unexpected obstacles.
2. I maintain equanimity during periods of career uncertainty or transition.
3. I can separate professional setbacks from my sense of personal worth.

4. I'm able to accept workplace realities without resentment or excessive frustration.
5. I can hold professional goals without making my wellbeing dependent on specific outcomes.

Layer 3: Philosophical Transcendence

1. I recognise that my professional identity is a role I play rather than who I fundamentally am.
2. I can engage fully in work without being defined by achievements or setbacks.
3. I experience periods where action flows naturally without the sense of being a separate "doer."
4. I can see how professional situations that seemed disastrous often contained hidden opportunities.
5. I maintain perspective on work within the larger context of human experience.

Relationships

Layer 1: Strategic Control

1. I communicate clearly about needs and expectations in relationships.
2. I develop multiple approaches to addressing relationship challenges.
3. I'm able to recognise and interrupt unhelpful patterns in my interactions.
4. I create and maintain appropriate boundaries with others.
5. I can strategically navigate difficult conversations with preparation and structure.

Layer 2: Mental Preparedness

1. I maintain emotional balance when others don't meet my expectations.
2. I can accept people as they are without trying to change their fundamental nature.

3. I navigate relationship uncertainty without excessive anxiety or control attempts.
4. I can hold preferences for how others behave without becoming rigid or demanding.
5. I respond to relationship challenges with flexibility rather than fixed reactions.

Layer 3: Philosophical Transcendence

1. I recognise that my sense of being a separate self interacting with other separate selves isn't the complete picture.
2. I experience moments of genuine connection that transcend usual boundaries of identity.
3. I can see how relationship challenges often reflect universal human patterns rather than just personal stories.
4. I hold relationships as sacred while not identifying completely with particular roles or dynamics.
5. I can love fully while recognising that who I fundamentally am isn't dependent on any relationship.

Health/Body

Layer 1: Strategic Control

1. I have structured approaches to maintaining physical wellbeing.
2. I develop multiple strategies for health goals rather than relying on single approaches.
3. I gather relevant information before making health decisions.
4. I create specific plans for addressing health challenges when they arise.
5. I set clear metrics to track progress toward health objectives.

Layer 2: Mental Preparedness

1. I maintain equilibrium when facing health uncertainties or limitations.

2. I can accept bodily realities without excessive resistance or denial.
3. I adapt flexibly when health plans require modification.
4. I maintain perspective during physical discomfort or challenge.
5. I can work with health professionals collaboratively rather than with anxiety or avoidance.

Layer 3: Philosophical Transcendence

1. I recognise that while I have a body, my fundamental nature isn't limited to physical form.
2. I can experience physical sensations without being completely identified with them.
3. I maintain perspective on health within the larger context of the human condition.
4. I can face mortality and impermanence with equanimity rather than denial.
5. I experience moments where the boundary between "self" and "body" relaxes or dissolves.

Scoring Guide

For each section, add your circled numbers to get a score for that layer in that domain.

5-11: Beginning development in this layer
12-18: Moderate development in this layer
19-25: Strong development in this layer

Your scores indicate where you're currently operating in each life domain. Remember that development typically builds sequentially—Layer 1 creates the foundation for Layer 2, which in turn creates conditions for Layer 3. However, you might find yourself more developed in different layers across different domains.

Appendix B

Practice Guide for the Three Layers

This guide provides focused practices for developing each layer of resilience. For optimal results, work primarily with practices from your current layer of development while also exploring the next layer.

Layer 1 Practices: Developing Strategic Control

Strategic Delta Development:

1. For an important goal, identify three completely different approaches to achieving it.
2. For each approach, list the first three concrete steps you could take.
3. Develop at least two contingency responses for potential obstacles in each approach.
4. Create a structured timeline for advancing all paths simultaneously, even at different paces.
5. Establish clear metrics to evaluate progress across all paths.

Strategic Cycle Practice:

1. Identify a recurring challenge in your life.
2. Create a structured four-phase approach:
   - Assessment: Gather objective information about the current situation
   - Options: Generate at least three distinct approaches
   - Selection: Choose an approach based on clear criteria
   - Implementation: Create specific action steps with timelines

3. Apply this cycle consistently to similar challenges, refining it based on results.

Quantum Possibility Mapping:

1. Select a situation where you feel stuck or limited.
2. List assumptions you're making about what's possible in this situation.
3. For each assumption, ask: "What if this isn't completely true? What becomes possible then?"
4. Identify "weak signals"—subtle patterns or anomalies that might indicate emerging possibilities.
5. Design small experiments to test expanded possibilities without major commitment.

Pattern Interruption Protocol:

1. Identify habitual reactions that create unwanted outcomes.
2. Design specific pattern interruptions—deliberate actions that break automatic sequences:
   - Physical interruption (changing posture, location, or movement)
   - Cognitive interruption (asking a specific question or reframing the situation)
   - Temporal interruption (introducing a deliberate pause before responding)
3. Practice these interruptions until they become automatic responses to triggering situations.

Layer 2 Practices: Developing Mental Preparedness

Acceptance Cultivation:

1. Identify a current reality you're resisting.
2. Distinguish between the factual situation and your interpretations about it.
3 Practice the statement: "This is what's happening right now. I can accept that this is the reality I'm working with."

4. Notice physical tension that signals resistance and consciously release it.
5. Ask: "How might my response change if I fully accepted this reality without requiring it to be different?"

Uncertainty Navigation:

1. Identify a situation involving significant uncertainty.
2. Notice your habitual response to this uncertainty (anxiety, control attempts, avoidance).
3. Practice reframing uncertainty as a field of possibilities rather than a threat.
4. Ask: "What opportunities might exist precisely because the future isn't fixed?"
5. Develop comfort with provisional knowing—holding understanding as a working hypothesis rather than fixed truth.

Flexibility Training:

1. Deliberately expose yourself to minor novelty and change regularly:
   - Take different routes to familiar destinations
   - Rearrange your environment
   - Engage with perspectives that challenge your assumptions
   - Try new approaches to routine activities
2. When facing disruption, practice the question: "How might this change be beneficial in ways I can't currently see?"
3. Develop comfort with both-and thinking rather than either-or limitations.

Response Diversification:

1. Identify situations where you have limited or automatic responses.
2. For each situation, generate at least five completely different possible responses.

3. Practice mentally rehearsing these alternatives until they feel genuinely available.
4. In daily life, deliberately choose non-habitual responses to build this capacity.
5. After interactions, reflect: "What other responses might have been effective here?"

Layer 3 Practices: Developing Philosophical Transcendence

Awareness Recognition:

1. Several times throughout your day, pause and notice that you are aware.
2. Direct attention to the awareness itself rather than its contents.
3. Notice that this awareness remains unchanged regardless of what appears within it.
4. Ask: "What is aware of my current experience?" without answering conceptually.
5. Rest in the recognition of awareness as your fundamental nature rather than as a capacity you possess.

Identity Inquiry:

1. When thoughts, emotions, or sensations arise, ask: "Who/what is experiencing this?"
2. Notice how the "I" sense shifts location and quality as you investigate it directly.
3. Recognise how the sense of being a separate self is constructed from thought, memory, and sensation rather than existing as a fixed entity.
4. In daily activities, experiment with holding identity provisionally rather than solidly.
5. Practice the question: "What if who I am is not limited to the story I tell about myself?"

Time Investigation:

1. Notice how the concepts of "past" and "future" always appear as present thoughts.
2. When caught in regret or anxiety, recognise: "This is a present experience about an imagined time, not a journey to another time."
3. Practice full engagement with present experience without the psychological division into past, present, and future.
4. Notice how the sense of duration is constructed rather than fundamental.
5. Experiment with the recognition: "This eternal now is the only reality I ever experience."

Non-Dual Contemplation:

1. With any perceptual experience (seeing, hearing, feeling), notice both the perception and the awareness of that perception.
2. Recognise how perception and awareness of perception aren't actually two separate things but aspects of a unified experience.
3. Notice how boundaries between "inside" and "outside" are more conceptual than actual in direct experience.
4. In interactions, experiment with the recognition that apparent separation between "self" and "other" is constructed rather than fundamental.
5. Allow activities to unfold naturally without the sense of a separate controller directing them.

Appendix C

Reading List by Layer

This curated reading list provides resources aligned with each layer of resilience. These selections have been chosen for their practical value and accessibility rather than academic complexity.

Layer 1: Strategic Control

1. *Thinking in Bets: Making Smarter Decisions When You Don't Have All the Facts* by Annie Duke
   - Explores decision-making under uncertainty, emphasising probabilistic thinking and outcome independence.
2. *Range: Why Generalists Triumph in a Specialized World* by David Epstein
   - Presents research on why developing multiple paths and diverse capabilities creates strategic advantage in complex environments.
3. *Antifragile: Things That Gain from Disorder* by Nassim Nicholas Taleb
   - Introduces systems that don't merely withstand disruption but actually benefit from it—a cornerstone of strategic resilience.

Layer 2: Mental Preparedness

1. *The Obstacle Is the Way* by Ryan Holiday
   - Draws from Stoic philosophy to present practical approaches for converting obstacles into opportunities through perception, action, and will.

2. *Radical Acceptance* by Tara Brach
   - Offers accessible practices for developing acceptance as a foundation for effective action rather than resignation.
3. *Comfortable with Uncertainty* by Pema Chödrön
   - Provides practical guidance for developing equanimity amid life's inherent uncertainties and challenges.
4. *The Surrender Experiment* by Michael Singer
   - Chronicles a personal journey of releasing resistance to life's flow while maintaining active engagement.
5. *Man's Search for Meaning* by Viktor Frankl
   - Explores developing meaning and purpose even in the most challenging circumstances—the foundation of **Layer 2 resilience**.

Layer 3: Philosophical Transcendence

1. *I Am That* by Nisargadatta Maharaj
   - Offers direct pointing to your fundamental nature beyond the separate self through dialogues that cut through conceptual understanding.
2. *The Power of Now* by Eckhart Tolle
   - Explores practical approaches to recognising the illusory nature of time and the freedom found in present awareness.

Born in Jamshedpur, India, in 1979, **Amar B. Singh** grew up in the township of Telco Colony. His early schooling was at the Chinmaya Vidyalaya which helped shape his interest in Hindu Vedanta philosophy. In 1997, he went to Bihar Institute of Technology, where he studied metallurgical engineering. It was also the period where he excelled as the senior editor of his college magazine and a prominent member of the college literary society. He pursued his MBA at XLRI, Jamshedpur, with a focus on finance and strategy. Later, he added an LLB degree to his academic credentials.

Throughout his career, Amar has worked with various companies in the areas of finance, marketing, and strategy. However, he resists being confined to any particular title or function, as his writing continually explores the existential question of identity. His works aim to cultivate a more perceptive society, one that does not live blindly. Amar's poetry and narratives seamlessly blend the ancient wisdom of religion and culture